Mac® OS X For Dummies®

D0473923

Cheat Sheet

Five Awesome Web Sites for Mac OS X Lovers

`http://til.info.apple.com`: The Apple Tech Info Library is a treasure trove of tech notes, software update information, and documentation.

`www.macfixit.com`: Ted Landau has created perhaps the greatest Mac troubleshooting site of all time. Don't miss it.

`www.versiontracker.com`: VersionTracker is the place to go to find freeware, shareware, and software updates. If VersionTracker doesn't have it, it probably doesn't exist.

`www.maccentral.com`: This site is where those in the know go for up-to-the-minute Mac news (and co-author Bob LeVitus' bi-weekly "Ask Dr. Mac" column).

`www.apple.com/macosx`: Check this official Apple Mac OS X Web site often for updates, news, and info on your favorite operating system.

Keyboard Shortcuts

All these shortcuts work in the Finder, and many of them work in other application programs as well. See those perforations over there? That's so you can tear this cheat sheet out so that you don't have to memorize all these shortcuts. Ready? RIP!

Command	Keyboard Shortcut	Command	Keyboard Shortcut
Close All	⌘+Option+W	Show Info	⌘+I
Close Window	⌘+W	Make Alias	⌘+M
Copy	⌘+C	New Folder	⌘+Shift+N
Cut	⌘+X	Open	⌘+O
Duplicate	⌘+D	Paste	⌘+V
Eject Disk	⌘+E	Print	⌘+P
Find (Sherlock)	⌘+F	Select All	⌘+A
Find Again	⌘+G	Undo	⌘+Z

For Dummies®: Bestselling Book Series for Beginners

Mac® OS X For Dummies®

Cheat Sheet

Do You Need an Antivirus Program?

You do if you're at risk. How do you know if you're at risk? You're at risk if you

- Download files from the Internet
- Receive e-mail with attachments (and open the attachments)
- Are on a network and share files with others
- Use disks — floppy, Zip, Jaz, Orb, CD-R, or other — that have ever been inserted in anyone else's Mac

These are the ways that viruses spread, so if any or all of the preceding apply to you, you'd be well served to run an antivirus program, such as Virex or Norton AntiVirus for Macintosh.

Top Six Things You Should Never Do

1. Keep only one copy of your important documents. Make at least two back-up copies and keep one of them in a safe place. Period.

2. Get up from your Mac without saving your work. Just before your butt leaves the chair, your fingers should be pressing ⌘+S. Make it a habit.

3. Shut off your Mac by pulling the plug or flipping the power switch. Always use the Shut Down command from the Apple (🍎) menu.

4. Bump, drop, shake, wobble, dribble, drop kick, or play catch with a hard drive while it's running. Don't forget that your Mac has a hard drive inside it, too.

5. Pay attention to anyone who says that Windows is just like the Mac. Yeah, right. And Yugo is the Eastern-European cousin of BMW.

6. Pay list price for any hardware or software. What lists for $499 at Pierre's Chrome and Glass Computer Boutique may only cost $275 at Bubba's Mail-Order Warehouse and Chili Emporium.

Hungry Minds™

Copyright © 2001 Hungry Minds, Inc.
All rights reserved.

Cheat Sheet $2.95 value. Item 0706-0.

For more information about Hungry Minds,
call 1-800-762-2974.

For Dummies®: Bestselling Book Series for Beginners

 TM

References for the Rest of Us! ®

BESTSELLING BOOK SERIES

Are you intimidated and confused by computers? Do you find that traditional manuals are overloaded with technical details you'll never use? Do your friends and family always call you to fix simple problems on their PCs? Then the For Dummies® computer book series from Hungry Minds, Inc. is for you.

For Dummies books are written for those frustrated computer users who know they aren't really dumb but find that PC hardware, software, and indeed the unique vocabulary of computing make them feel helpless. For Dummies books use a lighthearted approach, a down-to-earth style, and even cartoons and humorous icons to dispel computer novices' fears and build their confidence. Lighthearted but not lightweight, these books are a perfect survival guide for anyone forced to use a computer.

> *"I like my copy so much I told friends; now they bought copies."*
>
> *— Irene C., Orwell, Ohio*

> *"Quick, concise, nontechnical, and humorous."*
>
> *— Jay A., Elburn, Illinois*

> *"Thanks, I needed this book. Now I can sleep at night."*
>
> *— Robin F., British Columbia, Canada*

Already, millions of satisfied readers agree. They have made For Dummies books the #1 introductory level computer book series and have written asking for more. So, if you're looking for the most fun and easy way to learn about computers, look to For Dummies books to give you a helping hand.

Mac® OS X

FOR

DUMMIES®

Mac® OS X
FOR
DUMMIES®

by Bob Levitus and Shelly Brisbin

Hungry Minds™

HUNGRY MINDS, INC.

New York, NY ◆ Cleveland, OH ◆ Indianapolis, IN

Mac® OS X For Dummies®

Published by
Hungry Minds, Inc.
909 Third Avenue
New York, NY 10022
www.hungryminds.com
www.dummies.com

Library of Congress Control Number: 00-103653

ISBN: 0-7645-0706-0

Printed in the United States of America

10 9 8 7 6 5 4 3 2

1O/RQ/QZ/QR/IN

Distributed in the United States by Hungry Minds, Inc.

Distributed by CDG Books Canada Inc. for Canada; by Transworld Publishers Limited in the United Kingdom; by IDG Norge Books for Norway; by IDG Sweden Books for Sweden; by IDG Books Australia Publishing Corporation Pty. Ltd. for Australia and New Zealand; by TransQuest Publishers Pte Ltd. for Singapore, Malaysia, Thailand, Indonesia, and Hong Kong; by Gotop Information Inc. for Taiwan; by ICG Muse, Inc. for Japan; by Intersoft for South Africa; by Eyrolles for France; by International Thomson Publishing for Germany, Austria and Switzerland; by Distribuidora Cuspide for Argentina; by LR International for Brazil; by Galileo Libros for Chile; by Ediciones ZETA S.C.R. Ltda. for Peru; by WS Computer Publishing Corporation, Inc., for the Philippines; by Contemporanea de Ediciones for Venezuela; by Express Computer Distributors for the Caribbean and West Indies; by Micronesia Media Distributor, Inc. for Micronesia; by Chips Computadoras S.A. de C.V. for Mexico; by Editorial Norma de Panama S.A. for Panama; by American Bookshops for Finland.

For general information on Hungry Minds' products and services please contact our Customer Care Department within the U.S. at 800-762-2974, outside the U.S. at 317-572-3993 or fax 317-572-4002.

For sales inquiries and reseller information, including discounts, premium and bulk quantity sales, and foreign-language translations, please contact our Customer Care Department at 800-434-3422, fax 317-572-4002, or write to Hungry Minds, Inc., Attn: Customer Care Department, 10475 Crosspoint Boulevard, Indianapolis, IN 46256.

For information on licensing foreign or domestic rights, please contact our Sub-Rights Customer Care Department at 212-884-5000.

For information on using Hungry Minds' products and services in the classroom or for ordering examination copies, please contact our Educational Sales Department at 800-434-2086 or fax 317-572-4005.

Please contact our Public Relations Department at 212-884-5163 for press review copies or 212-884-5000 for author interviews and other publicity information or fax 212-884-5400.

For authorization to photocopy items for corporate, personal, or educational use, please contact Copyright Clearance Center, 222 Rosewood Drive, Danvers, MA 01923, or fax 978-750-4470.

Hungry Minds™ is a trademark of Hungry Minds, Inc.

About the Authors

Bob LeVitus, often referred to as "Dr. Macintosh," has written 35 popular computer books, including *Mac OS 9 For Dummies* for Hungry Minds, Inc., *Mac Answers: 2nd Edition* for Osborne/McGraw Hill (with Shelly Brisbin), *Stupid Mac Tricks* and *Dr. Macintosh*, both for Addison-Wesley, as well as recent titles such as *Macworld Microsoft Office 2001 Bible* (with Dennis Cohen, who technically edited this book) and *Internet For iMacs For Dummies*, (with Natanya Pitts) both for Hungry Minds, Inc. His books have sold more than a million copies worldwide. While his first love will always be the Mac, he's also written more than half a dozen popular books for Windows users.

Bob is presently a syndicated newspaper columnist *(Dr. Mac)* for the Houston Chronicle, Austin American-Statesman, and writes a bi-weekly question and answer column for legendary Mac web site MacCentral. He's also been published in more than two dozen computer magazines over the past twelve years. A tireless publicity hound, Bob's achievements have been documented in major media around the world. He's known for his expertise, trademark humorous style, and ability to translate "techie" jargon into usable and fun advice for regular folks.

Always a popular speaker at computer user groups and trade shows, Bob has spoken at more than 200 seminars here and abroad, presented keynote addresses in three countries, and produced a series of training seminars in five cities. (He also won the Macworld Expo MacJeopardy World Championship three times before retiring his crown.)

Bob is one of the world's leading authorities on the Mac OS. From 1989 to 1997 he was a contributing editor/columnist for *MacUser* magazine, writing the *Help Folder, Beating the System, Personal Best,* and *Game Room* columns at various times in his illustrious career. He was the host of Mac Today, a half-hour television show syndicated in over 100 markets, which aired in late 1992.

Prior to giving his life over to computers, Bob spent almost seven years at Kresser/Craig/D.I.K., a Los Angeles advertising agency and marketing consultancy and its subsidiary L & J Research. He holds a B.S. in Marketing from California State University.

Bob LeVitus lives in Austin, Texas with his wife Lisa, children Allison and Jacob, and a small pack of Welsh Springer Spaniels and Vizslas.

Dedication

This book is dedicated to my father, Jim LeVitus, a huge Mac fan who taught me everything I know about almost everything except computers.

Author's Acknowledgments

Special thanks to everyone at Apple who helped us turn this book around in record time: Keri Walker, Nathalie Welch, Ken Bereskin, Alicia Awbrey, Matt Hutchison, and all the rest. We couldn't have done it without you.

Thanks also to superagent Carole "I-Look-*nothing*-like-Swifty-Lazar" McClendon, for dealmaking beyond the call of duty. You're a treasure.

Super-geeky thanks to Shelly "I'll do the geeky stuff" Brisbin, whose help was invaluable in getting this book out the door on time.

Big-time thanks to the gang at Hungry Minds: Mike "Let's-make-a-deal!" Roney, Tom "Is it done yet?" Heine, Kyle "the whipcracker" Looper, James "whipcracker-on-steroids" Russell, Teresa "Can you rewrite this?" Artman, and all the others. And, of course, the big guy himself, John Kilcullen. Nobody does it better than you guys.

Extra special thanks to my technical editor, Dennis R. Cohen: You rock, dude!

Thanks for my family and friends for putting up with me during my all-too-lengthy absences during this book's gestation.

Thanks to Saccone's Pizza, Lucky Dog, Iron Works BBQ, Taco Cabana, Bass Ale, and Eli's Cheesecake for providing sustenance as I worked.

And finally, thanks to you, gentle reader, for buying this book.

Publisher's Acknowledgments

We're proud of this book; please send us your comments through our Online Registration Form located at www.dummies.com.

Some of the people who helped bring this book to market include the following:

Acquisitions, Editorial, and Media Development

Project Editor: James H. Russell

Acquisitions Editor: Tom Heine

Copy Editor: Teresa Artman

Technical Editor: Dennis R. Cohen

Editorial Manager: Kyle Looper

Editorial Assistant: Jean Rogers

Production

Project Coordinator: Dale White

Layout and Graphics: Joe Bucki, Brian Drumm, John Greenough, Brent Savage, Jacque Schneider, Brian Torwelle, Erin Zeltner, Jeremey Unger

Proofreaders: Mary Lagu, Susan Moritz, Angel Perez, Nancy Price, Marianne Santy, Charles Spencer

Indexer: Sharon Hilgenberg

Special Help
Apple Computer, Inc.

General and Administrative

Hungry Minds, Inc.: John Kilcullen, CEO; Bill Barry, President and COO; John Ball, Executive VP, Operations & Administration; John Harris, CFO

Hungry Minds Technology Publishing Group: Richard Swadley, Senior Vice President and Publisher; Mary Bednarek, Vice President and Publisher, Networking and Certification; Walter R. Bruce III, Vice President and Publisher, General User and Design Professional; Joseph Wikert, Vice President and Publisher, Programming; Mary C. Corder, Editorial Director, Branded Technology Editorial; Andy Cummings, Publishing Director, General User and Design Professional; Barry Pruett, Publishing Director, Visual

Hungry Minds Manufacturing: Ivor Parker, Vice President, Manufacturing

Hungry Minds Marketing: John Helmus, Assistant Vice President, Director of Marketing

Hungry Minds Production for Branded Press: Debbie Stailey, Production Director

Hungry Minds Sales: Roland Elgey, Senior Vice President, Sales and Marketing; Michael Violano, Vice President, International Sales and Sub Rights

◆

The publisher would like to give special thanks to Patrick J. McGovern, without whom this book would not have been possible.

◆

Contents at a Glance

Cartoons at a Glance

By Rich Tennant

page 277

page 7

page 227

page 77

page 131

Cartoon Information:
Fax: 978-546-7747
E-Mail: richtennant@the5thwave.com
World Wide Web: www.the5thwave.com

Table of Contents

Introduction

· ·

*Y*ou made the right choice twice: Mac OS X and this book.

Take a deep breath and get ready to have a rollicking good time. That's right. This is a computer book, but even so it's going to be fun. What a concept! Whether you're brand-spanking new to the Mac or a grizzled old Mac-vet, we guarantee that discovering the ins and outs of Mac OS X will be fun and easy. Hungry Minds, Inc. (the publisher of this book) couldn't say it on the cover if it weren't true!

About This Book

This book's roots lie with Bob's international bestseller *Macintosh System 7.5 For Dummies,* an award-winning book so good that it was offered by now-deceased Mac cloner Power Computing in lieu of a system software manual. Now Bob's back with *Mac OS X For Dummie*s, written with the able assistance of his former *MacUser* editor Shelly Brisbin. This book combines all the old, familiar features of the previous books (*Mac OS 8 For Dummies, Mac OS 8.5 For Dummies,* and *Mac OS 9 For Dummies*) with updated information about the latest, greatest offering from Apple.

Why write a *For Dummies* book about Mac OS X? Well, Mac OS X is a big, complicated personal computer operating system. So we made *Mac OS X For Dummies* a not-so-big, not-very-complicated book that shows you what Mac OS X is all about without boring you, confusing you, or poking you with sharp objects.

In fact, you'll be so darned comfortable that Bob wanted to call this book *Mac OS X without the Discomfort,* but the publishers wouldn't let him. Apparently we *For Dummies* authors have to follow some rules, and using the word *Dummies* in the title is one of them. Bob also wanted to call this book *Mac OS X For People Smart Enough to Know They Need Help,* but you can just imagine what Hungry Minds thought of that.

And speaking of dummies, remember that it's just a word. We don't think that you're dumb. Quite the opposite! (If you're reading this in a bookstore, approach the cashier with your wallet in your hand, buy the book, and we'll know you're even smarter!)

This book is chock-full of information and advice and explains everything you need to know about Mac OS X in language you can understand. We also supplemented it with tips, tricks, techniques, and steps, all served up in generous quantities.

Conventions Used in This Book

To get the most out of this book, you need to know how we do things and why. So, here are a few conventions we use in this book to make your life easier:

- When we want you to open an item in a menu, we write something like "choose File⇨Open," which means, "Pull down the File menu and choose the Open command."

- When we refer to the menu, we're referring to the menu in the upper-left corner of the Finder's menu bar that looks like a blue Apple (called the *Apple menu*). For example, we may say, "From the menu, choose File⇨Open." We do *not* use the symbol to refer to the key on your Mac keyboard that may or may not have both the ⌘ and symbols on it. We refer to that key (called the *Command key*) with the equally funky ⌘ symbol and say something like, "press the ⌘ key." So, when you see , think Apple menu.

- For keyboard shortcuts, we write something like ⌘+*A*, which means to hold down the ⌘ key (the one with the little pretzel and/or symbol on it) and press the letter A on the keyboard. If you see something like ⌘+*Shift*+*A*, that means to hold down the ⌘ and Shift keys while pressing the A key. Again, for absolute clarity, we will never refer to the ⌘ key with the symbol. We reserve that symbol for the menu *(Apple menu)*. For the Command key, we use only the ⌘ symbol.

- Stuff you're supposed to type appears in bold type, **like this.**

- Sometimes an entire a sentence is in bold, as you'll see when we present a numbered list of steps. **In those cases, we debold what you're supposed to type,** like this.

- Web addresses, programming code (not much in this book), and things that appear onscreen are shown in a special monofont typeface, `like this.`

What You're Not to Read

The chapters in the first part of this book are where we describe the basic everyday things that you need to understand to operate your Mac effectively.

Even though OS X is way different from previous Mac operating systems, this first part is so basic that if you've been using a Mac for long, you may think you know it all. But hey! — not-so-old-timers need a solid foundation. So here's our advice: Skip through stuff that you know to get to the stuff *you* need faster.

Other stuff that you can skip over if you're so inclined are sidebars and any section marked with a Technical Stuff icon, which we talk about in a moment.

Foolish Assumptions

While we know what happens when you make assumptions, there are a few we've made anyway. First, we assume that you, gentle reader, know nothing about using Mac OS X. What we do assume is that you know what a Mac is, that you want to use OS X, that you want to learn about OS X without digesting an incomprehensible technical manual, and that you made an excellent choice selecting this particular book.

In any case, we do our best to explain each new concept in full and loving detail. Maybe that's foolish, but . . . oh well.

Oh, and we also assume that you can read.

How This Book Is Organized

Mac OS X For Dummies is divided into five logical parts, numbered (surprisingly enough) Parts 38 through 43. Just kidding — we wanted to see if you were paying attention; they're actually numbered Parts 1 through 5, except that they're numbered using those stuffy old Roman numerals instead of Arabic numerals.

You may want to read them in order, especially if you're a beginner, but if you already know a lot — or think you know a lot — feel free to skip around and read the parts that interest you most.

Part 1: Desktop Madness: Navigating Mac OS X

This first part is very, very basic training. From the mouse to the Desktop, from menus, windows, and icons to the snazzy new Dock, it's all here. A lot of what you need to know to navigate the depths of Mac OS X safely and sanely is in this section. And while old-timers may just want to skim through it, you newbies should probably read every word. Twice.

Part II: Rounding Out Your Basic Training

In this part, we build on the basics of Part 1 and really get you revving with your Mac. Here we cover additional topics every Mac user needs to know, coupled with some hands-on, step-by-step training. We start with a look at each and every OS X Finder menu in full and loving detail; then we move on to talk about the all-important Finder in depth. Next up is a chapter about how to open and save files (a skill you're sure to find handy), and finally we take a look at how to manage removable media (which means *ejectable disks*).

Part III: Doing Stuff with Your Mac

This part is chock full of ways to do cool stuff with your Mac. You'll discover the Internet first — how to get it working on your Mac, and what to do with it after you do. Next, we show you the ins and outs of printing under OS X. You also read about many of the applications that come with OS X, plus how to make your copy of OS X look and feel just as you like it. That's all followed by the low-down on the Classic Environment, and possibly the most useful chapter in the whole book, Chapter 15, which details each and every gosh-darned System Preference.

Part IV: U 2 Can B a Guru

Here we get into the nitty-gritty underbelly of Mac OS X, where we cover more advanced topics such as file sharing, backing up your files, and the all-important troubleshooting chapter, Chapter 18.

Part V: The Part of Tens

Last, but not least, it's The Part of Tens, which is mostly a Letterman rip-off, although it does include heaping helpings of tips, optional software, great Mac Web sites, and hardware ideas.

Appendix

Last, but certainly not least, here we cover installing Mac OS X. The whole process has become quite easy with this version of the system software, but if you have to install OS X yourself, it would behoove you to read this helpful appendix first.

Icons Used in This Book

You'll see little round pictures (icons) off to the left side of the text throughout this book. Consider these icons miniature road signs, telling you a little something extra about the topic at hand. Here's what the different icons look like and what they all mean.

Look for tip icons to find the juiciest morsels: shortcuts, tips, and undocumented secrets about OS X. Try them all; impress your friends!

When you see this icon, it means that this particular morsel is something the authors think you should memorize (or at least write on your shirt cuff).

Put on your propeller beanie hat and pocket protector; this icon points out the truly nerdy stuff. It's certainly not required reading, but it must be interesting or informative or we wouldn't have wasted the space.

Read these notes very, very, very carefully. Did we say *ver*-y? Warning icons flag important information. The author and publisher will not be responsible if your Mac explodes or spews flaming parts because you ignored a Warning icon. Just kidding! Macs don't explode or spew (with the exception of a few choice PowerBook 5300s, which won't run OS X anyway). But we got your attention, didn't we?

These icons represent Bob or Shelly ranting or raving about something that just bugs 'em. (Imagine your authors foaming from the mouth.) Rants are required to be irreverent, irrelevant, or both. We also try to keep them short, more for your sake than ours.

Well, now, what could this icon possibly be about? Named by famous editorial consultant Mr. Obvious, this icon highlights all things new and different in Mac OS X. Now, can someone tell us how to get to the Rocket Science Department?

Where to Go from Here

Go to a comfortable spot (preferably not far from your Mac) and read the book.

We didn't write this book for ourselves. We wrote it for you and would love to hear how it worked for you. So please drop us a line or register your comments through the Hungry Minds Online Registration Form located at `http://my2cents.dummies.com`.

Did this book work for you? What did you like? What didn't you like? What questions were unanswered? Did you want to know more about something? Did you want to find out less about something? Tell us! Bob has received more than 100 suggestions about previous editions, most of which are incorporated here. So keep up the good work! You can send the authors snail mail care of Hungry Minds, Inc. (the mailroom there will see that we receive it), or send e-mail to Bob directly at `boblevitus@boblevitus.com`. We appreciate your feedback, and Bob will *try* to respond to all e-mail within a few days. (Unlike some authors, he makes no promises, though.)

So what are you waiting for? Go enjoy the book!

Part I

Desktop Madness: Navigating Mac OS X

The 5th Wave — By Rich Tennant

"A BRIEF ANNOUNCEMENT, CLASS — AN OPEN-FACED PEANUT BUTTER SANDWICH IS NOT AN APPROPRIATE REPLACEMENT FOR A MISSING MOUSEPAD."

In this part . . .

Mac OS X sports tons of new goodies and features. We'll get to the hot new goodies soon enough, but you have to crawl before you walk.

In this part, you discover the most basic of basics, such as how to turn your Mac on. Next, we acquaint you with the Mac OS X Desktop: windows, icons, the Dock, the Finder — the whole shmear.

So get comfortable, roll up your sleeves, fire up your Mac if you like, and settle down with Part I, a delightful little section Bob likes to think of as "The Hassle-Free Way to Get Started with Mac OS X."

Chapter 1

Mac OS X 101
(Prerequisites: None)

In This Chapter

▶ Checking out Mac OS X

▶ Finding help if you're a beginner

▶ Turning on your Mac

▶ Knowing what you should see when you turn on your Mac

▶ Shutting down your Mac without getting chewed out by it

▶ Taking a refresher course on using a mouse

*C*ongratulate yourself on choosing Mac OS X (which stands for Macintosh Operating System X — and that's the Roman numeral *ten*, not the letter *X*). You made a smart move because you scored more than just an operating system upgrade. Mac OS X includes dozens of new or improved features to make using your Mac easier, as well as dozens more that help you do more work in less time. Now you can use these new features to be more productive, have fewer headaches, reduce your cholesterol level, and fall in love with your Mac all over again.

In this chapter, we start at the very beginning and talk about Mac OS X in mostly abstract terms. You can turn your Mac on if you like, but most of the chapter has no hands-on material. What you will find, however, is a bunch of important stuff that you need to know to proceed. If you're a total beginner to the Mac experience, you should probably read every word in this chapter. Even if you are past the beginner stage, you may want to skim these sections anyway to refresh your memory.

Those of you who are upgrading from an earlier version of Mac OS to Mac OS X should read the Appendix right about now for installation information.

Of education and burgers

Most of the world's PCs use Windows, poor schmucks. You're among the lucky few to have a computer with an operating system that's intuitive, easy to use, and, dare we say, fun. If you don't believe us, try using Windows for a day or two. Go ahead. You probably won't suffer any permanent damage. In fact, you'll really begin to appreciate how good you have it. Feel free to hug your Mac. Or give it a peck on the CD-ROM drive slot — just try not to get your tongue caught.

Mac OS X makes a Mac even more of a Mac. "How so?" you ask. Well, think of it this way: If any old operating system is an education, Mac OS X is an Ivy League education (and a PC running Windows dropped outta high school in the tenth grade and flips burgers for a living!). With Mac OS X, your Mac becomes an elegant,

powerful tool that's the envy of the rest of the computer industry.

Here's why we can say that: Unix is widely regarded as the best "industrial strength" operating system, and Mac OS X is based on Unix. For now, just know that being based on Unix means that a Mac running OS X will crash less often than an older Mac or a Windows machine, which means less downtime. But perhaps the biggest advantage OS X has over most flavors of Windows is that when an application crashes, it doesn't crash your entire computer and you don't have to restart to continue working. Yes, friends and neighbors, the Mac can finally legitimately claim to have a superior, more stable operating system than Windows.

Gnawing to the Core of Mac OS X

Along with the code in its read-only memory (ROM), the operating system (that is, the "OS" in "Mac OS X") is what makes a Mac a Mac. Without it, your Mac is a pile of silicon and circuits — no smarter than a toaster.

"So, what does an operating system do?" you ask. Good question. The short answer is that an *operating system* controls the basic and most important operations of your computer. In the case of Mac OS X and your Mac, the operating system

- ✔ Manages memory
- ✔ Controls how windows, icons, and menus work
- ✔ Keeps track of files
- ✔ Manages networking
- ✔ Does lots of housekeeping chores (just kidding!)

Other forms of software, such as word processors and Web browsers, rely on the operating system to create and maintain the environment in which that software works its magic. When you create a memo, for example, the word processor provides the tools for you to type and format the information. In the background, the operating system is the muscle for the word processor, performing crucial functions like:

- Providing the mechanism for drawing and moving the window in which you write the memo

- Helping the word processor create drop-down menus and dialog boxes for you to interact with

- Keeping track of a file when you save it

- Communicating with other programs

- And much, much more (stuff that only geeks could care about)

So, now that you have a little background in operating systems, take a gander at the next section before you do anything else with your Mac.

A Safety Net for the Absolute Beginner (Or Any User)

In this section, we deal with the stuff that the manual that came with your Mac doesn't cover, or doesn't cover in nearly enough detail. If you're a first-time Macintosh user, please, *please* read this section of the book carefully — it could save your life. Okay, okay; perhaps we're being overly dramatic. What we mean to say is that reading this section could save your *Mac.* Even if you're an experienced Mac user, you may want to read this section anyway. Chances are that you need a few reminders.

Turning the dang thing on

Okay. This is the big moment — turning on your Mac! Gaze at it longingly first and say something cheesy like, "You're the most awesome computer I've ever known. . . ." If that doesn't turn your Mac on (it probably won't), please read on.

If you actually thought flattery would turn on your Mac, you should probably read *Self-Psychotherapy For Dummies* before you continue with this book. (And if you think that book exists, maybe you should check out *Gullibility For Dummies*).

If you don't know how to turn your Mac on, don't feel bad, just look in the manual that came with your Mac. Apple, in its infinite wisdom, has manufactured Macs with power switches and buttons on every conceivable surface: on the front, side, and back of the CPU, and even on the keyboard or monitor. Some Macs (including most older PowerBooks) even hide the power button behind a little plastic door. Because of the vast number of different configurations, we can't tell you where the switch is without devoting a whole chapter just to that topic (can you say booooo-ring?).

What you should see on startup

When you finally do turn on your Macintosh, you set in motion a sophisticated and complex series of events that culminates in the loading of Mac OS X and the appearance of the new Mac Desktop. After a small bit of whirring, buzzing, and flashing (meaning that the operating system is loading), one of the following three icons appears in the center of your screen:

✔ **Happy Mac:** Each time you first start up your Mac, it first tests all your hardware — slots, ports, disks, random-access memory (RAM) — and so on. If everything passes, you hear a pleasing musical chord and see the cheerful little happy Mac in the middle of your screen (like the one shown in the margin).

Next you see the soothing blue Mac OS logo, with the message Mac OS X, followed by a status indicator and messages that tell you that the Mac is going through its normal startup motions. Makes you feel kind of warm and fuzzy, doesn't it? If all this fanfare shows up on your screen, Mac OS X is loading properly. In the unlikely event that you don't see the smiling Mac, soothing messages, and the familiar Desktop, see Chapter 18 where we show you how to troubleshoot your system.

Then, you may or may not see the Mac OS X log-in screen, where you enter your name and password. If you do (you'll only see it if your Mac is set up for multiple users; don't worry, we tell you all about this in Chapter 16), type in your user name and password; then press the Enter key and away you go.

Either way, the new Mac Desktop soon materializes before your eyes. If you haven't customized, configured, or tinkered with your Desktop, it should look something like Figure 1-1. Now is a good time to take a moment for positive thoughts about the person who convinced you that you wanted a Mac. That person was right!

If you don't want to have to type your name and password every time you start or restart your Mac (or even if you do), check out Chapter 15 for the scoop on how to turn the log-in screen on or off.

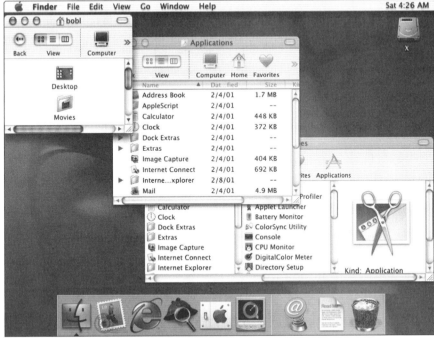

Figure 1-1:
The Mac OS X Desktop as it appears after a brand, spanking new installation of OS X.

🖙 **Sad Mac:** If any of your hardware fails when it's tested, you see a black screen with the dreaded sad Mac icon (shown in the margin) and hear a far less pleasing musical chord known by Mac aficionados as the *Chimes of Doom*. The fact that something went wrong is no reflection on your prowess as a Macintosh user. Something inside your Mac is broken, and it probably needs to go in for repairs (usually to an Apple dealer). See Chapter 18 to try and get your Mac well again.

If your computer is under warranty, dial 1-800-SOS-APPL and a customer service person can tell you what to do. Before you do anything, though, skip ahead to Chapter 18. It's entirely possible that one of the suggestions there can get you back on track without your having to spend even a moment on hold.

🖙 **Flashing question mark folder:** Although it's unlikely that you'll ever see the sad Mac, most users eventually encounter the flashing question-mark-on-a-folder icon (which looks something like the one shown in the margin) in place of the usual happy Mac. This icon means that your Mac can't find a startup disk, hard drive, or CD-ROM containing a valid Macintosh operating system. See Chapter 18 to try and ease your Mac's ills.

How do you know which version of the Mac OS your computer has? Simple. Just choose About This Mac from the menu in the upper-left corner of the Finder's menu bar. The About This Mac window pops up in the middle of your screen, as shown in Figure 1-2. In the upper-right corner of this window, you find the version number of the Mac OS you're using.

Figure 1-2:
About This Mac tells you which version of Mac OS X you're running.

Shutting down properly

Turning off the power without shutting your Mac down properly is one of the worst things you can do to your poor Mac. Not shutting down your Mac properly can really screw up your hard drive, scramble the contents of your most important files, or both.

The legend of the boot

Boot this. Boot that. "I booted my Mac and...." or "Did it boot?" and so on. Talking about computers for long without hearing the boot word is nearly impossible. But why boot? Why not shoe or shirt or even shazam?

Back in the very olden days — maybe the 1970s or a little earlier — starting up a computer required you to toggle little manual switches on the front panel, which began an internal process that loaded the operating system. The process became known as *bootstrapping* because if you toggled the right switches, the computer would "pull itself up by its bootstraps."

This phrase didn't take long to transmogrify into *booting* and finally to *boot*.

Over the years, booting has come to mean turning on almost any computer, or even a peripheral device such as a printer. Some people also use it to refer to launching an application: "I booted Excel."

So the next time one of your gearhead friends says the b-word, ask whether he knows where the term comes from. Then dazzle him with the depth and breadth of your (not quite useful) knowledge!

Eternally yours . . . *now*

Mac OS X is designed so you never have to shut it down. You can configure it to sleep after a specified period of inactivity (see Chapter 15 for more info on the Energy Saver features of OS X). If you do so, your Mac will consume very little electricity when it's sleeping and will be ready to use just a few seconds after you awaken it by pressing any key or clicking the mouse. On the other hand, if you're not going to be using it for a few days, you may want to shut it down anyway.

Note: If you leave your Mac on constantly and you're gone when a lightning storm or rolling blackout hits, your Mac may well get wasted. So be sure you have adequate protection if you decide to leave your Mac on and unattended for long periods. See the next section for more info on lightning and your Mac.

If there's a thunderstorm nearby, or if you're unfortunate enough to live where there are rolling blackouts, you *really* should shut your Mac down (see the next section where we briefly discuss lightning and your Mac).

To turn off your Mac, always use the Shut Down command on the menu, or press the Power key once and then click the Shut Down button. On new Apple Pro keyboards, which don't have a Power key, press Ctrl+Eject and then click the Shut Down button.

Of course, most of us have broken this rule several times without anything horrible happening. Don't be lulled into a false sense of security, however. Break the rules one time too many or under the wrong circumstances, and your most important file *will* be toast. The only times you should turn off your Mac without shutting down properly is if your screen is frozen or if you crash and can't do anything else. This doesn't happen often, but when it does, turning your Mac off and then back on is the only solution. Sometimes even that doesn't work, and you may have to unplug the computer from the power outlet to get it to reboot.

A few things you should definitely NOT do with your Mac

In this section, we deal with the bad stuff that can happen to your computer if you do the wrong things with it. (If something bad has already happened to you, see Chapter 18.)

✔ **Don't unplug your Mac when it's turned on.** Very bad things can happen, such as having your operating system break. See the preceding section where we discuss shutting your system down properly.

✔ **Don't use your Mac when lightning is near.** Here's a simple life equation for you: Mac + lightning = dead Mac. 'Nuff said. Oh, and don't place much faith in inexpensive surge protectors. A good jolt of lightning will fry the surge protector right along with your computer. Some surge protectors can withstand most lightning strikes, but these warriors are not the cheapies you buy at your local computer emporium. Unplugging your Mac from the wall during electrical storms is safer and less expensive. (Don't forget to unplug your external modem, network hubs, or other hardware that plugs into the wall as well — lightning can fry them, too.)

✔ **Don't jostle, bump, shake, kick, throw, dribble, or punt your Mac, especially while it's running.** Your Mac contains a hard drive that spins at 5,400+ *revolutions per minute* (rpm). A jolt to a hard drive while it's reading or writing a file can cause the head to crash into the disk, which can render many or all the files on it unrecoverable.

✔ **Don't forget to back up your data!** If the stuff on your hard drive means anything to you, you must back it up. Not maybe. You must. Even if your most important file is your last saved game of *Myth II: Soulblighter,* you still need to realize how important it is to back up your files.

In Chapter 17, we discuss how to back up your files, and we *strongly* recommend that you read Chapter 17 sooner rather than later — preferably before you do any significant work on your Mac.

Dr. Macintosh sez: "There are only two kinds of Mac users: those who have never lost data and those who will." Which kind will you be?

✔ **Don't kiss your monitor while wearing stuff on your lips.** For obvious reasons!

Point-and-click boot camp

Are you new to the Mac? Just learning how to move the mouse around? Now is a good time to go over some fundamental stuff you need to know for just about everything you'll be doing on the Mac. Spend a few minutes reading this section, and soon you'll be clicking, double-clicking, pressing, and pointing all over the place. If you think you've got the whole mousing thing pretty much figured out, feel free to skip this section. We'll catch you on the other side.

Still with us? Good. Now for some basic terminology.

✔ **Point:** Before you can click or press anything, you have to *point* to it. Place your hand on your mouse and move it so that the cursor arrow is over the object you want — like on top of an icon or a button — then click it to select it or double-click it to open it (if it's an application, or an icon that starts up an application). You point and then click — or *point-and-click*, in computer lingo.

✔ **Click:** (Also called *single-click.*) Use your index finger to push the mouse button all the way down and let go, so that it produces a satisfying click-ing sound. (If you have one of the new optical Apple Pro mice you push down the whole thing to click.) Use a single-click to highlight an icon, press a button, or activate a check box or window.

✔ **Double-click:** *Click twice* in rapid succession. With a little practice, you can perfect this technique in no time. Use a double-click to open a folder or to launch a file or application.

✔ **Drag:** *Dragging* something usually accompanies clicking it first. With the mouse button held down, move the mouse on your desk or mouse pad so that the cursor — and whatever you select — moves across the screen. The combination of pressing the mouse and dragging it is usu-ally referred to as *click-and-drag*.

✔ **Press:** A *press* is half a click. Instead of letting go of the mouse button to finish the click, keep holding it down. In most cases, your next step is to drag the mouse somewhere — down a menu to choose a command, or across the screen to move an object, for example.

✔ **Choosing an item from a menu:** To get to Mac OS menu commands, you must first open a menu and then pick the option you want. Point at the name of the menu you want with your mouse cursor, and then do one of the following:

  • Press your mouse button down (but don't let up yet) and then drag your mouse until you select the command you want. When the command is highlighted, finish selecting by letting go of the mouse button.

  • Click once (on the menu's name). The menu drops down and remains open. Now drag your mouse down until the command you want is highlighted and then click.

A pop quiz on mousing

For those of you who need to hone your mousing skills, here's a little quiz:

1. **How do you select an icon?**

   A. Stare at it intently for five seconds.

   B. Point to it with your finger, slap the side of your monitor, and say "That one, stupid!"

   C. Move the mouse pointer on top of the icon and click once.

2. **When do you need to double-click?**

   A. Whenever you find yourself saying, "There's no place like home."

   B. When you're using both hands to control the mouse.

   C. When you want to open a file or folder.

3. **How do you select multiple items or blocks of text?**

   A. Get several people to stare intently at the items you want to select.

   B. Attach multiple mice to your Mac.

   C. Slide the mouse, moving the on-screen pointer to the location where you want to begin selecting. Press and hold down the mouse button. Drag the pointer across the items or text that you want to select. Then let go of the mouse button.

4. **How do you move a selected item?**

   A. Call U-Haul.

   B. Pick up and tilt your monitor until the item slides to the proper location.

   C. Point to the item and hold down (press) the mouse button. With the mouse button still held down, drag the pointer to the new location and let go of the mouse button.

If you haven't figured it out by now, the correct answer to each of these questions is C. If any other answer sounded remotely plausible, sit down with your Mac and just play with it for a while. If you have kids at your disposal, watch them play with your Mac. They'll show you how to use it in no time.

Chapter 2

Meet the Desktop

· ·

· ·

*T*his chapter — about the Macintosh Desktop — is where we get down to the nitty-gritty about the nifty new Mac OS X Desktop: the place where you start doing stuff with your Mac.

Those of you who've been using Mac OS for awhile may find some of the information in this chapter repetitive; some features we describe have not changed from earlier versions of the Mac OS. But in Mac OS X, much more is new than the version number. Although you still use the Desktop for many of the same tasks, it looks very different, with lots of new tools and features and terminology that you need to know before you can call yourself truly Mac OS X savvy. Besides, if you decide to skip this chapter — just because you think you have all the new stuff figured out — we assure you you'll miss out on sarcasm, clever wordplay, shortcuts, awesome techniques, a bad pun or two, and lots of good advice on making the Desktop an easier place to be. If that's not enough to convince you, we also provide a bunch of stuff Apple didn't bother to tell you (as if you read the manual anyway!).

Tantalized? Let's rock.

Clearing Off the Desktop

Just about everything you do on your Mac begins and ends with the Desktop; this is where you manage files, store documents, launch programs, adjust the way your Mac works, and much more. If you ever expect to master your Mac, the first step is to master the Desktop.

The terms *Desktop* and *Finder* are sometimes used interchangeably to refer to the total Macintosh environment you see — icons, windows, menus, and all that other cool stuff. Just to make things confusing, the background you see on your screen — the backdrop behind your hard drive icon and open windows — is also called the Desktop. In this book, we refer to the Finder as the Finder, which we discuss in Chapters 7 and 8. When we say "Desktop," we're talking about the background behind your windows and dock, where your hard drive icon appears.

Got it? The Desktop is convenient and fast. Put stuff there. Figure 2-1 shows the default Mac OS X Desktop.

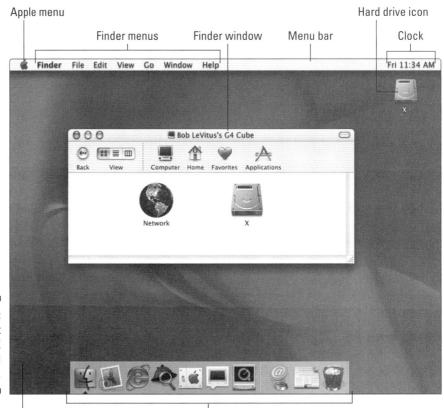

Figure 2-1:
The default
Mac OS X
Finder and
Desktop.

Touring the Desktop

Because the Desktop is the center of your Mac OS experience, before you go any further, check out its most prominent features:

- ✔ **The Desktop itself:** *The Desktop* is the area behind the windows and the Dock, where your hard drive icon lives. The Desktop isn't a window, yet it acts like one. Like a folder window or drive window, the Desktop can contain icons. But unlike most windows, which require a bit of navigation to get to, the Desktop is a great place for things you use a lot, such as folders, applications, or documents. The next section discusses the default icons you see on the Desktop when you first load up Mac OS X.

- ✔ **The Dock:** *The Dock* is the Finder's main navigation shortcut tool. It makes it easy to get to frequently used icons, even when you have a screen full of windows. Like the Desktop, the Dock is a great place for things you use a lot, such as folders, applications, or particular documents. It puts your frequently used icons at your fingertips, and, as we show in the Chapter 3, it's almost infinitely customizable, too.

  If you used an earlier version of Mac OS, think of the Dock as the OS X version of the Apple () menu in Mac OS versions of the past. Yes, the OS X Finder *does* have an menu, but it doesn't work at all like the menu in earlier versions of Mac OS (see Chapter 6 for more info on the menu).

- ✔ **Icons:** *Icons* are the little pictures you see in your windows and on your Desktop. All icons are containers that hold things that you work with on your Mac, such as programs and documents. In Chapter 4, we cover icons in detail, and the next section discusses the icons that you see on the OS X Desktop when you first boot up Mac OS X.

- ✔ **Windows:** Opening most icons (by double-clicking them) makes a window appear. *Windows* in the Finder show you the contents of hard drive and folder icons, and windows in applications usually show you the contents of your documents. For the full scoop on windows, check out Chapter 5.

- ✔ **Menus:** *Menus* let you choose to do things, such as create new folders, duplicate files, cut, copy or paste text, and so on. You can find out all about them in Chapter 6.

- ✔ **Aliases:** *Alias* icons help keep things organized. When you open an alias icon, it automatically opens some other icon (which is known as its *parent icon*). Use aliases of things you use often so that you can keep the originals tucked away in one of your perfectly organized folders. You can check out aliases in Chapter 4.

  If all these new terms such as aliaes, Dock, and so on seem strange to you, don't worry — these will be explained in detail in the rest of the chapters in Part I.

Sniffing out the default Desktop icons

Icons on the Desktop behave the same as icons in a window (we discuss icons in Chapter 4). You move them and copy them in the same way you would an icon in a window. The only difference is that Desktop items are not in a window; they're on the Desktop, which makes them more convenient to use.

Actually, if you look at your home directory (click the Home button on the toolbar) you see a folder named `Desktop` that contains the same icons you placed on the Desktop. The reason for this folder is that each user has an individual Desktop. But we're getting ahead of ourselves. Read more about your home directory, users, and all that jazz in later chapters of this book.

To move an item to the Desktop, simply click its icon in a window and drag it onto the Desktop.

- **Hard drive icon:** The first icon you should become familiar with is the icon for your hard drive. You can usually find it on the upper-right side of your Finder window when you first start your Mac (refer to Figure 2-1). Look for the name Macintosh HD, iMac HD, or something like that (unless you've renamed it).

- **Disk icons:** Disk icons always appear on the Desktop. When you insert a CD-ROM or DVD disc, its icon appears on the Desktop just below your hard drive icon (space permitting).

  If you don't see a disk icon on your Desktop, skip ahead to Chapter 6, where we discuss Finder preferences. That's where you can choose whether to see disks on your Desktop.

- **All and sundry:** In Figure 2-2, you see two new icons (just below Bob's two hard drive icons on the right): `a picture.tiff`, which is a picture document, and Grab, which is an alias for a program. (Check out more info about aliases in Chapter 4.)

Picture this: A picture on your Desktop

We'd be remiss if we didn't mention that you can change the background picture of your Desktop. If you're sick of the default Desktop picture, here's how to change your Desktop picture:

1. **Choose Finder⇨Preferences from the Finder menu.**

   The Finder Preferences window appears.

2. **Click the Select Picture button; if the only button you see reads** Remove Picture, **click it once and it changes back to** Select Picture.

3. **Choose a new picture for your Desktop.**

   If you don't know how to choose a picture using the Open File dialog box, find out how in Chapter 8.

In Figure 2-3, see Bob's Desktop with a background picture of his son Jacob standing on the field of a Miami Fusion soccer game. (If you want a reminder of what the default Desktop background looks like, refer to Figure 2-1.)

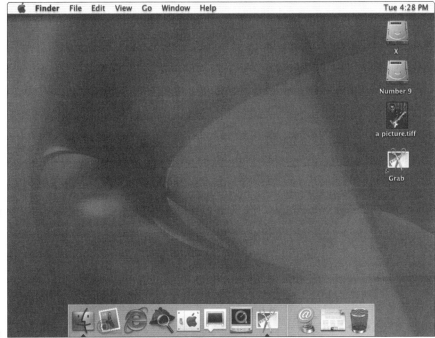

Figure 2-2: The Desktop is a good place to keep oft-needed icons.

Figure 2-3:
Bob's
beautified
Desktop.

Chapter 3

"What's Up, Dock?"

*I*n this chapter, we take a look at the *Dock*, a section of the Desktop that gives you both quick access to frequently used applications and a quick way to bring a file or application that's already open to the front so that you can work with it. Read on to discover how to use the Dock and how to customize it so that it works and looks just the way you want.

Running Down the Dock

We show you how to work with icons in the next section, but first take a minute to look at the row of pictures at the bottom of the your Mac OS X Finder screen. That row, ladies and gentlemen, is the Dock (as shown in Figure 3-1), and those individual pictures are known as *icons* (which we discuss in Chapter 4). When you click a dock icon, you:

🖊 **Open applications, files, or folders**

or

🖊 **Bring an open application, file, or folder to the front of all others**

Figure 3-1:
The Dock and all its default icons.

By default, the Dock contains a number of commonly used Mac OS X applications, and you can also store your own applications, files, or folders there. We show you how to do that in the "Adding icons to the Dock" section later in this chapter.

Most of the items that you find on the Dock when you first use Mac OS X are probably familiar to you already. If they aren't, they certainly will be in time. In the following sections, we give you a brief description of each, moving from left to right along the Dock, and we point you to other parts of this book where we cover an item in more detail.

The Dock is a great place to store your favorite icons and have quick access to them, but don't confuse the Dock with Favorites — you know, those files, folders, or URLs that you see when you click the Favorites button in the toolbar at the top of Finder windows. Adding to Favorites does not affect the Dock's inventory; likewise, putting an item on the Dock does not add it to your list of Favorites.

Finder

The Finder application (which we discuss at length in Chapters 7 and 8) is always open. Click the Finder icon (shown in the margin) to open a Finder window. If a Finder window is already open and you click the Finder icon on the Dock, a new Finder window will open in front of it. You can open as many Finder windows as you like by choosing File⇨New Finder Window or using the keyboard shortcut ⌘+N.

Mail

Click this icon to launch Apple's OS X e-mail application, appropriately named *Mail,* with which you can send and receive e-mail. We describe Mail in glorious detail in Chapter 11.

Internet Explorer

Microsoft's Internet Explorer is the Web browser included with Mac OS X. Click this Dock icon to launch Internet Explorer, which we discuss in detail in Chapter 11. You may have seen its lowercase *e* icon before — especially on Windows machines.

Sherlock

 Use the Sherlock application to find things — on your hard drive, on a server, or on the Internet. Sherlock can search your hard drive for lost files, use Internet search engines to find Web sites, and search for people, product prices, and even keywords in the news. Track down more info on Sherlock in Chapter 11.

System Preferences

 Click the System Preferences icon on the Dock to open the System Preferences application. System Preferences (which we describe in Chapter 15) gives you access to all sorts of settings that you use to configure your Mac just the way you like it. Clicking the Dock icon (as shown in Figure 3-1) is just the same as choosing System Preferences from the Apple ()menu.

QuickTime Player

 QuickTime is Apple's multimedia application, providing you with a format for recording and playing movies, audio programs, and streaming audio and video. Open QuickTime by clicking the QuickTime Player icon. From the QuickTime viewer window that appears, you can view QuickTime TV over the Internet or view QuickTime movies from disks or CD-ROMs.

Apple — Mac OS X

 The Apple — Mac OS X icon launches your Web browser (Internet Explorer by default) and takes you to the Mac OS X section of Apple's Web site.

Late Breaking News

 This icon launches the Apple Help Viewer and displays any information Apple wants to make available to you about the software you installed. For more info on Mac Help, check out Chapter 5.

Trash

 The Trash icon is unique among Dock items: It's not a file or application that you open. Instead, you drag things to this icon to get rid of them.

Don't want it? Trash it

The Trash is a special container where you put stuff that you no longer want on your hard drive or removable media storage devices (such as a Zip disk or SuperDisk). Got four copies of TextEdit on your hard drive? Drag three of them to the Trash. Tired of tripping over old letters that you don't want to keep? Drag them to the Trash, too. To put something in the Trash, just drag its icon on top of the Trash icon and watch it disappear. Then you just have to empty the trash (see the next section).

Like other icons, you know you've connected with the Trash while dragging when the trash icon is highlighted. And like other Dock icons, the Trash icon's name appears when you move the cursor over the icon.

Taking out the trash

You know how the garbage in the trash can sits there until the sanitation engineers come by and pick it up each week? The Mac OS X Trash works the same. When you put something in the Trash, it sits there until you choose Finder⇨Empty Trash or press ⌘+Shift+Delete.

Think twice before you invoke the Empty Trash command. After you empty the Trash, the files it contained are (usually) gone forever. Our advice: Before you get too bold, read this book's Appendix and back up your hard drive several times. After you get proficient at backups, even though the files are technically gone forever from your hard drive, you can get them back if you like (we hope).

While items sit in the Trash, waiting for you to empty it, the Trash basket shows you that there are files waiting for you there . . . just like in real life, your unemptied Trash is full of garbage.

You can also empty the Trash by pressing the mouse button and holding it down while hovering your mouse cursor over the Trash icon on the Dock for a second or two. The Empty Trash menu pops up like magic. Move your mouse over it to select it and then release the mouse button.

Digging stuff out of the Trash (yech!)

As with all icons, you can open the Trash to see what's in there — just click its icon in the Dock. If you decide that you don't want to get rid of an item that's already in the Trash, just drag it back out, either onto the Finder or back into the folder where it belongs.

Use a utility program to retrieve a trashed file after you empty the Trash: DiskWarrior, Norton Utilities, and Tech Tool Pro are the three most popular. They don't have a 100-percent success rate, though, so you should still consider using the Empty Trash command as fatal to your files. Also, as of this writing, none of them were Mac OS X compatible, though they should all be by the time you read this.

Workin' the Dock

The Dock is a convenient way to get at oft-used icons. By default, the Dock comes pre-stocked with icons that Apple thinks you'll need most frequently (we show you these in the previous section), but can be customized to contain any icons you choose. In this section you'll learn all about the Dock — how to use it, how to customize it, how to resize it, and more.

Of mice and Dock icons

Dock icons work just like other icons except that instead of double-clicking them, you only single-click them. (We discuss icons in Chapter 4.) Note that when you single-click a Dock icon, the chosen Dock icon moves up and out of its place on the Dock for a moment, letting you know that you've activated it. Check out Figure 3-2 to see an animated Dock icon — it's still on the Dock, but it's raised higher than the inactive ones.

Figure 3-2:
A raised
Dock icon:
selected
and
opening.

Black triangle indicates an active icon.

When an application on the Dock is open, an up arrow (it looks like a small black pyramid) appears below its Dock icon, just like you see in Figure 3-2.

To discover the name of a Dock icon, just move your cursor over any item on the Dock and the item's name appears above it (as shown in Figure 3-3). This feature is quite handy because you can't view Dock items as a list in the same the way that you can with icons that are stored in windows. And, as you can read in the "Resizing the Dock" section later in this chapter, you can resize the Dock to make the icons smaller (which does make them more difficult to see). Hovering your mouse cursor to discover the name of a teeny icon makes this feature even more useful.

Figure 3-3:
Move your
cursor over
a Dock icon
to display
its name.

Adding icons to the Dock

You can customize your Dock with favorite applications, a document you update daily, or maybe a folder containing your favorite recipes — whatever you need quick access to. The following sections tell you what kind of stuff to put on the Dock and how to add an icon to the Dock.

Knowing what to put on the Dock

Put things on the Dock that you need quick access to and that you use often, or add items that aren't quickly available from menus or the toolbar. If you like using the Dock better than the Go menu or the Finder window toolbar, for example, add your Documents folder to the Dock.

We suggest adding these items to your Dock.

- ✔ **A word processing application:** Most people use word processing software more than any other application.

- ✔ **A project folder:** Suppose that you follow our advice and store all the files that you create in the Documents folder, or subfolders thereof. One of those subfolders contains all the documents for your thesis, or the biggest project you have at work, or your massive recipe collection . . . whatever. Add that folder to the Dock and then you can access it much more quickly than if you have to open your Documents folder first.

- ✔ **A special utility or application:** The Grab application is an essential part of our work with Mac OS X because we use it to take screen shots. You may prefer to have handy a file transfer protocol (FTP) application (used to download files from the Internet), a graphics application such as Photoshop, or a calendar program. (We talk about some Mac OS X applications in Chapter 13.)

- ✔ **Your favorite URL:** Save a link to a site that you visit every day — one that you use in your job, or a favorite news site, or your personalized page from an Internet service provider (ISP). Sure, you can make one of these pages your browser's start page, but the Dock lets you add one or more additional URLs.

Here's how to quickly add a URL to the Dock. Open Internet Explorer (IE) and go to the page with a URL that you want to save on the Dock. Click and drag the small icon you find at the left of the URL in the Address bar (see Figure 3-4) to the right side of the Dock, and then release the mouse button. Your URL is now in place. When you click the URL icon that you move to your Dock, IE opens to that page. You can add several URL icons to the Dock, but bear in mind that the Dock and its icons shrink to accommodate added icons, making them harder to see. Perhaps the best idea if you want easy access to several URLs is to create a folder full of URLs and put the folder on the Dock. Then you can just hover your mouse cursor over the folder and then press and hold the mouse button to pop up a menu with all your URLs.

Figure 3-4:
Drag a URL's
icon from
the IE
Address bar.

Keep in mind that even though you can make the Dock smaller, you're still limited to one row of icons. The smaller that you make the Dock, the larger the crowd of icons that you can amass. You have to determine for yourself what's best for you: having lots of icons available on the Dock that may be difficult to see because they're so tiny; or having less clutter but fewer icons on your Dock.

Adding an icon to the Dock

Adding an application, file, or folder to the Dock is as simple as dragging it there. Follow these steps to add an icon to the Dock:

1. **Open a Finder window containing an application, file, or folder that you use frequently.**

   As you can see in Figure 3-5, we chose the Grab application (it's high-lighted); we use Grab constantly to take the pictures of Mac OS you see throughout this book. (Find the Grab application, if you're interested, in the Utilities folder inside your Applications folder, which we discuss in Chapter 13.)

2. **Click the item that you want to add to the Dock and drag it out of the Finder window and onto the Dock as in Figure 3-5.**

   An icon for this item now appears on the Dock.

Figure 3-5:
Dragging an
icon onto
the Dock to
add it.

You can add several items at the same time to the Dock by selecting them all and dragging the group to the Dock. However, you can delete only one icon at a time from the Dock (see the next section).

Removing an icon from the Dock

To remove an item from the Dock, just drag its icon onto the Desktop. It disappears with a cool *poof* animation. By moving an icon out of the Dock, you aren't moving or copying the item itself — you're just removing its icon from the Dock. It makes no sense to us, but hey, that's how it works.

When you open an application with an icon that doesn't ordinarily appear on the Dock, its icon magically appears on the Dock until you quit that application. When you do, its icon magically disappears from the Dock. In other words, you'll see a temporary Dock icon for every program that's currently open; these temporary icons disappear when you quit the program.

Setting Dock preferences

You can change a few things about the Dock to make it look and behave just the way you want it to. To do so, just choose Dock⟹Dock Preferences from the menu in the upper-left corner of the Finder's menu bar) on your Desktop. In the Dock window that opens (see Figure 3-6), you can adjust your Dock with the following preferences:

✔ **Dock Size:** Note the slider bar here. Move this slider to the right (larger) or left (smaller) to adjust the size of the Dock on your Finder. As you move the slider, watch the Dock change size. Now *there's* a fun way to spend a Saturday afternoon!

As you add items to the Dock, each icon — and the Dock itself — shrinks to accommodate the new ones.

✔ **Magnification:** This slider controls how big icons grow when you pass the arrow cursor over them. Or you can deselect this check box to turn off magnification entirely.

✔ **Automatically hide and show the Dock:** Don't like the Dock? Maybe you want to free up the screen real estate at the bottom of your monitor? Then select the Auto Hide and Show check box; after that, the Dock displays itself only when you move the cursor to the bottom of the screen where the dock would ordinarily appear. It's like magic! (Okay, it's like Windows, but we hate to admit it.)

If the Dock is not visible, deselect (that is, uncheck) this Auto Hide and Show check box to bring it back. The option remains turned off unless you change it or choose Dock⇨Turn Hiding Off from the menu or press ⌘+Option+D.

✔ **Animate Opening Applications:** Mac OS X animates (bounces) Dock icons when you click them to open an item. If you don't like that option, deselect this check box and the bouncing animation will cease evermore.

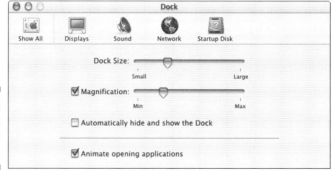

Figure 3-6:
The Dock
Preferences
window.

Resizing the Dock

If the default size of the Dock bugs you, you can make the Dock smaller and save yourself a lot of screen real estate. This space comes in especially handy when you add your own stuff to the Dock.

Shrink or enlarge the Dock (and its icons) by dragging its sizer handle. To make it appear, move your cursor over the thin white line that appears on the right side of the Dock (as you see in the margin). Drag the sizer down to make the Dock smaller, holding onto the mouse button until you find the size you like. The more you drag this control down, the smaller the Dock gets (see Figure 3-7). To enlarge the Dock again, just drag the sizer back up. Poof! Big Dock! You can enlarge the Dock until it fills your screen from side to side.

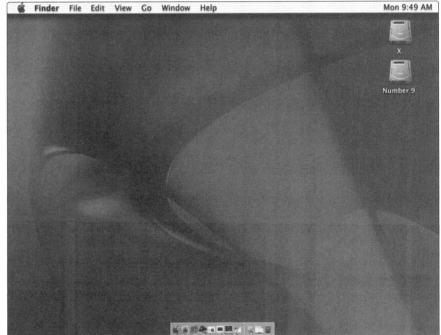

Figure 3-7:
The Desktop
with a cute
little Dock.

Check out the teeny tiny Dock.

Chapter 4

I Think Icon! I Think Icon!

*I*f you're going to use a Macintosh, you're going to use icons. Period. They are a fundamental part what makes a Mac a Mac. We discuss icons some in Chapters 2 and 3, but now we're going to get down to the real nitty gritty and explain them in great detail.

Trust us: By the time you finish this chapter, you'll be so familiar with all the different types of icons Mac OS X has to offer that you'll probably dream of them tonight.

Introducing . . . Icons!

Icons are those funny little pictographs in your windows. Icons represent things that you work with on your Mac, such as programs, documents, and folders.

Icons come in several shapes and sizes. After you've been around the Macintosh for a while, you get a sixth sense about what an icon contains just by looking at it. You'll find three main types of icons: applications, documents, and folders. Well, there are actually four types — aliases are an icon type in their own right. Don't worry; we take a look at all four icon types in the following sections.

Don't confuse icons with buttons; they're sort of alike, but they're different. When you click a button, something (such as a file, an application, or a folder) opens — *buttons* are simply pointers. *Icons* actually represent things on your hard drive, like folders and applications. You can only move buttons to a limited number of places (such as the toolbar or Dock, but you can't move a button onto the Desktop, or into a window). You can move icons almost anywhere in the Finder — in a window or on the Desktop — but you can't move an icon into the menu bar. And although you double-click icons to open them, you single-click buttons. The toolbar items in the Finder (see Figure 4-1; we discuss these in detail in Chapter 6) are good examples of buttons. And while it may be a stretch to call items in the Dock "buttons," they act like buttons in that you single-click them to open them.

Application icons

Application icons are linked to programs — the software that you use to accomplish tasks on your Mac. Your word processor is an application. So are AOL and Adobe Photoshop. Myth II and Quake III are also applications (and great games to boot).

Application icons come in a variety of shapes. For example, *application* (*application* means program) *icons* are often square-ish. Sometimes, though, they're diamond-shaped, rectangular, or just oddly shaped. In Figure 4-1 you can see icons of various shapes).

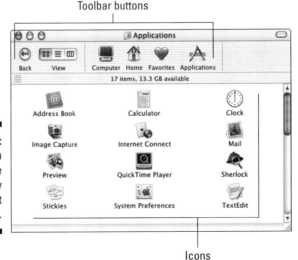

Figure 4-1: Application icons come in many different shapes.

Document icons

Document icons are files created by applications. A letter to your mom, which you can create in AppleWorks (formerly known as ClarisWorks) or Microsoft Word, is a document. So are Bob's latest column and his Quicken Data file. Document icons are almost always reminiscent of a piece of paper, as shown in Figure 4-2.

Figure 4-2: Four typical document icons.

Folder icons

Folder icons are the Mac's organizational containers. You put icons, usually application or document icons, into folders. You can also put folders inside other folders. Folders look like . . . well, folders . . . and can contain just about any other icon. You use folders to organize your files and applications on your hard drive. You can have as many folders as you want, so don't be afraid to create new ones. The thought behind the whole folders thing is pretty obvious — if your hard drive is a filing cabinet, then folders are its drawers and folders (duh!). Figure 4-3 shows some typical folder icons.

Figure 4-3: A couple run-of-the-mill folder icons.

Aliases

Aliases are wonderful — no, *fabulous* — organizational tools that Apple introduced in the days of Mac OS 7. (Although Mac OS 7 was originally called *System* 7, Apple didn't begin the Mac OS designation until version 7.6.) We like aliases so much, in fact, we thought they deserved their very own section. See the next section for more info on this ultra-useful tool and see Figure 4-4 to check out what an alias icon looks like.

Figure 4-4:
An alias icon (right) and its parent (left).

Aliases: The Greatest Invention Since Sliced Bread

An *alias* is a tiny file that automatically opens the file it represents. While an alias is technically an icon, it's actually an icon that opens another icon automatically. You can put aliases in convenient places, such as the Desktop, to help you open programs and files that you access often easily.

Microsoft stole the alias feature from Apple (if you've used Windows, you may know aliases as *shortcuts*). But what else is new?

An alias is different from a duplicated file. For example, Microsoft's Word 2001 word processor uses 9.7 megabytes (MB) of disk space. If we duplicate it, we have two files, each using 9.7 MB of disk space. An alias of Microsoft Word, on the other hand, uses a mere 4 kilobytes (KB).

So why do we think that aliases are so great? Well, here's a few good reasons:

✔ **Aliases enable you to make items appear to be in more than one place, which on many occasions is exactly what you want to do.** For example, keeping an alias of your word processor on your Desktop and another on the Dock is convenient. You may even want a third alias of it in your Documents folder for quick access. Aliases enable you to open your word processor quickly and easily without navigating into the depths of your Applications folder each time that you need it.

✔ **You can create aliases and store them simultaneously to represent the same document in several different folders.** This is a great help when you need to file a document that could logically be stored in any one of several files. For example, if you write a memo to Fred Smith about the Smythe Marketing Campaign to be executed in the fourth quarter, which folder does the document go in? Smith? Smythe? Marketing? Memos? 4th Quarter? With aliases, it doesn't matter. You can put the actual file in any folder, and then create aliases of the file, placing them in any other applicable folder. Now you can search for a specific document in several places; whichever pertinent folder you open, you can find the memo.

✔ **Some programs need to remain in the same folder as their supporting files and folders, but with aliases, you can pretend to move.** Many Classic programs, for example, won't function properly unless they're in the same folder as their dictionaries, thesauruses, data files (for games), templates, and so on. Thus, without an alias, you can't put those programs on the Desktop without impairing their functionality.

Creating aliases

When you create an alias, its icon looks the same as the icon it represents, but the suffix `alias` is tacked onto its name and a tiny arrow called a *badge* appears in the lower left corner of its icon. Look back at Figure 4-4 to see both an alias and its *parent icon* (that is, the icon that will open if you open the alias).

To create an alias for an icon, do one of the following:

✔ **Click the parent icon and choose File➪Make Alias.**

✔ **Click the parent icon and press ⌘+L.**

✔ **Click any file or folder, press and hold down the ⌘ and Option keys, and drag the file or folder to either another folder or to the Desktop while holding down the ⌘ and Option keys.** Presto! An alias appears in the target folder (or Desktop) immediately. Better still, aliases created this way don't have that pesky `alias` suffix tacked onto them.

✔ **Choose File➪Add to Favorites (or press ⌘+T) to automatically create an alias and place it in the Favorites folder. Henceforth, that alias appears when you click the Favorites button from the toolbar or choose Go➪Favorites➪Go To Favorites.**

✔ **Click an icon while holding down the Control key and choose the Make Alias command from the *contextual menu* that appears.** The alias appears in the same folder as its parent. (We explore contextual menus — which are very cool context-sensitive pop-up menus — in Chapter 6.)

The temporary alias theory

The Desktop is an excellent place to keep the things you need most often — whether you use aliases of documents or save the actual files on the Desktop until you figure out where you want to store them. For example, when Bob first creates a file, he saves it in its proper folder inside the Documents folder somewhere. If it's a document that he plans to work on for more than a day or two, such as a magazine article, he makes an alias of the document (or folder) and plops it on the Desktop. After he finish the article and submits it to an editor, he trashes the alias, leaving the original file stashed away in its proper folder.

Of course, you can place that same folder in the Dock as well, so you can use the press-and-hold trick to open its subfolders. But nothing says you can't have an item appear several places at once for maximum convenience.

Incidentally, a similar technique can be used without the aliases. Just save all your new documents on the Desktop (yourhomefolder/ Library/Desktop). Later, when you're finished with the documents, you can file them away in their proper folders.

Deleting aliases

This is a short section because this is such an easy chore. To delete an alias, drag it onto the Trash icon on the Dock. That's it!

Deleting an alias does *not* delete the parent item (if you want to do delete the parent item, you'll have to go hunt it down and kill it yourself).

Finding an alias's parent

Say you create an alias of a file, and later want to delete both the alias and its parent file. But you can't find the parent file! What to do? Well, you could use Sherlock to find it (we discuss Sherlock in Chapter 11), but the fastest way to find the parent icon of an alias is to select the alias (single-click) and then choose File⇨Show Original or press ⌘+R.

Playing with Icons

After checking out the different types of icons, it's time to see what you can do to them! In the upcoming sections, we show you how to open, rename, get rid of, and select icons. In a matter of moments, you'll be an icon pro!

Open sez me! Opening icons

You can open any icon in the following four ways:

- ✔ Click the icon once to select it, and then choose File⇨Open.
- ✔ Double-click the icon by clicking it twice in rapid succession. If it doesn't open, you double-clicked too slowly.
- ✔ To open an icon without having to use your mouse, select the icon, and then press either ⌘+O or ⌘+↓.
- ✔ Click the icon while holding down the Control key and use the contextual menu's Open command.

Of course, you can also open any folder or document icon from within an application — skip ahead to Chapter 8 for more on that.

Getting rid of icons

To get rid of an icon — any icon — merely drag it to the Trash on your Dock. (See Chapter 3 for more info on the Dock and the Trash.)

Playing the icon name game (renaming icons)

Icon, icon-a, bo-bicon, banana fanna fo-ficon. Betcha that you can change the name of any old icon!

Navigating icons like a supergeek

In addition to the old point-and-click method of navigating icons, you can also move among icons by using the keyboard. In an active window, make sure that no icons are selected and then type the first letter of a file's name. In all views, the first icon that starts with that letter is selected. To move to the next icon alphabetically, press the Tab key. To move to the icon in previous alphabetical order, press Shift+Tab.

If more than one icon begins with the same letter, type in more than one letter to further restrict the possible results. Suppose you have three folders in the same window that all begin with *A: Applications, Abstracts,* and *Aunt* Mary's Stuff. To isolate the Applications folder, type **app**.

If no window is active, typing a letter selects the first icon on the Desktop that starts with that letter.

That's not entirely true. If an icon is locked (see the upcoming section "Information"), busy (an application that's currently open), or you don't have the administrator's permission to rename that icon (see Chapter 16 for details about permissions), you won't be able to rename it. Similarly, you can't rename certain *reserved* icons, such as the Library or Desktop folders.

To rename an icon, you can either click the icon's name directly (don't click the icon itself because that selects the icon) or you can click the icon and then press Return (or Enter) on your keyboard once.

Either way, the icon's name is selected, the icon is surrounded with a box, and you can now type in a new name (as in Figure 4-5). In addition to selecting the name, the cursor changes from a pointer to a text-editing I-beam. An *I-beam cursor* (shown in the margin) is the Mac's way of telling you that you can type now. At this point, if you click the I-beam cursor anywhere in the name box, you can edit the icon's original name. If you don't click the I-beam cursor in the name box but just begin typing, the icon's original name is replaced by what you type.

If you've never changed an icon's name, give it a try. And don't forget: If you click the icon itself, the icon is selected and you won't be able to change its name. If you do accidentally select the icon, just press Return (or Enter) one time to edit the name of the icon.

Figure 4-5:
Changing an icon's name by typing over the old one.

Selecting multiple icons

Sometimes you want to move or copy several items into a single folder. The process is pretty much the same as it is when you copy one file or folder (that is, you just drag the icon to where you want it and drop it there). But you first need to select all of the items you want before you can drag them, en masse, to their destination. You'll find the following method a lot more convenient than selecting and copying files one at a time.

1. **To select more than one icon in a folder, do either one of the following:**

   • Click once within the folder window (don't click on any one icon) and drag your mouse while continuing to hold down the mouse button. You see an outline of a box around the icons as you drag, and icons within or touching the box become highlighted. (See Figure 4-6.)

   • Click one icon and then hold down the Shift key as you click others. As long as you hold down the Shift key, each new icon you click and every icon beween it and the first icon you clicked is added to the selection.

   • Click one icon and then hold down the Command (⌘) key as you click others. The difference between using the Shift and ⌘ keys is that the ⌘ key will not select everything between it and the first icon you clicked. Instead, only items you actually click on are added to the selection.

   To deselect an icon selected in any of these three ways, click it while holding down the ⌘ key.

2. **When you've selected all the items you want, click one of them (don't click anywhere else, or you'll deselect the icons you just selected) and drag (or Option+drag) them to the location where you want to move (or copy) them.**

Figure 4-6:
Selecting more than one icon with your mouse.

Be careful with multiple selections, especially when you drag icons to the Trash. You can easily and accidentally select more than one icon, so watch out that you don't put an icon in the Trash accidentally by not paying close attention.

Info-mation

Every icon has an Info window that gives you (surprise!) information about that icon and enables you to choose which other users (if any) you want to have the *privilege* of using this icon. (We discuss sharing files and privileges in detail in Chapter 16.) The Info window is also where you lock an icon so that it can't be renamed or dragged to the Trash.

To see an icon's Info window, click the icon and choose File⟳Show Info (or press ⌘+I) The Info window for that icon appears, as in Figure 4-7, which shows the Info window for the QuickTime Player icon.

Documents, folders, and disks each have slightly different Info windows.

The Show pop-up menu determines what information the Info window shows about an icon. The Show pop-up menu contains the following four options.

✔ **General Information:** This option (you guessed it!) shows general information about an icon, including the following information:

- **Kind:** Shows you what kind of file this is — an application, document, disk, folder, and so on.
- **Size:** Tells you how much disk space this file uses.
- **Where:** Shows you the path to the folder that contains this file.
- **Created:** Tells you the date and time this file was created.
- **Modified:** Tells you the date and time this file was last modified (that is, saved).
- **Version:** Shows copyright information and the file's version number.

✔ **Applications:** Manages the language that the application uses for menus and dialog boxes. Note that this option only appears if you're using an Info window to look at certain application programs.

✔ **Preview:** When you select a document icon, you can see a glimpse of what's in that document.

You can also see this preview when you select a document icon in Columns view — it magically appears in the rightmost column.

✔ **Privileges:** Governs which users have access to this icon. We discuss privileges in Chapter 16.

In addition to the Show pop-up menu, you also see the following features in the Info window:

✔ **The Locked check box:** Shows you whether you can change an icon's name or drag it to the Trash. When an application is *locked* (this check box will be checked), you can't change its name or drag it to the Trash. (We discuss the Trash in Chapter 3.)

Folders and disks can't be locked by merely clicking a check box (see the following tip); documents and applications can.

Folders and disks can be locked by merely selecting the Locked check box in the Info window. In previous versions of Mac OS, you had to open the Sharing panel of the Info (formerly known as Get Info) window, but Mac OS X conveniently allows you to lock a folder by selecting the Locked check box in the General Information area of the Info window. Yea!

✔ **The Comments text box:** Gives you the opportunity to enter (type in) your comments about the icon.

Figure 4-7:
A typical
Info window
for an
application
(QuickTime
Player, in
this case).

Chapter 5

Looking through Finder Windows

In This Chapter

▶ Of gumdrops and windows

▶ Keeping it small with scroll bars (not to be confused with whiskey bars)

▶ Knowing your active windows from your passive windows

▶ Dealie-boppers in windows

▶ Resizing, moving, and closing windows

*W*indows are and have always been an integral part of Macintosh computing. Windows on the Desktop show you the contents of hard drive and folder icons; windows in applications usually show you the contents of your documents. Along with the Desktop, Dock, icons, and menus, windows are just part of what makes your Mac a Mac, and so knowing how to use them is essential.

This chapter focuses on Finder windows. But after you get the hang of Finder windows, you pretty much know how all the windows you'll ever see on your Mac work. So don't worry. At the end of this brief chapter, you'll know all you need to operate any Mac window like a pro.

Anatomy of a Window

For the most part, windows are windows. As you use different programs, you'll probably notice that some of them (Adobe Photoshop or Microsoft Word, for example) take liberties with windows by adding features like pop-up menus, zoom percentage, and file size to the scroll bar area. Don't let it bug you. That extra fluff is just window dressing (pun intended).

Windows in programs running in the Classic environment look different — like Mac OS 9 windows. (We cover the Classic environment in Chapter 14.)

And so, without further ado, the following list gives you a look at the main features of a typical Finder window (shown in Figure 5-1). We discuss these features in greater detail in later sections of this chapter.

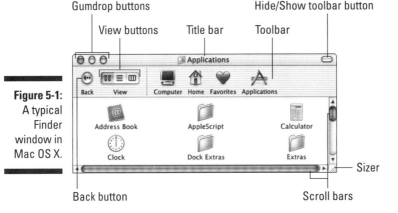

Gumdrop buttons · Hide/Show toolbar button · View buttons · Title bar · Toolbar

Figure 5-1: A typical Finder window in Mac OS X.

Back button · Scroll bars · Sizer

- ✔ **Title bar:** Shows the name of the window.
- ✔ **Scroll bars:** For moving around windows.
- ✔ **Toolbar:** Where frequently used items live.
- ✔ **Back button:** Takes you to the last folder you viewed.
- ✔ **View buttons:** Choose from three exciting views of your window.
- ✔ **Gumdrop buttons:** Shut 'em, shrink 'em, and make 'em grow. These buttons close, minimize, or expand a window, respectively.
- ✔ **Hide/Show toolbar button:** Causes your computer to melt into a puddle of molten silicon slag. Just kidding! This button actually does what its name implies — hides or shows the toolbar of a window.

Top o' the window to ya!

Take a gander at the top of a window — any window. You see three buttons in the upper-left corner and the name of the window in the top center. This section is called the *title bar*. These three buttons (called *gumdrop buttons* by some folks because they look like, well, gumdrops) are known as Close, Minimize, and Expand, and are colored red, yellow, and green. Here's what they do (from left to right):

✔ **Close (red):** Click this button to *close* the window.

✔ **Minimize (yellow):** Click this button to *minimize* the window. Minimizing appears to close the window, but instead of making it disappear, Minimize adds an icon for the window on the Dock. To view the window again, click the Dock icon for a window you minimized. If the window happens to be a QuickTime movie, the movie continues to play, albeit at postage stamp size, in its icon on the Dock. (We discuss the Dock in Chapter 3.)

✔ **Expand (green):** Click this button to make the window larger or smaller, depending on its current size. If you're looking at a standard size window, clicking Maximize makes it bigger. Click it again to return the window to its original size. If the window is larger than its contents, clicking this button shrinks the window to the smallest size that can completely enclose the contents without scrolling.

A scroll new world

Yet another way to see more of what is in a window is to scroll through it. Scroll bars appear at the bottom and right sides of any window that contains more stuff — icons, text, pixels, or whatever — than you can see in the window. In Figure 5-2, dragging the scroll bar on the right side of the window reveals the items above Clock and below QuickTime Player, depending on whether you scroll up or down. And dragging the scroll bar on the bottom of the window (which moves left to right) reveals the Kind column, which is to the right of the Size column.

And yes, the scroll bars also look a bit gumdrop-like. The best we can tell, Steve Jobs (Apple's charismatic CEO) has a thing for gumdrops.

You can scroll in the following four ways:

✔ **Click a scroll bar and drag.** The content of the window scrolls proportionally to how far you drag the scroll box.

✔ **Click in the scroll bar area but not on the scrollbar itself.** The window scrolls either one page up (if you click above the scrollbar) or down (if you click below the scrollbar). If the scroll bar is white (that is, it doesn't have a blue scroll box showing), you have no items to scroll to — which means that everything that window contains is already visible.

For what it's worth, the Page Up and Page Down keys function the same as clicking the grayish scroll bar area (the vertical scroll bar only) in the Finder and many applications. But these keys don't work in some programs, so don't get too dependent on them.

✓ **Click a scroll arrow at the top or bottom of a scroll area.** The window scrolls a little. Press and hold a scroll arrow and the window scrolls a lot.

✓ **Use the keyboard.** In the Finder, click an icon in the window first and then use the arrow keys to move up, down, left, or right. Using an arrow key selects the next icon in that direction and automatically scrolls the window, if necessary. In other programs, you may or may not be able to use the keyboard to scroll. The Page Up and Page Down keys work in most programs, but many programs don't use the arrow keys for scrolling their windows. The best advice we can give you is to try it — it'll either work or it won't.

In the Finder, you can also press the Tab key on the keyboard to select the next icon (in the current window) alphabetically.

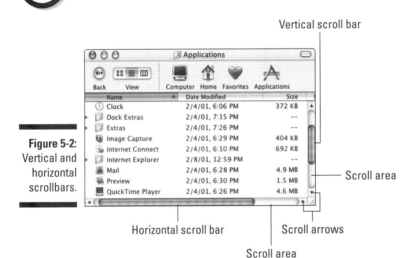

Vertical scroll bar

Figure 5-2: Vertical and horizontal scrollbars.

Scroll area

Horizontal scroll bar · Scroll arrows

Scroll area

(Hyper) Active Windows

To work within a window, the window must be *active.* The active window is always the frontmost window, and inactive windows always appear behind the active window. Only one window may be active at a time. To make a window active, click it anywhere — in the middle, on the title bar, or on a scroll bar — it doesn't matter where, with one proviso — you can't click the red, yellow, or green gumdrop buttons of an inactive window to activate it.

When you move your mouse *over* the red, yellow, or green gumdrop buttons of an inactive window but don't click your mouse button, the gumdrops light up, enabling you to Close, Minimize, or Expand an inactive window without first making it active.

Look at Figure 5-3 for an example of an active window (the Applications window) in front of an inactive window (the Utilities window).

Following is a list of the major visual cues between active and inactive windows:

✔ The active window's title bar gumdrop buttons — the red, yellow, and green ones — are, well, red, yellow and green. The inactive window's buttons are gray.

REMEMBER

If you move your mouse over an inactive window's gumdrop buttons, they light up in their usual colors so that you can close, minimize, or expand an inactive window without first making it active.

✔ Other buttons and scroll bars in an active window look different, too — they are bright; in an inactive window, these features are grayed out and more subdued.

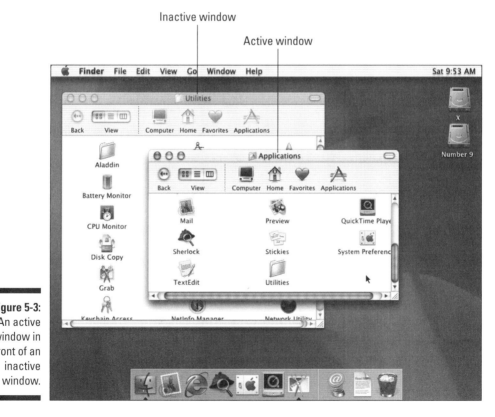

Figure 5-3:
An active window in front of an inactive window.

Dialog Box Dealie-boppers

A dialog box is a special kind of window that pops up over the active window. You generally see them when you select a menu item that ends in an ellipsis (...). You can read more about ellipses in Chapter 6.

Dialog boxes may contain a number of standard Macintosh features (Bob calls them *dealie-boppers*), such as radio buttons, pop-up menus, text entry boxes, and check boxes. You see these features again and again in dialog boxes. Take a moment to check out each of these dealie-boppers in Figure 5-4, and then see the following list where we describe how to use them.

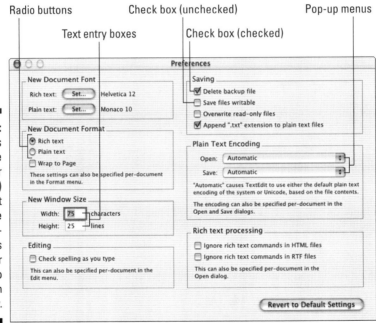

Figure 5-4: This Preference window (for TextEdit) offers most of the dealie-boppers you're ever likely to encounter in a window.

✔ **Radio buttons:** *Radio buttons* are so named because like the buttons on your car radio (assuming you have a very old car), only one can be active (when they're active they appear to be pushed in, just like old radio buttons) at a time. Radio buttons always appear in a group of two or more; when you select one, all the others are automatically deselected. Eggheads call this setup *mutually exclusive.*

As you see in Figure 5-4, the first radio button (Rich Text) is selected. If you were to now select the radio button for Plain Text, you deactivate (deselect) Rich Text. Got it? Good.

Here's a nifty and undocumented shortcut: You can usually select check boxes and radio buttons by clicking their names (instead of the buttons or boxes), too. Didn't know that, did you?

✔ **Pop-up menus:** These menus are appropriately named — that's what they do: pop up when you click them. You can always tell a pop-up menu because it appears in a slightly rounded rectangle and has double-ended arrow symbol (or, a pair of back-to-back triangles if you like) on the right. For an example, check out Figure 5-4 (the two pop-up menus both read `Automatic`).

Have you figured out yet what radio buttons and pop-up menus have in common? *Hint:* They both enable you to make a single selection from a group of options.

✔ **Text entry boxes:** In text entry boxes (sometimes called *fields*), you type in text (including numbers) from the keyboard. When a text entry box (or boxes) appears with a selected radio button, only when that radio button is selected can you make an entry in that box. In Figure 5-4, the New Window Size options are both text entry boxes.

✔ **Check boxes:** The last dealie-bopper you see frequently is the check box. In a group of check boxes, you can select or deselect each one individually. Check boxes are *selected* when they contain a check mark, and they are *deselected* when they're empty. Unlike radio buttons, which force you to choose one and only one item, check boxes are independent. Each one can be either selected or deselected. In Figure 5-4, you see three check boxes, two of which are selected.

Working with Windows

In this section, we give you a closer look at windows themselves: how you move them, size them, and use them. Although Mac OS X windows are similar to the windows you've used in other versions of Mac OS, you'll find some new wrinkles.

If you're relatively new to the Mac, you may want to read this section while sitting at your computer, trying the techniques as you read them. You may find it easier to remember something you read if actually do it.

Resizing windows

If you want to see more (or less) of what's in a window, use the sizer in the extreme lower-right corner of a window (we call out the sizer back in Figure 5-1; it has little diagonal grippy lines on it). Just drag the sizer downward and to the right to make a window larger; or drag it upward and to the left to make a window smaller. In other words, once you grab the sizer you can make a window whatever size you like.

Moving windows

To move a window, click anywhere in a window's title bar and drag the window to wherever you want it. The window moves wherever you move the mouse, and stops dead in its tracks when you release the mouse button.

Shutting yo' windows

Now that we've gone on and on about windows, maybe we should tell you how to close them. You can close an active window in one of three ways (the last two require the window to be active, by the way):

✔ Click the red close button in the upper-left corner of the title bar.

✔ Choose File⇨Close Window from the Finder menu.

✔ Press ⌘+W.

TIP

Hunting the seldom-seen Close All Windows command

If you're like us, by the end of the day, your Desktop is scattered with open windows — sometimes a dozen or more. Wouldn't you love to be able to close them all at once with a single *Close All* windows command? But you don't see a Close All command in any of the menus, do you?

Well, even though Apple (in its infinite wisdom) has hidden this useful command from mere mortals, you can make it come out and play by doing one of the following:

✔ Hold down the Option key and click any window's red gumdrop Close button.

✔ Hold down the Option key and choose File⇨Close All. (The Close All command usually reads Close Window, but becomes Close All when the Option key is held down; release the Option key and it changes back to Close Window.)

✔ Press ⌘+Option+W.

Chapter 6

A Bevy of Delectable Menus

*L*ike icons and windows, menus are a quintessential part of the Macintosh experience. In this chapter, we start with a few menu basics and then move on to the Finder's menus. We try to provide an appropriate level of detail based on the menu item's importance, and in many cases we direct you to another part of the book where that feature is discussed in greater detail.

Menu Basics

Mac menus are often referred to as *pull-down menus*. To check out the Mac OS X menus, click the Finder button in the Dock to activate the Finder, and then look at the top of your screen. From left to right you see the Apple menu, the Finder menu, and six other menus that we discuss throughout this chapter. To use an OS X menu, you click its name to make the menu appear and then pull (drag) down to select a menu item. Piece of cake! Figure 6-1 shows the Go menu dropped down.

Ever since Mac OS 8, menus stay down after you click their names until you either select an item or click outside the menu's boundaries. They also close if you click and hold on a menu for too long — about 15 seconds — without doing anything. Nice touch, eh?

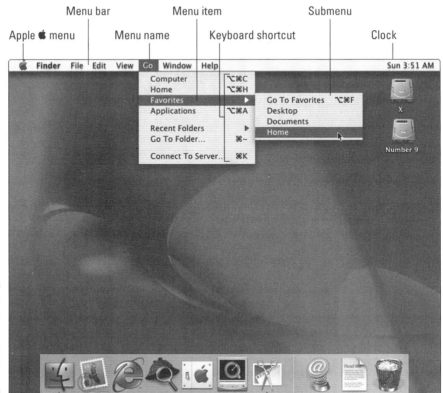

Figure 6-1:
The Finder's
menu bar
with the Go
menu pulled
down.

Musical menus

Before you start working with OS X menus, you really, really should know this about menus in general — they may change unexpectedly. Why? Well, the menus that you see in the menu bar at the top of the screen always reflect the program that's active at the time. When you switch from the Finder to a program, or from a program to another program, the menus change immediately to match whatever you switched to.

For example, when the Finder is active, the menu bar looks like Figure 6-1. But if you launch TextEdit, the menu bar changes to what you see in Figure 6-2.

An easy way to tell which program is active is to look at the left-most menu with a name (the one just to the right of the menu). When you're in the Finder, of course, that menu reads Finder. But if you switch to another program or launch a new program, that menu changes to the name of the active program.

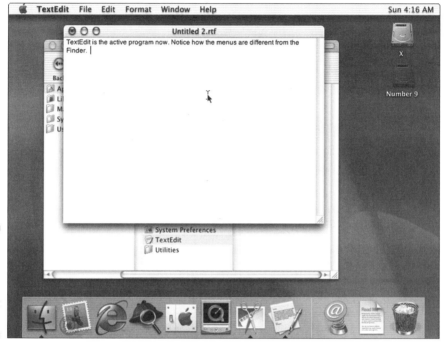

Figure 6-2:
The menu
bar changes
when
TextEdit
is active.

We cover only the menus that are part of OS X here in this chapter. The menus that come with other programs are beyond the purview of this book — this chapter alone would be a set of encyclopedias if we tried to cover them all!

Contextual menus (they're sooo sensitive)

Contextual menus are a neat feature Apple introduced in Mac OS 8. A *contextual menu* lists commands that apply to the item the cursor is over. Contextual menus appear in windows, on icons, and most places on the Desktop when you hold down the Control key and click — what we like to call a Control+Click. (See Figure 6-3, which shows the contextual menu that appears when you Control+click a document icon.) Actions appear in contextual menus only if they make sense for the item you Control+Click. For example, if you Control+Click inside a window but not on any icon, the contextual menu contains actions that you perform on a window. If you Control+Click an icon inside a window, by contrast, you see a contextual menu for that icon. So, you see, a contextual menu for a document differs from the contextual menu for a window. That's why they call 'em contextual!

Figure 6-3:
Only
relevant
items
appear in a
contextual
menu.

Don't believe us? Control+Click the Desktop (that is, click somewhere that's not in any window and not on any icon) and you see a contextual menu with different commands.

Contextual menus are also available in many applications. Open your favorite app and try Control+Clicking to find out if they're there. In most cases, a contextual menu is a quick way to avoid going to the menu bar to choose a command. Get in the habit of Control+Clicking items. Before you know it, using contextual menus will become second nature to you.

Disabled options

Menu items that appear in black on a menu are currently available. Menu items not currently available are grayed out, meaning they're disabled. You cannot select a disabled menu item. In Figure 6-4, the File menu is pulled down while nothing is selected in the Finder, and this is why many of the menu items are disabled. These items are disabled because an item (such as a window or icon) must be selected in order for you to use one these menu items. For example, the Show Original command is grayed out because it works only if the selected item is an alias.

Figure 6-4:
A menu with
disabled
items.

Submenus

A *submenu* is just that: a menu under a menu item. You can tell if a menu item has a submenu if it has a black triangle to the right of its name. To use a submenu, click a menu name once to drop down the menu, and then slide your cursor down to any item with a black triangle. When the item is highlighted, move your mouse to the right just slightly. The submenu should pop out of the original menu's item. If you refer to Figure 6-1, you can see the Favorites submenu open underneath the Go menu. If you were to release the mouse button while doing exactly what is pictured, a Finder window would pop open and show you a Finder window displaying your home folder.

Submenus used to be called *hierarchical menus,* but that's just a mouthful. For a while, people liked to call them *pull-right* menus. But these days just about everyone refers to them as submenus.

Keyboard shortcut commands

Most menu items, or at least the most common ones, have keyboard shortcuts to help you quickly navigate your Mac without having to haggle so much with the mouse. These key combinations indicate that you can activate the menu items without using the mouse by pressing the Command key and then pressing another key before releasing the Command key. Memorize the shortcuts you use often.

Some people refer to the Command key as the Apple key. That's because on most keyboards that key has both the pretzel-looking Command key symbol (⌘) *and* an Apple logo (⬤) on it. To avoid confusion with ⬤ menu, we'll stick with calling it Command key.

Following are four things you need to know to grasp keyboard shortcuts:

- ✔ **Keyboard shortcuts are shown in menus.** If you refer to Figure 6-4, you can see that the keyboard shortcut for the Find command (⌘+F) appears on the menu after the word Find. Any menu item with one of these pretzel-symbol-letter combinations after its name can be executed with that keyboard shortcut. Just press the ⌘ key and the letter shown in the menu — N for New Finder Window, F for Find, and so on — and the appropriate command is executed.

- ✔ **Capital letters don't mean you have to press Shift as part of the short-cut.** Although the letters next to the ⌘ symbol in the Finder's menus are capital letters, you don't have to press the Shift key to use the keyboard shortcut. If you see ⌘+P, for example, this means that you hold down the ⌘ key and press P. Some programs have keyboard combinations that require the use of ⌘+Shift, but these programs let you know by calling the key combination something like ⌘+Shift+S or ⌘+Shift+O. Other programs — including the Finder — indicate that you need to use the Shift key with a little up-facing arrow in the shortcut. For example, in Figure 6-4 the keyboard shortcut for creating a new folder (which we describe throughout this book as ⌘+Shift+ N)uses a little up-facing arrow to denote the Shift key.

✔ **Recognizing the funky looking Option key symbol.** You'll see one other symbol sometimes used in keyboard shortcuts: it represents the Option key (sometimes abbreviated in keyboard shortcuts as *Opt*). Although difficult to describe, you can refer back to Figure 6-1 to see it — it's the symbol just to the left of the Command symbol in the top three shortcuts. What this freakish symbol means in the Computer menu item (the top shortcut in Figure 6-1), for example, is that if you press both the ⌘ and Option keys and then press the C key, a Finder window showing *Computer* appears.

✔ **If it makes sense, it's probably a shortcut.** Most keyboard shortcuts have a mnemonic relationship to their names. For example, here are some of the more basic keyboard shortcuts: New Finder Window is ⌘+N; New Folder is ⌘+Shift+N; Open is ⌘+O; Show Info is ⌘+I; and Duplicate is ⌘+D. Maybe that's why Help displays its shortcut as ⌘+? even though the actual shortcut for Help is ⌘+Shift+/.

It's elliptical

Another feature of Mac menus is the ellipsis after a menu item's name. Ellipses, in case your English teacher forgot to mention them, are the three little dots (. . .) that appear in place of missing text. They basically mean that there are more options to be had by clicking the menu item.

So, when you see ellipses after a menu item, choosing that item displays a dialog box or sheet (we discuss dialog boxes in Chapter 5 and sheets in Chapter 8) in which you can make further choices. If you refer back to Figure 6-1, for example, you can see that the Go To Folder and Connect To Server commands both have ellipses. If you choose either command, the appropriate dialog box opens.

Choosing a menu item with an ellipsis never actually makes anything happen other than to open a dialog box or sheet; from there you make further choices and then click a button to make things happen.

Underneath the Apple (*) Menu Tree*

The Macintosh interface has sported an *Apple* ( ) *menu* since time immemorial (well, the 1980s anyway). So, when the Mac OS X Public Beta appeared without one, Mac users everywhere crawled out of the woodwork to express

their outrage. The bruised Apple ultimately relented and now OS X has an 
menu, just like every version of Mac OS before it. The following sections discuss the differences between the old  menu and the new, and also take you
through its main menu items.

What's in . . . and what's out

This new  menu isn't like any  menu before it, though; the biggest differences being

➔ The  symbol in the  menu is now blue instead of rainbow striped.

➔ It's not customizable anymore. You used to be able to add items — applications, folders, documents, aliases, or whatever your heart desired —
   to your  menu. You can't do that in the OS X  menu. What you see on
   the OS X  menu is what you get. But it's not a big issue because the OS
   X Dock *is* customizable and does let you add items — applications, folders, documents, aliases, or whatever your heart desires. (We discuss the
   Dock in Chapter 3.)

Tiptoeing through the  menu items

You won't find any programs available from the new OS X  menu — no calculator, no scrapbook, no programs at all. Instead, the  menu provides a set
of useful commands, described below, that are always available no matter
what program is active.

From top to bottom, the Apple menu's items are

➔ **About This Mac:** Choose this item to see what version of Mac OS X
   you're running and how much memory your Mac has.

➔ **Get Mac OS X Software:** Launches your Web browser and takes you to
   Apple's Web site.

➔ **System Preferences:** Choose this item to open the System Preferences
   window (which we discuss in great detail in Chapter 15).

➔ **Dock (submenu):** Lets you mess with, well, the Dock! Scour Chapter 3
   for more info on the Dock.

➔ **Location (submenu):** Enables you to quickly switch network configurations. We describe locations and network configurations in Chapter 11.

We're getting a little bit ahead of ourselves, but because you're probably wondering, a *location* reflects all the settings made in the Network System Preferences pane. They're mostly useful to PowerBook users, who often have different network configurations (locations) for different places they might use their Mac, such as the office (to connect to an Ethernet network), home (to connect to an DSL or cable connection), and out of town (to connect using the internal modem). Each configuration — office, home, and out of town — is known as a location; you can switch from one location to another quickly and painlessly using this menu item. Got it? If not, read Chapter 11.

✔ **Recent Items (submenu):** Your Mac keeps track of the applications and documents you've used recently. Expand this menu item to choose one of them.

✔ **Force Quit:** When a program misbehaves — either crashes, freezes, or otherwise becomes recalcitrant — this is the command for you. Choosing this brings up the Force Quit Applications dialog box that lets you choose which application you want to quit (shown in Figure 6-5).

Figure 6-5:
Use Force
Quit
Applications
to get out of
a badly
behaved
program.

This command is so handy that there's even a semisecret keyboard shortcut for it: ⌘+Option+Esc. It's not on the menu, although it is displayed on the Force Quit Applications window. (You can see it in the lower-left of Figure 6-5.)

Unlike in earlier versions of Mac OS, you don't need to reboot to continue working after you force a program to quit. If a program ever freaks out on you, Force Quit can almost certainly put it out of its misery and allow you to continue using your Mac.

✔ **Sleep:** Puts your Mac into its low-powered sleep mode. We talk more about sleep in Chapter 15. (Yawn!)

✔ **Restart:** Choose this to reboot your Mac, which is essentially the same as shutting down your machine and then turning it back on.

✔ **Shut Down:** Use this to turn off your Mac safely.

✔ **Log Out (⌘+Shift +Q):** Because OS X is a multi-user operating system, you can have multiple users on one Mac. This command enables you to switch users without restarting or shutting down.

Logging out means that the current user, as identified by username and password, is leaving the scene. The next person to use the Mac (even if it's you) has to enter a username and password to regain entry. All this sharing stuff can be found in Chapter 16.

Your Constant Companion: The Finder Menu

The very first menu on the Mac OS X menu bar is the *Finder menu* — so named because it includes commands that enable you to control the way lots of things work in the Finder. But it's really much more than a command center for the Finder.

When you have an application open, the Finder menu changes to the name of that application, and the commands available change — but just a little bit. (We discuss this unusual phenomenon in the "Musical menus" section earlier in this chapter.) What makes this cool is that you have access to some Finder menu items even when you're running an application such as AppleWorks or Internet Explorer. We have more to say about that as we work our way through the Finder menu in the list below.

The following list gives you a gander at the main items in the Finder menu. It's not too long, but it's packed with useful goodies, such as:

✔ **About The Finder:** Choose this to find out which version of the Finder is running on your Mac.

Okay, so this menu item isn't particularly useful, or at least not for very long. But when an application is running, the About The Finder item becomes About *application_name* and usually gives information about the program's version number, the company, and the people who worked on the program, and any other tidbits that the developers decide to throw in. Sometimes *these* tidbits are useful.

✔ **Preferences:** Choose this to control how the Desktop looks and acts. When you choose it, the Finder Preferences window appears, as shown in Figure 6-6. (Read all about perferences in Chapter 15.)

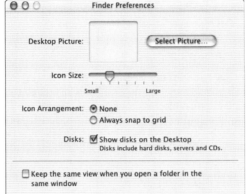

Figure 6-6:
Take a
gander at
the Finder
Preferences
window.

Select the Disks check box to choose whether hard drives, CDs, DVDs, and other types of disks appear on the Desktop. OS X selects this option by default (which mimics earlier versions of Mac OS). But if you don't want disk icons cluttering your beautiful Desktop, deselect this check box. If it's deselected, you can still work with CDs, DVDs, and other types of disk. You'll just have to open a Finder window and click the Computer button to access them.

✔ **Empty Trash (⌘+Shift+Delete):** Deletes all items in the Trash from your hard drive — period. We talk about the Trash in Chapters 3 and 4.

We've said it before and we'll say it again: Use this command with a modicum of caution. After a file is trashed and the Trash emptied, it's *gone*. (Okay, maybe Norton Utilities can bring it back, but don't bet the farm on it.)

✔ **Hide Finder (⌘+H):** Use this command when you've got Finder windows open and they're distracting you. Choosing it makes the Finder inactive (another currently running program becomes active) and hides any open Finder windows. To make the Finder visible again, either choose Show All from the Finder menu (or whatever it's called in the active application — the command should still be there) or click the Finder button on the Dock. The advantage to hiding the Finder — rather than closing or minimizing all your windows to get a clean screen — is that you don't have to open them all again when you're ready to get the windows back. Instead, you just choose Show All or click the Finder button in the Dock.

✔ **Hide Others:** This command hides all windows associated with all running programs except the active program.

✔ **Show All:** Use this as the antidote to both hide commands. Choose this and nothing is hidden anymore.

You used to find these show and hide commands in the Application menu (that menu on the right side of the menu bar, that displayed the icon of the active application) of older versions of Mac OS. If you're using the Classic environment or a Classic application (which we discuss in Chapter 14), that's where you'll still find them.

File Management and More: Meet the File Menu

The File menu contains many commands that enable you to manipulate your files and folders. We discuss file management in Chapter 10, but here we give you the lowdown on the actual File menu itself.

You'll probably use these commands frequently, so it would behoove you to memorize their keyboard shortcuts.

- **New Finder Window (⌘+N):** Opens a new Finder window. We discuss the Finder window in Chapter 7.
- **New Folder (⌘+Shift+N):** Creates a new, untitled folder in the active window. If no window is active, this command creates a new folder on the Desktop.

In every version of Mac OS since the beginning of time, the New Folder keyboard shortcut has been ⌘+N — just like the New Document keyboard shortcut in most applications is also ⌘+N. When creating a shortcut for the New Finder Window command in OS X, Apple decided to add the Shift key to the New Folder keyboard shortcut. We admit this decision kind of makes sense: Opening a new Finder window and opening a new document both create a new window, while creating a new folder simply displays a new icon. But if you're a veteran Mac user, you better get used to adding the Shift key to ⌘+N to create a folder.

- **Open (⌘+O):** Opens the selected item, be it icon, window, or folder.
- **Close Window (⌘+W):** Closes the active window. If no windows are open, or if none are selected, the Close Window command is grayed out and cannot be chosen.

Most menu commands are intuitive. So how did Apple come up with ⌘+W as a shortcut for Close Window? You think Apple would assign the letter *c*, for *C*lose. However, ⌘+C is the shortcut for *copy*. If you really want someone to blame for this, it was Microsoft that originally married Close with ⌘+W.

Close All Windows (⌘+Option+W): If you hold down the Option key before you click the File menu, the Close Window command changes to Close All, which enables you to close all open Finder windows. Flip to the sidebar at the end of Chapter 5 to read all about this command.

✔ **Show Info (⌘+I):** Opens an Info window for the selected icon. (We tell you all about the Info window in Chapter 4.)

✔ **Duplicate (⌘+D):** Makes a copy of the selected icon, adds the word *copy* to its name, and then places the copy in the same window as the original icon. You may use the Duplicate command on any icon except a disk icon.

You can't duplicate an entire disk onto itself. But you can copy an entire disk (call it Disk 1) to any other disk (call it Disk 2). Just drag the Disk 1 onto Disk 2's icon. The contents of Disk 1 will be copied to Disk 2 and will appear in a folder named Disk 1 on Disk 2.

✔ **Make Alias (⌘+L):** Creates an alias for the selected icon in the same folder as the selected icon (or on the Desktop if the selected icon is on the Desktop). We cover aliases in detail in Chapter 4.

✔ **Show Original (⌘+R):** Suppose you make and use an alias; you put it on your Desktop or in your Favorites folder, and everything's peachy. But now you want to delete or move the original file or folder as part of a little spring cleaning. Where is that original? You've been using the alias so long you can't remember. To find it, click the alias and then choose File➪Show Original. Quick as a flash, the Finder window switches to the folder that contains the parent icon. You can now delete, copy, move, or change the parent icon.

✔ **Add To Favorites (⌘+T):** Creates an alias of the selected item and puts it in the Favorites folder. You can now reach the item by clicking the Favorites button on the Finder window toolbar. And remember, the Favorites folder is easily available from both Open and Save sheets (see Chapter 8), making it even more useful.

✔ **Move To Trash (⌘+Delete):** Moves the selected icon to the Trash.

The icon (that is, the item the icon represents) that you move to the trash is not deleted from your hard drive until you choose the Empty Trash command from the Finder menu, the Trash's pop-up menu, or the contextual menu.

✔ **Find (⌘+F):** Use the File➪Find command when you need to find a file or folder on your hard drive and you can't remember where you put it. This command is a Mac OS X feature that really kicks butt. We discuss Sherlock (which, by the way, can do much more than find stuff on your hard drive) in detail in Chapter 12.

The Edit Menu (Which Shoulda Been Called the Clipboard Menu)

In contrast to the File menu, which has commands that mostly deal with file management and are exclusive to the Finder window, the Edit menu's commands and functions are available in almost every Macintosh program ever made.

Because almost every program has an Edit menu and because almost every program uses the same keyboard shortcuts on its Edit menu, it behooves you to know the Edit menu keyboard shortcuts by heart, even if you remember no others.

Personally, we think that the Edit menu should have been called the Clipboard menu because most of its commands deal with the Macintosh Clipboard.

Comprehending the Clipboard

The *Clipboard* is a holding area for the last thing you cut or copied. That copied *item* can be text, a picture, a portion of a picture, an object in a drawing program, a column of numbers in a spreadsheet, or just about anything that can be selected. In other words, the Clipboard is the Mac's temporary storage area.

The Clipboard commands in the Edit menu are only enabled when they can actually be used. If the currently selected item can be cut or copied, the Cut and Copy commands in the Edit menu are enabled. If the selected item can't be cut or copied, the commands are unavailable and are dimmed (gray). And when nothing is selected, the Cut, Copy, Paste, and Clear commands are also dimmed.

Copying or cutting to the Clipboard

To cut or copy something to the Clipboard, select the item and then choose Cut or Copy from the Edit menu or use the keyboard shortcuts ⌘+X (cut) or ⌘+C (copy). Choosing Cut *deletes* the selected item and puts it on the Clipboard; choosing Copy *copies* the selected item to the clipboard but does not delete the selected item.

As a storage area, the Clipboard's contents are temporary. *Very* temporary. When you cut or copy an item, that item remains on the Clipboard only until you cut or copy something else. When you do cut or copy something else, the new item replaces the Clipboard's contents and in turn remains on the Clipboard until you cut or copy something else, and so on.

Of course, whatever's on the Clipboard heads straight for oblivion if you crash, lose power, log out, or shut your Mac down, so don't count on it too heavily.

Pasting from the Clipboard

To place the item that's on the Clipboard, click where you want the item to go and then paste what you copy or cut (choose Paste from the Edit menu or use the keyboard shortcut ⌘+V). Pasting doesn't purge the contents of the Clipboard. In fact, an item stays on the Clipboard until you cut, copy, clear, crash (these used to be called the four Cs of Macintosh computing, but Mac OS X almost never crashes), restart, shut down, or log out. That means you can paste the same item over, and over, and over again, which can come in pretty handy at times.

Almost all programs have an Edit menu and use the Macintosh Clipboard, which means that you can usually cut or copy something in a document in one program and paste it into a document from another program. Usually.

Checking out the main Edit menu items

The previous section gives you probably 75 percent of what you need to know about the Edit menu. Still, because we get paid to be thorough and because the Finder's Edit menu has a few commands that aren't Clipboard-related, in this section we go through the Edit menu's commands one by one.

✔ **Undo/Redo (⌘+Z):** This command undoes the last thing you did. For example, if you change the name of a folder and then choose this command, the name of the folder resorts back to what it was before you changed it.

The Undo command toggles (that is, switches back and forth) between the new and old states as long as you don't do anything else. Say you name a file *Undo Me* and choose Edit➪Undo; the file name reverts to its previous name. If you pull down the Edit menu now, the Undo command reads Redo instead of Undo. Select Redo, and the name of the file changes back to *Undo Me*. You can continue to Undo and Redo until you click somewhere else.

Don't forget about this command because it can be a lifesaver. Almost every program has an Undo command. Now for the bad news: The Undo command is ephemeral, like the Clipboard: You can only use Undo to reverse your last action, and as soon as you do something else — even just clicking a lousy icon — you lose the ability to undo the original action. At least, this is true in the Finder. Some programs, such as Microsoft Word and Adobe Photoshop, allow multiple undos.

Here's a cool new feature — the Undo command works with certain actions it never worked with before, such as moving icons. That's way cool because sometimes you drag an icon somewhere and drop it accidentally. Finding it is a hassle. Now you can just undo the move. Kewl beans.

As you find out more about your Mac and OS X, you'll no doubt discover actions that you can't undo. Still, Undo is a great command when available, and we urge you to get in the habit of trying it often.

- **Cut (⌘+X):** Removes the selected item and places it on the Clipboard. You can then paste the item from the Clipboard to another document, text box, or other valid destination. For more info on Cut and the Clipboard, see the previous section.

- **Copy (⌘+C):** Makes a copy of the selected item and places it on the Clipboard. However, the original is not removed, as it is when you cut something. For more info on Copy and the Clipboard, see the previous section.

- **Paste (⌘+V):** Places the contents of the Clipboard at the place you last clicked. For more info on Paste and the Clipboard, see the previous section.

- **Select All (⌘+A):** Selects all icons in the active window. Or, if no window is active, Select All selects every icon on the Desktop. If a window is active, choosing Select All selects every icon in the window, regardless of whether you can see them on screen.

The Select All command has nothing whatsoever to do with the Clipboard, so why is it on the Edit menu? Who knows? The Powers That Be at Apple put it there once upon a time, and there it remains.

- **Show Clipboard:** Summons the Clipboard window, which lists the type of item (such as text, picture, or a sound) on the Clipboard and a message letting you know whether the item on the Clipboard can be displayed.

A View from a Window: The View Menu

The View menu controls what the icons and windows look like, how icons and windows are arranged and sorted, and the look of your windows. The View menu affects the icons in the active window or, if no window is active, it affects the icons on the Desktop.

The following list gives you a brief description of each of the menu items on the View menu:

- **as Columns:** Changes the active window to Columns view. Choosing Columns view is a new way (added in Mac OS X) to view your files in a Finder window where the folders on your computer are displayed in a column at the left of the Finder window and the contents of those folders are displayed in a larger window pane on the right. See Chapter 7 for more info on Columns view.

✔ **as Icons:** Icon view is the traditional Macintosh view — the one most closely associated with the Macintosh experience. We admit, icons in Mac OS X are far more beautiful than they've ever been in previous versions of Mac OS. But we still feel that this view is least useful — those big honking icons, beautiful or not, take up far too much valuable screen real estate. We discuss Icon view in Chapter 7.

✔ **as List:** In List view, you can copy or move items from different folders with a single motion, without opening multiple windows. In either Icon view or Columns view, on the other hand, moving files from two or more different folders requires opening several windows and two separate drags. See Chapter 7 for more on List view.

✔ **Clean Up:** Choose this to align icons to an invisible grid; you use it to keep your windows and Desktop neat and tidy. (If you like this invisible grid, don't forget that you can turn it on or off for the Desktop and individual windows by using View Options.) Clean Up is available only in Icon view or when no windows are active. If no windows are active, the command instead cleans up your Desktop. (To deactivate all open windows, just click anywhere on the Desktop.)

If you're like us, you have taken great pains to place icons carefully in specific places on your Desktop. Cleaning up your Desktop destroys all your beautiful work and moves all your perfectly arranged icons. And alas, cleaning up your Desktop is not undo-able.

✔ **Arrange by name:** Rearranges your icons in alphabetical order. Like Clean Up, it's only available for windows viewed as icons, and it's not undo-able.

✔ **Hide/Show toolbar (⌘+B):** Shows or hides the buttons on the toolbar of the active window. Suppose that you want to see more files and fewer buttons. Because the buttons on this toolbar are also available from the Go menu (see the next section), you're safe in hiding them. Just choose Hide Toolbar to make the toolbar go away, or Show Toolbar to bring it back. (As we detail in Chapter 5, the gray oval button in the upper right corner of every Finder window does the same thing.)

You should also note that when the toolbar is hidden, opening a folder opens a *new* Finder window rather than reusing the current one (which is what happens when the toolbar is showing unless you've changed this preference in Finder Preferences).

Go to Chapter 7 for more about the toolbar in Finder windows.

✔ **Customize Toolbar:** This one is way cool — use it to design your own Finder window toolbar. We discuss this nifty feature in Chapter 7.

✔ **Hide/Show Status bar:** Shows or hides the status bar for the active window. The status bar tells you how many items are in each window, how much space is available on your hard drive, and what permissions you have for this window's contents. (Read about permissions in Chapter 16.)

✔ **Show View Options (⌘+J):** Here's where you can soup up the way one or all of your windows looks and behaves. You can do this either globally (so that all windows use the same view when opened) or on a window-by-window basis. We discuss Show View Options more in Chapter 7.

Going Places

The Go menu is chock full of shortcuts. The items on this menu take you places on your Mac — many of the same places you can go with the Finder window toolbar — and a few other places.

Checking out Go menu items

The following list gives you a brief look at the items on the Go menu.

See the next section for info on some items that aren't listed here, such as Computer, Home, and Favorites.

✔ **Recent Folders:** Use this submenu to quickly go back to a folder you recently visited. Every time you open a folder, Mac OS X creates an alias to it and stores it in the Recent Folders folder. You can open any of these aliases from the Recent Folders submenu of the Go menu.

✔ **Go to Folder (⌘+~):** Summons the Go to Folder dialog box, as shown in Figure 6-7. Look at your Desktop. Maybe it's cluttered with lots of windows, or maybe it's completely empty. Either way, suppose that you're several clicks away from a folder you want to open. If you know the path from your hard drive to that folder, you can type the path to the folder you want in text box (separating each folder name with a forward slash [/]) and click Go to move (relatively) quickly to the folder you need. This method is definitely nerdy, but can save you some time.

The first character you type must also be a forward slash, as shown in Figure 6-7.

✔ **Connect to Server (⌘+K):** If your Mac is connected to a network or to the Internet, use this command to reach these remote resources.

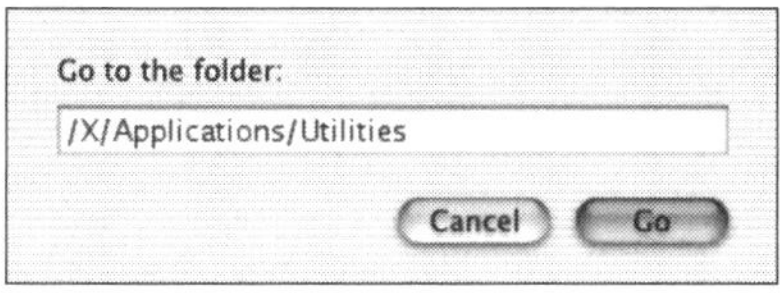

Figure 6-7:
Getting
there the
geeky way.

Go to the folder:

/X/Applications/Utilities

Cancel   Go

Go, go, go . . . to Chapter 7

Note that the Go menu lists keyboard shortcuts for commands you also find on the Finder window toolbar. We cover these in detail in Chapter 7 as buttons, and the commands do the same things. But if you want to know the commands and keyboard shortcuts to these commands, here ya go:

Command	Keyboard Shortcut
Computer	⌘+Option+C
Home	⌘+Option+H
Favorites	⌘+Option+F
Applications	⌘+Option+A

The Go menu also has a Favorites menu item that parallels the use of the Favorites button on the Finder toolbar. The submenu shows your favorite items — the ones you mark using the Add to Favorites command from the File menu — but it shows them as a submenu instead of in a window, as the Finder's Favorites button does. It's up to you whether you like the menu better than the button, but we think they both have their moments.

Window Dressing

Again with the windows! (We spend a lot of pages in Chapter 5 giving you the scoop on how to work with windows.) The commands on the Window menu provide you with tools that you can use to manage your windows. Following is a brief look at each of the menu items on the Window menu.

✔ **Minimize Window (⌘+M):** Use this command to unclutter your Desktop.

With a Finder window selected (the command will be unavailable — grayed out — if you don't have an active Finder window), using the Minimize Window command makes a file disappear, as it were: The file or folder is still open, but it's not active, and you don't see it on your screen. You do see, however, an icon representing it in the Dock. (Read all about the Dock in Chapter 3.)

✔ **Bring All to Front:** In previous versions of Mac OS, when you clicked a window belonging to an application, *all* that application's windows came to the front — that is, windows moved within layers and as layers. Under

OS X, windows interleave. For example, you could have a Finder window, a Word window, a Photoshop window, a Word window, and another Finder window in a front-to-back order. Choosing Bring All to Front enables you to have all the Finder windows move to the front of those belonging to other applications (while keeping their own relative ordering). This essentially allows an emulation of the layering to which Mac (and Windows) users are accustomed.

If you hold down the Option key when you pull down the Window menu, the Bring All to Front command changes to the useful Arrange in Front, which arranges all your Desktop windows neatly starting in the upper-left corner of the Desktop, as shown in Figure 6-8.

✔ **Other items:** The remaining items on the Window menu are the names of all currently open Finder windows. Click a window's name to bring it to the front.

The names of windows that you minimize (the ones with icons appearing on the Dock) remain on the Window menu. You can view the window by choosing its name from the Window menu.

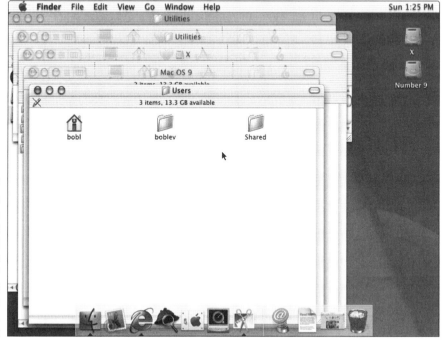

Figure 6-8:
The Arrange in Front command stacks up your windows neatly in the corner.

Not Just a Beatles Movie:
Help and the Help Menu

One of the best features about all Macs since System 7.*x* is the system's excellent built-in help. And Mac OS X doesn't cheat you on that legacy: This system has online help in abundance. When you have a question about how to do something, the Mac Help Center is the first place you should visit (after this book, of course).

The sole item in the Help menu — Mac Help (⌘+?) — opens the Mac Help window, as shown in Figure 6-9.

The one exception to the rule we mention earlier in this chapter — that you don't have to press Shift for capital letters in a keyboard shortcut on a menu — is the keyboard shortcut for Help. This shortcut appears on the Help menu as ⌘+?, and you do have to hold down the Shift key to type the question mark. In fact, if you type ⌘+/ (which is what you get when you type a lowercase question mark), nothing happens. This is different from earlier version of Mac OS. In other words, the shortcut for Help *should be* ⌘+Shift+/ even though the menu says ⌘+?. Got it? If you're wondering why this is, you'll have to ask Apple. Personally, we think it's lame.

Figure 6-9: Mac Help is nothing if not helpful.

To use Mac Help, simply type a word or phrase into the text field at the top of the Help Center window and then click the Ask button. In a few seconds, your Mac provides you with one or more articles to read, which (theoretically) is related your question. For example, if you type **menus** and click the Ask button, you'll get five pages of help articles, as shown in Figure 6-10.

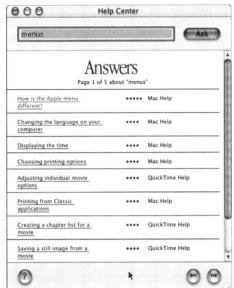

Figure 6-10:
You got
questions?
Mac's got
answers.

While you don't have to be connected to the Internet to use Mac Help, you do need an Internet connection to get the most out of it. That's because OS X only installs certain help articles on your hard drive. If you ask a question that isn't answered by the help articles on your hard drive, Mac Help will connect to Apple's Web site and download the answer (assuming you have an active Internet connection). While this may sometimes be inconvenient, it is also smart. This way, the help system can be updated at any time by Apple without requiring any action from you.

After you've asked a question and Mac Help has grabbed the answer from the Apple Web site, that answer remains on your hard drive forever. If you ask for it again (even in a later date), your computer won't have to download it from the Apple Web site again.

Part II
Rounding Out Your Basic Training

The 5th Wave   By Rich Tennant

"My God! I've gained 9 pixels!"

In this part . . .

Peruse the chapters in this part to discover how to perform important hands-on tasks. But don't get all worked up: This stuff is easy. In fact, we think of this part as "The Lazy Person's How-To Guide."

First we show you each and every Mac OS X menu, in full and loving detail. Then, it's time to learn more about the all-important Finder, followed by a pair of all-important skills: saving and opening files. You also discover how to use removable media with your Mac — a good thing to know!

Chapter 7

New-fangled Finder

*B*elieve it or not, all the stuff on your Mac can fit in one window — *the Finder window.* In this window, you can double-click your way to your favorite application, your documents, or out onto the Internet. In fact, the Finder is the place you are when you haven't yet gone anyplace at all. The Finder window appears on the Desktop when you start up your Mac, and it's always available. Even if you're an old hand with Mac OS, we show you how to get the most from the new Finder in this chapter.

Finding the Finder

If you don't see the Finder window on the Desktop when your Mac finishes the start-up process, you probably closed it the last time the Mac was on. So, how do you find the Finder window again? Well, there are a couple ways you can do it:

✔ Choose File⇨New Finder window, and a Finder window appears. New Finder windows always open up showing the top level of your drives. In other words, they open up reading Computer, the same as if you choose Go⇨Computer or clicked the Computer button in the toolbar.

You'll probably open a lot of new windows, so consider memorizing this command's keyboard shortcut: ⌘+N. This shortcut is good to know because most software programs use the ⌘+N shortcut to create a new document. If your memory is bad, use this mnemonic device: N is for New.

✔ Click the Finder icon in the Dock (it's the left-most one, with a smiley Mac face on it).

The Finder is at its core a very talented window. If you need the low-down on windows in general, see Chapter 5.

Getting to Know the Finder

A Finder window is a handy friend. Use the Finder to navigate through disks and folders, to documents and applications on your hard drive, or to connect to other Macs and Internet servers — right from your Desktop. In Figure 7-1, you can see a typical Finder window, which includes the following main features:

- ✔ **Toolbar:** From here you can open frequently used items.

- ✔ **Back button:** Takes you to the last folder you viewed in this window. This is sort of like in a Web browser, where the back button takes you to the page you were viewing before the current one, but this Back button takes you back one folder instead of one Web page.

- ✔ **Icons:** Click these to open your stuff — applications, files, folders, and remote resources, such as Web sites.

- ✔ **Status bar:** Just below the toolbar is the status bar, which tells you the amount of space available on this hard drive and the number of items in the current folder.

You can turn the Status bar on and off by choosing View➪Show Status Bar (which changes to View➪Hide Status Bar when the Status bar is showing).

- ✔ **View buttons:** Use these buttons to view the contents of your Finder window by icons, list, or columns. Read about these views in the "Customizing Finder Windows with Views" section later in this chapter.

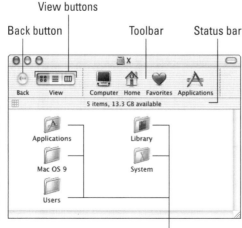

Figure 7-1: The contents of the mysterious drive X.

Hey, I know you!

If you're an experienced Mac user, you know the Finder well. Every version of Mac OS before Max OS X has included the Finder, and its appearance has remained pretty much the same since the Mac was introduced in 1984. What's new in Mac OS X is that you can use a single window in the Finder — instead of multiple windows — to view just about everything stored on your hard drive. Instead of opening a new window for each folder, the Finder can display everything in the same window, shifting your view of items as you click or select them with buttons in the window.

You still have the option to use multiple windows. If you *really* like multiple Finder windows onscreen the way many long-time Mac users do, just hold down the ⌘ key when you double-click any folder, and it'll open in a separate window (with the toolbar hidden).

Note: If you've hidden the toolbar by clicking a Finder window's Hide/Show Toolbar button, new windows open automatically when you open a folder — you don't have to hold down the ⌘ key at all. It can be disconcerting when all of a sudden the Finder starts behaving differently. If you want to use the new "one window" approach when you've hidden the Toolbar, hold down the Option key when you double-click a folder. The folder will open in the same window, as if you had never hidden the toolbar.

Belly Up to the Toolbar

Right below the title bar, you find the Finder window toolbar (refer to Figure 7-1). On it are buttons that take you all sorts of places, whether you're on your own hard drive, in the wider world of the Internet, or on a network you may be connected to. To activate a toolbar button, click it once.

You say you don't want to see the toolbar at the top of the window? Okay! Just choose View➪Hide Toolbar or click the little gray gumdrop-looking thing in the upper-right corner of every Finder window, and it's gone. If only life were always so easy!

From left to right, here's the lowdown on the toolbar's default buttons:

If you've customized your toolbar, as we show you how to do later in this chapter, it won't look exactly like this.

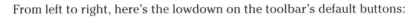

   ✔ **Back:** The Back button takes you to the last folder you viewed in this
      window. For more on this nifty navigation device, see the next section.

✔ **View buttons:** The three view buttons change the way the window displays its contents. Stay tuned for an entire section on views coming up in just a few pages.

✔ **Computer:** Click this button to see what hard drives, CD/DVD-ROM or Zip drives, and servers are connected to your Mac. Or maybe you just want to see everything you've got in one place. Either way, click here to see the list of your mounted disks (see Figure 7-2). You can double-click on any of the drives or disks you see there to get to their contents. Finally, the other icon you see — the Network icon — reveals all available servers on your network (if any).

Figure 7-2:
Checking
out your
computer's
storage
devices and
servers.

✔ **Home:** There's no place like it, is there? At least no place *we* know. The Home button leads to your private *home folder* on the Mac (think of it as your own personal storage facility). You find other folders there, including: `Desktop`, `Documents`, `Library`, `Movies`, `Music`, `Pictures`, `Public`, and `Sites`. Use these folders to store your personal stuff and you'll never lose track of it — because it's conveniently located within folders that are available with just a single click in the Finder.

Click Home if you've lost your bearings while cruising around your Mac in the Finder window. You may or may not share your Mac with others, but every user who works on this computer has his or her own home folder. Rest easy, though — only your folders and your files appear when you click the Home button on a shared Mac. Read all about sharing Macs in Chapter 16.

You can set up a portion of your home folder so that others can drop stuff in, or take stuff out. Chapter 16 has the scoop.

✔ **Favorites:** Click the Favorites button to see items you use a lot, such as files, folders, or links to Web sites. You can quickly add items to a folder with the Add To Favorites command (⌘+T) on the File menu. See Chapter 6 for more on the Add To Favorites command or if you need more info on menus in general.

Favorites are *aliases*: that is, pointers that you double-click to open items that are stored somewhere else (usually on your Mac). When you install Mac OS X, two folders — your home folder and your Documents folder — are already in your Favorites folder.

✔ **Applications:** Click the Applications button on the toolbar to reach the Applications folder, which contains applications that come with Mac OS X. In this folder, you can (and probably should) put any new applications you install so that you can easily keep track of them. We discuss most of these programs in various places throughout the rest of the book, especially in Chapter 13.

If you share a computer with others, you'll need appropriate permissions to add things to the Applications folder; if you're the only one who uses your computer, you're the administrator by default and can add all the programs you like to it. If that doesn't make sense to you at this time, you should read Chapter 16, which is all about sharing.

Navigating the Finder: Up, Down, and Backwards

In addition to the toolbar icons described above and some good old-fashioned double-clicking, the Mac OS X Finder window offers a nifty new navigation tool: the aptly named Back button in the toolbar. We also talk a bit about the current folder pop-up menu, so that you can always find where you're at in a jiffy.

"Where am I?": The current folder pop-up menu

In the center of a window's title bar (refer to Figure 7-1), you can see the name of the folder you're currently viewing. To see more folder names, ⌘+Click (hold the mouse button down) the folder name. First, you see the one that contains the current folder (Applications in Figure 7-3); then, below that one, you see its parent folder or drive (X, in Figure 7-3). Move down the menu to move higher in your Mac's folder hierarchy until you're where you want to be. You read that right: Move your mouse down to go up.

It's easier to see than to explain, so here's Figure 7-3.

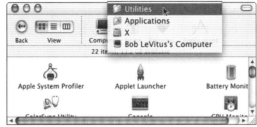

Figure 7-3:
Navigate
through
folders with
this pop-up
menu.

Use this pop-up menu to move from your current folder all the way to the Computer folder. Now click the Back button. Hey, you're right back where you were before you touched that pop-up menu.

"Web integration, man!": The Back button

Suppose that you're fiddling around in the Finder window, opening stuff, and maybe even looking for a particular file. You realize that the item you want is in the folder you just left. D'oh! What to do? Click the Back button — yes, just like with a Web browser. The Back button (shown in the margin) is the left-pointing arrow at the left end of the Finder window toolbar. If you want to move to the last folder you were at, just click Back, and there you are! If you use a Web browser (and who doesn't these days?), you're probably a pro at this already.

Here's an example of how the Back button works. Say you're in your home folder, you click the Favorites button, and then a split-second later you realize that you actually need something in your home folder. Just a quick click of the Back button and poof! You're back home.

Customizing Finder Windows with Views

You have three ways to view a window — Column view, Icon view, and List view. Some people like columns, some like icons, and others love lists. To each her own. The following sections give you a look at each view. Play with the different Finder views and see which one works best for you. (For what it's worth, we both prefer Column view.)

Column view

The Column view is new; previous versions of Mac OS didn't have it. It's quickly become the favorite way for both of us to display windows in the Finder and almost everyone we've talked to about this new view thinks it's a darn handy way to quickly look through a lot of folders at once.

To display a window in the Column view, either click the Column view button in the toolbar (shown in the margin) or choose View⇨as Columns from the Finder's menu bar.

You can have as many columns as your screen can handle. Just use the window sizer in the lower-right corner to enlarge your window horizontally so that new columns have room to open.

See what a Finder window displayed with in Column view looks like in Figure 7-4. Here's how it works: When you click the Applications folder in the leftmost column, its contents appears in the next column to the right. When you click the Internet Explorer folder in the second column, its contents appear in the third column. And when you clicked the Read Me.rtf document in the third column, a big icon plus some information about the file (its kind, size, and creation and modification dates) appears in the fourth column.

Figure 7-4:
A Finder
window in
Column
view.

Icon view: The ol' stick-in-the-mud view

If there's a view that's a dead-ringer for the old Finder interface, it's Icon view. In all fairness, we must say that many perfectly happy Macintosh users love the Icon view and refuse to even consider anything else. Fine. But as the number of files on your hard drive increases (as it does for every Mac user), screen real estate becomes more and more valuable. Too, the only benefit that the Icon view has over the column or List views is the capability to arrange the icons anywhere you like within the window. Big deal.

We offer this solution as a compromise. If you still want to see your files and folders in Icon view, here's how to make them smaller so that more of them fit in the same space onscreen.

To change the size of a window's icons, choose View⇨Show View Options. In the View Options

window that appears, click the Window tab. Drag the Icon Size slider you find there to the left. This makes the icons in the active window smaller. Conversely, you could make 'em all bigger by dragging the Icon Size slider to the right. Bigger icons make us crazy, but if you like them that way, your Mac can accommodate you.

If you want to make the icons in *every* window bigger or smaller, click the Global tab in the View Options window and drag the Icon slider right or left. This affects all windows displayed in Icon view. (Read more on the View Options window coming up in a page or two. . . .)

Note: if you like Icon view, consider purchasing a larger monitor — we hear that monitors now come in a 24-inch size.

Icon view

Icon view is a free-form view that allows you to move big icons around within a window to your heart's content. Check out the Finder window in Figure 7-5 to see what Icon view looks like.

 To display a window in Icon view, either click the Icon view button in the toolbar (as shown in the margin) or choose View⇨as Icons from the Finder's menu bar.

Figure 7-5: Icon view is pretty and very Mac-like, but a total waste of screen real estate.

Easy copying and moving in List view

Here's a slick advantage for viewing folders and files in List view with the disclosure triangles. Because you can easily see folders and files with just one window open, you can copy or move items from separate folders with a dragging single motion. You're spared having to open multiple windows, as you must do in the Icon view or Column view; in those views, moving files from two or more different folders requires opening several windows and two separate file-dragging motions.

It's easier to do than to explain, but here goes. In Figure 7-6, you can move any or all of the three files in the Documents folder into the Desktop, Library, Movies, Music, Pictures, Public, or Sites folders without opening another window.

List view

Finally, we come to the view we both loved and used most in Mac OS 9 (but have forsaken since meeting the Column view): the List view (shown in Figure 7-6). The main reason we liked List view so much was the little triangles to the left of each folder, known as *disclosure triangles*, which let you view the contents of a folder without actually opening the folder. The Documents folder is shown collapsed in Figure 7-6.

To display a window in List view, either click the List view button in the toolbar (as shown in the margin) or choose View➪as List from the Finder's menu bar.

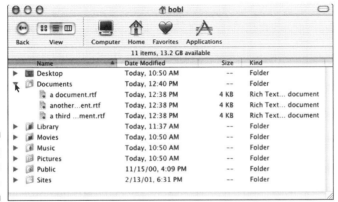

Figure 7-6:
A window in
List view.

A little triangle appears next to the name of the selected column in a List view window. (In Figure 7-7 you can see it in the Size column.) If this little arrow is pointing up, the items in that column will be sorted in descending order. If you click the little triangle once, it will point down, and the column will be sorted in ascending size order. This behavior is true for all columns in List view windows.

To change the order in which columns appear in a window, press and hold on a column's name, and then drag it to the left or right until it's where you want it. Release the mouse button, and the column will move where you want it.

Figure 7-7:
Sorting
items in
descending
order in
List view.

Name	Size ▲	Date Modified	Dat...ated	Kind
▶ Utilities	38.6 MB	Today	2/16/01	Folder
▶ Internet Explorer	19.6 MB	Today	2/16/01	Folder
▶ Dock Extras	10.7 MB	Today	2/16/01	Folder
▶ AppleScript	1.1 MB	2/16/01	2/16/01	Folder
Clock	372 KB	2/16/01	2/16/01	Application
System Preferences	424 KB	2/16/01	2/16/01	Application
Calculator	448 KB	2/16/01	2/16/01	Application
Image Capture	448 KB	2/16/01	2/16/01	Application
Internet Connect	788 KB	2/16/01	2/16/01	Application
Stickies	884 KB	2/16/01	2/16/01	Application
Chess	1.1 MB	2/16/01	2/16/01	Application
TextEdit	1.2 MB	2/16/01	2/16/01	Application
Address Book	1.7 MB	2/16/01	2/16/01	Application
Preview	1.9 MB	2/16/01	2/16/01	Application
QuickTime Player	4.6 MB	2/16/01	2/16/01	Application
Mail	5 MB	2/16/01	2/16/01	Application
Sherlock	6.6 MB	2/16/01	2/16/01	Application

(Window title: Applications — 17 items, 13.2 GB available — toolbar: Back, View, Computer, Home, Favorites, Applications)

Showing those View Options

To customize the way Finder windows look, use the View Options window. When you choose View➪Show View Options from the Finder menu bar (or press ⌘+J), you see the View Options window (see Figure 7-8).

Sharp-eyed readers may notice that the View Options window shown in Figure 7-8 reads `Applications` in its title bar. That's because the View Options window always bears the name of the active window (the one that will be affected if you click the Window tab instead of the Global tab).

Start by clicking the Global tab at the top of the View Options window. Now, whatever choices you set in this window affect *all* Finder windows for which you haven't specified explicit options (you can do this with the Window tab, which we'll get to in a moment).

First decide whether you want to modify the Global Icon view or Global List view and then choose one or the other from the View pop-up menu. If you choose Global Icon, your options apply to windows in Icon view; if you choose Global List, your choices apply to windows in List view. The choice you make determines what options you see in the Global tab. The following sections describe both choices.

Figure 7-8:
The Global
tab of the
View
Options
window.

The Global tab for Icon view

So you just can't kick that icon habit, eh? Okay . . . here's how to make global settings so all your windows look the same. (If this concept excites you, you really need to get out of the house more!)

In the Global tab of the View Options window, choose Global Icon from the View pop-up menu. Now you're really living on the edge — oooh — set how big you want your icons, how to arrange them in windows, and whether you want to insert a picture as a background for your folder windows (yup, *all* folders).

The following list describes the options you see on the tab after you choose Global Icon from the pop-up menu:

✔ **Icon Size:** Use the Icon Size slider to make icons larger or smaller. To save valuable screen real estate space, we recommend that you keep your icons small. The largest icon size is nothing short of huge. Make sure you have a Finder window open in which icons are visible as you move the slider: that way, you can determine icon size as they shrink or grow, depending on how far you move the slider.

✔ **Icon Arrangement:** Next, decide whether those icons should be penned up or free-range. If you leave the None radio button selected, your icons stay exactly as you place them. Selecting the Always Snap to Grid radio button creates nice, straight lines of icons. At least it usually does: If you drag the Icon Size slider all the way to the left, icon names move from beneath the icon to the right side of the icon. Unfortunately, that means that when you choose the Always Snap to Grid option, they line up in a way we find extremely ugly, as shown in Figure 7-9.

If you select the Keep Arranged By radio button, you can choose a sort order for your icons from the pop-up menu immediately below this button. Your choices are: By Name, By Date Modified, By Date Created, By Size, and By Kind.

Figure 7-9:
The Always
Snap to Grid
option looks
funky with
tiny icons.

✔ **Folder Background:** From this list of radio buttons, you can pick a color or picture for your windows, or opt for none at all. Look at Figure 7-10 to see what a folder looks like with a picture in it. We're not sure that windows should have pictures in them; as you can see in Figure 7-10, some pictures make icons and their names hard to discern. But if you like this feature, be our guest.

Whatever you choose — to insert a picture or choose a color or to choose neither — affects all your windows if you make these selections on the Global tab of the View Options window.

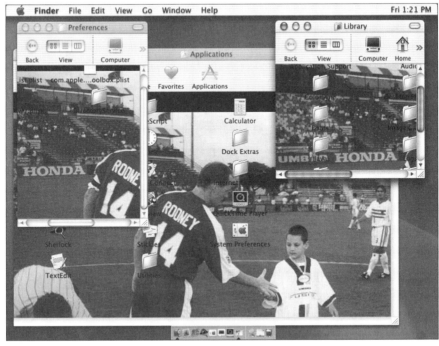

The Global tab for List view

Suppose you prefer List view (instead of Icon view). From the Global tab of the View Options window, choose Global List from the View pop-up menu. In Figure 7-11, you see a cluster of check boxes beneath the Show Columns heading. Most of the options here tell Mac OS X which column fields to display or hide. The choices you make should depend on what information you want displayed, such as:

- ✔ Date modified
- ✔ Date created
- ✔ Size
- ✔ Kind
- ✔ Label
- ✔ Version
- ✔ Comments

Figure 7-11:
Choose
which fields
to display in
List view.

Select the check boxes for the fields you want to see. You can sort items listed in windows by clicking these fields. You can always change your selections later if you find you aren't using a particular field.

There are two more options on this iteration of the global tab that may be useful to you. Near the bottom of this window you see two additional check boxes:

  ✔ **Use Relative Dates:** If you select this check box, Mac OS X intelligently substitutes relative word equivalents — such as yesterday or today — for numerical dates in List view.

    When you set your clock back a day and look at files that you updated that day before setting your clock back, the relative date reads *tomorrow*. Curious but true.

  ✔ **Calculate Folder Sizes:** Selecting this option instructs Mac OS X to do just that — view how much stuff is in each folder when you look at it in List view. The icons (including folder icons) in the active window are sorted in descending order from biggest to smallest when you sort by size.

    If you don't select the Calculate Folder Sizes check box, icons other than folders are sorted by size, with all folders — regardless of their size — appearing at the bottom of the list.

At the bottom of this dialog box, you find the Icon Size control. Select from two radio buttons here to choose between small and large icons in your List views. For our money, we think the smallest ones make windows appear noticeably faster; your mileage may vary.

Being really finicky and choosing your views window by window

Perhaps choosing a global look for your Finder windows is just too big of a commitment for you; or you have a set-up you like, but need a special view for a particular window. Here's how to adjust your window view settings individually.

1. **Open the window you want to set up.**

2. **Choose View⇨View Options from the menu bar.**

3. **Click the Window tab of the View Options window.**

4. **Make sure that the Use Global View Preferences check box is deselected so that you can get to the options for this window.**

   The options in the Window tab are conveniently the same as the global options we describe earlier in this chapter, so have at it and make this special window look just the way you like it.

Chapter 8

Mastering the Save Sheet and the Open Dialog Box

In This Chapter

▶ Navigating your folders

▶ Wandering along the path to any folder

▶ Saving your document

▶ Discovering the differences between the Save and Save As commands

▶ Mastering the Open dialog box

▶ Discerning the subtle differences between the Open dialog box and Save sheets

▶ Knowing what the Open dialog box doesn't show you

*B*eing well-known authorities on things Macintosh, Shelly and Bob receive many calls each year, from friends and relatives, that inevitably begin, "Well, I saved the file and now I don't know where it went." Mark our words, this chapter is one of the most important chapters in this book. If you don't understand the Open dialog box, the Save sheet, and the Save commands (there are two: Save and Save As — you see them when you choose File⇨Open or File⇨Save, respectively, in most programs) — you'll never quite get the hang of your Mac. Yet, mastering these essential techniques is perhaps the biggest problem that many Mac users have.

This chapter is your cure for your save and open woes. Hang with us and pay attention; everything will soon become crystal clear. And keep saying to yourself, "The Save sheet and the Open dialog box are just another view of the Finder," as we explain in this chapter.

You work with Open dialog boxes and Save sheets within applications. You only see them after you launch your favorite application or work within an open or newly created document. For more on launching applications, read through Chapter 4 on icons; for more on creating and opening documents, see the documentation for the program you're using.

Saving Your Document Before It's Too Late

You can create as many documents as you want, but all is lost if you don't save them to a storage device like your hard drive or some other disk. When you *save* a file, you are committing a copy to a disk — either a disk mounted on your Desktop, one available over a network, or wherever.

In this section, we show you how to save your masterpieces and prevent unnecessary pain in your life by developing good saving habits. If you take our advice, you'll save your work

- ✔ Every few minutes
- ✔ Before you switch to another program
- ✔ Before you print a document
- ✔ Before you stand up

If you don't heed this advice and the program you're using crashes while switching programs, printing, or sitting idle (which, not coincidentally, are the three most likely times for a crash), you lose everything you did since your last save.

The keyboard shortcut for Save in almost every program we know is ⌘+S. Memorize it. See it in your dreams. Train your finger muscles to do it unconsciously. Use it (the keyboard shortcut) or lose it (your unsaved work).

Checking out the Save sheet

When you choose to save a file for the first time (by choosing File⇨Save or pressing ⌘+S), a Save sheet appears in front of the window you're saving, as shown in Figure 8-1. You navigate folders in the Save sheet and Open dialog box the same way that you navigate folders in the Finder — by opening them to see their contents. The Save sheet works like the column view in the Finder. That is, you click an item on the left to see its contents on the right, and then click a folder in the right column to open and move it to the left. (See Chapter 7 for more info about navigating in column view.)

Before you can navigate the columns in a Save sheet, you need to click the downward pointing disclosure triangle (to the right of the Where menu, just above the Save button in Figure 8-1) to expand the sheet. Otherwise, you get a small, less functional version of the Save sheet, like you see in Figure 8-1. Click the disclosure triangle and the sheet expands, as you see in Figure 8-2.

○ ○ ○	Untitled.rtf

Save as: [   ]

Where: [Documents] [⬍] [▼]

(Cancel) (Save)

Figure 8-1:
The default
Save sheet
for TextEdit.

Like the column view in a Finder window, you can enlarge the Save sheet to see more. Just drag the lower-right corner of the sheet to the right. Then, when you click items in the current right column of the Save sheet (note that you must have the columns showing to have any columns to deal with here), their contents appear in a new, third column.

After you've saved a file one time, choosing File⇨Save or pressing ⌘+S doesn't bring up a Save sheet anymore. It just saves the file again without any further intervention on your part. Get in the habit of pressing ⌘+S often. It can't hurt, and it may just save your bacon someday.

In Figures 8-1 and 8-2, you can see respectively the Save sheets for the TextEdit program, default and expanded. In programs other than TextEdit, the Save sheet *may* contain additional options, fewer options, or different options, and therefore look slightly different. Don't worry. The Save sheet always works the same, no matter what options are there.

Unlike the Save dialog box in earlier version of Mac OS, in Mac OS X you can move the Save sheet around the screen, just as you can any window, by dragging the window's title bar around (first click on the title bar, and hold down the mouse button while you drag it wherever you desire). The Save sheet moves right along with the window. Also, a Save sheet in OS X doesn't prevent you from using other programs or windows when it's onscreen like older versions of Mac OS did.

Figure 8-2:
The
expanded
Save sheet
for TextEdit.

Wherefore art thou, Where drop-down menu?

Take some time and get to know the Where drop-down menu. It's a great navigation aid and a bit confusing for new users. With it, you can quickly move to a location on your hard drive and open or save a file stored there. Consider the Where drop-down menu a shortcut menu to frequently used folders, your Favorites, and folders you've used recently.

The Where drop-down menu looks a lot like the menu that appeared at the top of the Open/Save dialog boxes in earlier versions of Mac OS. But instead of tracing the folder path (as it did in versions of yore, and as the Finder window's drop-down menu still does), the Where drop-down menu lists four main places where you might save your files (Desktop, Home, Favorites, or iDisk) as well as more folders (under the Recent heading) where you have saved files recently. Therefore, if you move downward into a folder hierarchy and want to back up one, you have to choose an item on the drop-down menu (such as Documents, for example) and move back down the list from there. Yes, that is a pain, but understanding the Where menu can make it a little less confusing.

In this section, we run down the parts of the Where drop-down menu. In the process, we show you why it's best to store your files in certain places on your Mac and how to use the Where menu to quickly reach your favorite folders.

The Where menu works the same whether or not you've expanded the Save sheet by clicking the disclosure triangle.

Hiding your stuff under the right rock

If you've used previous versions of Mac OS, the rules about where to store things were a lot looser. Storing everything within your Documents folder wasn't at all important. But Mac OS X arranges its system files, applications, and other stuff a bit differently than older versions did.

We *strongly* advise you to store all your document files and the folders that contain them in the Documents folder within your home folder. Files that you place outside the Documents folder are very likely to get lost while you navigate through a maze of aliases and folders that belong and make sense to certain programs or parts of the system software — and not to you as a user.

If you have more than one user for your Mac, you could even save a file in another user's folder by accident, in which case you'd *never* find it again.

So, trust us when we say that Documents is the right place to start, not only because it's easy to remember but also because it's only a menu command (Go➪Favorites➪Documents) away, wherever you're working on your Mac.

Saving to the active folder

In the Save sheet, the name at the top in the Where drop-down menu is the name of the active item (be that item a folder, a drive, or the Desktop). In Figure 8-3, the active folder is Folder 2.

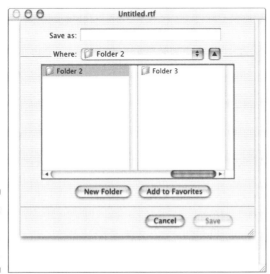

Figure 8-3:
Saving a
file in
Folder 2.

Think of the active item in a Save sheet as akin to the active window on the Desktop. That's where your file is saved by default if you click the Save button without changing the destination folder at all. This concept is important. In other words, if the Documents folder is the active item (as it is in both Figures 8-1 and 8-2), your document is saved in the Documents folder when you click the Save button. If Folder 2 is the active item (as it is in Figures 8-3 and 8-4), your document is saved in Folder 2 when you click the Save button. And so on.

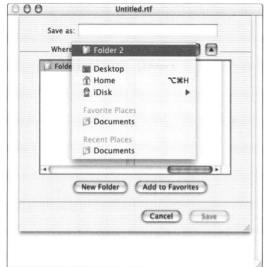

Figure 8-4:
The Where
drop-down
menu of the
Save sheet.

Knowing the best places to save

Mac OS X includes your Documents folder in the Favorite Places section by default, or you can add folders as Favorites by using the Add to Favorites button of the Save sheet. The four main storage areas that Mac OS X gives you are described in the following list:

✔ **Home:** This is your home folder on a Mac running Mac OS X. Every user of this Mac has their own home folder that contains all of his or her stuff — including documents, preferences, applications — everything. You can save documents to your home folder, which is named for you. To do this, choose Home from the Where menu and click the Save button.

We don't, however, recommend saving most of your stuff to your home folder. We find it easier to organize and find files in the Documents folder, away from the files that your Mac needs to operate and to keep track of preferences, fonts, and so forth.

✓ **Documents:** Located within your home folder, the Documents folder is the best place to store your files in our humble opinion. You can organize stuff inside your Documents folder by creating subfolders with meaningful names. For example, in Bob's Documents folder you'd find subfolders named Letters, Databases, Finances, Public Relations, Templates, Articles, and Books.

✓ **Desktop:** This is the root level of your Mac's folder structure. That is, items that you save here won't appear within any other folder, or within a Finder window — they're visible on the Desktop of your Mac.

Technically, files (or folders) on the Desktop are stored in your Desktop folder within your home folder (funny that!). But the exact same files or folders also appear on the Desktop. If that sounds redundant to you, it is — but with good reason. Because OS X is a multi-user operating system and each user has a personal home folder, your Desktop folder is how Mac OS X ensures that the icons you see on the Desktop are your icons and not some other user's.

Again, the Desktop is not a great place to store stuff. If you want to quickly reach an item, first save it in the appropriate folder, then create an alias for it and drag that alias to the Desktop or to the Dock. These items appear on the right when you choose Desktop from the Where drop-down menu.

✓ **iDisk:** If you use a Mac, Apple will provide you with a 20MB virtual disk, called an *iDisk*, at no cost to you. Your iDisk resides on an Apple servers and can only be used if you have an active Internet connection. Just know that if your Internet connection goes down, you won't have access to files you've saved on your iDisk.

One excellent use for your iDisk is to copy important files to it so you have a back-up copy if anything awful should happen to your hard drive or your Mac.

For more information — and to create your own iDisk — visit www.apple.com/itools.

✓ **Favorite Places:** When you designate a folder as a favorite, it appears in the Where drop-down menu. Just select the favorite folder where you want to store a file, and it opens in the Save sheet's rightmost column.

About Recent Places

When you save a file using the Save sheet, the folder containing it is added to the list of recent places. Check out the Recent Places submenu after you save files to several folders, and you'll see all of them on the list in the drop-down menu.

Getting active with the Save As field

When a Save sheet first appears, the Save As field is active and ready for you to type a name into it. If you press the Tab key, the Save As field becomes inactive and the file list box below (the one with the columns in it) becomes active. That's because the file list box and the Save As field are mutually exclusive. Only one can be active at any time. You either navigate the folder hierarchy or you name a file.

Look closely at Figure 8-5; you'll notice that the Save As field is active. You can tell which is active by the thin gray border that the Save As field has around it. In Figure 8-3, by contrast, the file list box is active (has the border) while the Save As field is inactive (has no border).

When you want to switch to a different folder to save a file, click anywhere in the file list box to make it active. In Figure 8-5, this box is displaying the folders (Desktop, Documents, Library, and so on) in the active item (a user's home folder, as in this example, boblev) but the file list box itself is not active. The Save As field is active, though — remember, they're mutually exclusive.

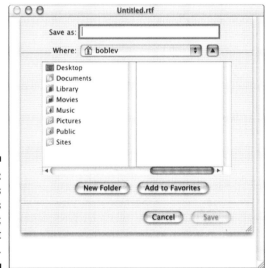

Figure 8-5:
The Save As field is active here; the file list box is not.

The following list discusses a few things to help you get ahold of this whole active/inactive silliness:

   ✔ Look for the thin border that shows you which part of the Save sheet is active. It's around the Save As field in Figure 8-5.

✔ If you type while the file list box is active, the list scrolls and selects the folder that most closely matches the letter(s) that you type. Go ahead and give it a try. For example, typing the letters **pu** in an active file list box selects the `Public` folder.

✔ When the file list is active, the letters that you type do not appear in the Save As field. If you want to type a file name, you have to activate the Save As field again to type in it.

✔ Regardless of which box or field is active at the time, when you press the Tab key on your keyboard, the other becomes active. So if the Save As field is active, it becomes inactive when you press Tab, and the file list box becomes active. Press Tab again, and they reverse — the Save As field becomes active again.

If you don't feel like pressing the Tab key, you can achieve the same effect by *clicking* either the file list box or the Save As field to make it active. Try it yourself and notice again how visual cues let you know which is active.

Putting your finger on the button

Most Save sheets contain the following four buttons: New Folder, Add to Favorites, Cancel, and Save. We describe them all briefly in the following list:

✔ **New Folder:** The New Folder button is a nice touch. Click this button, and you create a new folder inside the active folder in the Save sheet. You will first be given the opportunity to name the folder; then you can save your document there.

✔ **Add to Favorites:** If you find yourself saving a lot of files to a certain folder, it may very well become one of your favorite folders. Click the Add to Favorites button to designate the active folder as a favorite. After you do, you can quickly get to that folder from anywhere, but most especially from the Where drop-down menu in a Save sheet. Just select the folder from the Favorite Places section of the menu to open it.

✔ **Cancel:** Dismisses the Save sheet without saving anything anywhere. In other words, the Cancel button returns things to the way they were before you displayed the Save sheet.

The keyboard shortcut for Cancel is ⌘+. (that is, ⌘+ the period key). The Escape key usually (but not always) does the same thing. This shortcut is a good command to memorize because it cancels almost all dialog boxes, and it also cancels lots of other things. If a program is dragging — for example, your spreadsheet is calculating, your database is sorting, or your graphics program is rotating, and it's taking too long — try ⌘+. (It works — usually).

✔ **Save:** Saves the file to the active folder.

But wait! What if the Save button is grayed out? That only happens when you haven't yet typed a name for your file in the Save As field. Just typing a single character activates the Save button. Before you press Save, you have to name your file. Also, make sure that that you have navigated to the location where you want to save the file before you click the Save button.

It looks like Save and it acts like Save, so why is it called Save As?

The Save As command, which you can find in the File menu of almost every program ever made, lets you resave a file that has already been saved by giving it a different name.

Why would you want to do that? Here's a good (albeit slightly rude) example:

Suppose you have two sisters, Annabelle and Zelda. You write Annabelle a long, chatty letter, and save this document with the stunningly creative name `Letter to Annabelle`. At some point afterwards you decide that you want to send this same letter to Zelda, too, but you want to change a few things.

So you change the part about your date last night (Zelda isn't as liberated as Annabelle) and replace all references to Dick (Annabelle's husband) with Zeke (Zelda's husband; aren't computers grand?).

So you make all these changes to `Letter to Annabelle`, but you haven't saved this document yet. So while the document on your screen is actually a letter to Zelda, its file name is still `Letter to Annabelle`. If you were to save it now without using the Save As feature: `Letter to Annabelle` reflects the changes you just made (that is, the stuff in the letter meant for Annabelle is blown away, replaced by the stuff you wrote to Zelda). Thus, the file name `Letter to Annabelle` is inaccurate.

What you need to do is rename this file `Letter to Zelda`, and you use Save As to do so. Just choose File⇨Save As. A Save sheet appears, in which you can type a different file name. You can also navigate to another folder, if you like, and save the newly named version of the file there.

Now you have two distinct files — `Letter to Annabelle` and `Letter to Zelda`. Both contain the stuff they should, but both started life from the same file. *That's* what Save As is for.

Open (Sesame)

If you've read the earlier parts of this chapter, you probably already know how to use the Open dialog box — you just don't know you know yet. Open dialog boxes are so much like Save sheets that it's scary. To summon an Open dialog box, launch your favorite program and choose File⇨Open (or use the keyboard shortcut ⌘+O, which works in 98 percent of all programs ever made).

Check out a typical Open dialog box in Figure 8-6.

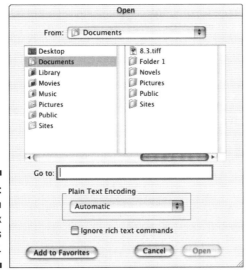

Figure 8-6:
The Open
dialog box
in all its
drab glory.

Getting there with the Go To field

Check out the Go To field near the bottom of the Open dialog box. This field lets you navigate through your folders by typing their folder names (separated by forward slashes — make sure to include the preceding slash) and clicking Open. For example, typing **/Number9/ Documents/Wordstuff** into the Go To field and clicking Open would move you directly to the Wordstuff folder within the Documents folder of your hard drive named Number9.

Given the graphical nature of the Mac interface, many Mac users will probably think this is kind of a lame feature (all that typing!). We must admit, though, that if you want to get to a folder quick and know right where it's at in your folder structure, this is a good way to do it.

Knowing the differences between Open dialog boxes and Save sheets

After you master navigating the Save sheet, you should have smooth sailing using an Open dialog box. They work the same except for a few minor differences:

- **There's no Save As field.** One isn't needed because this dialog box is the one you see when you want to open a file! Because you're not saving or naming a file here, you don't need the Save As field.

- **There's no Where drop-down menu.** In the Open dialog box, you find the From drop-down menu, instead. Why? Because you're opening a file *from* a certain folder, rather than telling your Mac *where* to save it. The From drop-down menu has the same basic job as the Where drop-down menu, and you see the same folders in it that you see in the Where drop-down menu, which we discuss in the "Wherefore art thou, Where drop-down menu?" section earlier in this chapter.

- **There's no New Folder button.** Why? Well, you can't open something that you haven't yet created, right? You don't need to create new folders when you're opening a file, basically, so there's no button to do so. Go figure!

You may notice a couple of other differences between the Save sheet (shown in Figures 8-1 to 8-4) and the Open dialog box (shown in Figure 8-6). Note in Figure 8-6 the Plain Text Encoding drop-down menu and the check box labeled `Ignore Rich Text Commands`. (Both are located near the bottom of the Open dialog box.) These are specific to TextEdit, and have to do with the format that TextEdit uses to save text files. Don't worry about these for now. Just remember that many applications add special items to their Open dialog boxes and Save sheets that help you select formats and other options specific to those programs.

Navigate through the Open dialog box just as you would in a Save sheet. Don't forget the mantra, "The Open dialog box and Save sheet are just another view of the Finder."

Knowing what the Open dialog box DOESN'T show you . . .

When you use a program's Open dialog box, only files that the program knows how to open appear in the file list. In other words, the program filters out files that it can't open, so you don't see them cluttering up the Open dialog box. This method of selectively displaying certain items in Open dialog boxes is a feature of most applications. So, when you're using TextEdit, its Open dialog box won't show you a bunch of spreadsheet files because TextEdit can only open text files. Pretty neat, eh?

On the other hand, not seeing every item in an Open dialog box can be a little disconcerting when you're trying to envision the correlation between the Finder and the Open dialog box.

Stuff that you see in the Finder doesn't always appear in the Open dialog box. That's why we show you the Save sheet first in this chapter: It always shows you everything. In a Save sheet, items that you can't select appear grayed, but they do appear. So . . . if you know that something is in a particular folder but you can't see it in the Open dialog box, consider the possibility that the program you're using isn't capable of opening that kind of document — not every program can open every document.

Chapter 9

Haggling with Removable Media

*I*n this chapter, we show you disk basics: how to format them; how to format them so that our less-fortunate Windows-using brethren (and sisteren) can use them; how to eject them; copying or moving files between disks; and much more. Onward!

Now, some of you with iMacs (or other Macintoshes that don't have a floppy disk drive, which these days is *all* Macs) may be thinking, "My Mac doesn't even have a floppy drive. Why should I read a whole chapter about disks?" Well, we'll tell ya. In this chapter, we tell you lots of info that applies to every Mac user, including folder management and moving or copying files. We also show you how to work with removable media, such as (but by no means limited to) Zip, Orb, Jaz, DVD-RAM, CD-RW, and SuperDisk disks, which many Mac owners also use. If you have a Power Mac G4, for example, you've probably got a Zip drive, CD-RW, or a DVD-RAM drive. And lots of Mac owners add SuperDisk drives, which read both standard 1.4MB floppies and 120MB SuperDisks, so that they can easily copy files for friends, or move their files between home and work.

Comprehending Disks

You should think of the disk icons that appear on the Desktop (and in the Finder window called *Computer*) as if they were folders. That's because disks are nothing but giant folders. When you double-click them, their contents appear in the Finder window just like a folder. You can drag stuff in and out of a disk's window, and you can manipulate the disk's window in all the usual ways. Just like a folder. In fact, for all intents and purposes disks *are* folders.

Is that a disk or a disc?

So how do you spell this critter, anyway? Sometimes you see it spelled d-i-s-k; other times you see it spelled d-i-s-c. If you're wondering what's up with that, here's the skinny.

In the good old days, the only kind of disk was a disk with a k: floppy disk, hard disk, Bernoulli disk, and so on.

Then, one day, the Compact Disc (you know, a CD) was invented. And the people who invented it chose to spell it with a c instead of a k, probably because it's round like a *discus* (think track and field).

Now some people will tell you that magnetic media (floppy, hard, Zip, Jaz, Orb, and so on) are called *disks* (spelled with a k). And that optical media — that is, discs that are read with a laser (such as CD-ROMs, audio CDs, DVDs, CD-RWs) — are called *discs* (spelled with a c).

In this book, that's the convention we follow, because it seems to make sense.

(And because our editors made us do it. <grin>)

The only exception Bob can think of is that you can't use the Duplicate keyboard shortcut (⌘+D) on a disk although you can use it on a folder.

Making Sure Your Disks Are Mac Disks

Brand-new disks sometimes need to be *formatted* — prepared to receive Macintosh files — before they can be used (this is especially true for floppy disks, if your Mac has a floppy drive). We say *sometimes* because you can buy new disks that are preformatted.

When you pop in any type of unformatted disk, your Mac pops up a dialog box that lets you format it. Formatting a disk takes only a few minutes to, so don't pay a whole lot more for preformatted disks unless you really believe that time is money.

Moving and Copying Disks

Moving an icon from one disk to another works the same as moving an icon from one folder to another with one notable exception: When you move a file from one disk to another, you automatically make a copy of it, leaving the original untouched and unmoved. If you want to move a file from one disk to another, you need to delete the original file by dragging it to the Trash.

Copying the contents of a removable disk (Zip and SuperDisk, among others) to your hard drive works a little differently. To do so, click the disk's icon and drag it onto the icon or window for the destination media (for example, your hard drive icon, your hard drive's open window, or onto any other folder icon or open folder window).

When the copy is completed, a folder bearing the same name as the copied disk appears in the destination folder. The new folder now contains each and every file that was on the disk of the same name.

Surprise! Your PC Disks Work, Too!

If you have friends unfortunate enough not to own Macs and you want to share files with them, one of the most excellent features of Mac OS X is that it reads both Mac- and MS-DOS-formatted disks without any user intervention. MS-DOS disks are formatted for use with personal computers (PCs) that run MS-DOS or Windows. If a friend has a Windows computer, you can read his or her disks by just sticking them in your disk drive. Your unfortunate friend, on the other hand, can't do diddly squat with your Mac-formatted disks — yet another reason why Macs are better. (This applies also to other types of disks, including Zip, Jaz, Orb, and SyQuest.)

Although PC-formatted disks will *work* in your Mac, the files on them may or may not. If the files are documents or images, one of your Mac programs can probably open them. But if the files are Windows programs (these often sport the `.exe` suffix, which stands for *executable*), your Mac won't be able to do anything with 'em.

Getting Disks out of Your Mac

You now know almost everything there is to know about disks except one important thing: how to eject a disk. Piece of cake, actually. There are several ways; all are simple to remember:

- Click the disk's icon to select it and then choose File➪Eject (or press ⌘+E).

- Drag the disk's icon to the Trash.

   This drives us nuts, and it has since forever. Anything else you drag into the Trash dies (or at least it does when you choose Finder➪Empty Trash). Why does dragging a disk to the Trash eject it?

- Click the disk icon while holding down the Control key and then choose Eject from the contextual menu.

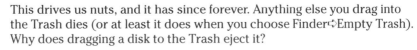

Chapter 10

File Management without Tearing Your Hair Out

*I*n other parts of this book, you can discover the basics about windows and icons and menus. Here, you begin a never-ending quest to discover the fastest, easiest, and most trouble-free way to manage the files on your Macintosh. Along the way, you'll discover what some of the special folders (most notably the multiple Library folders) in Mac OS X are all about.

If just thinking about files and folders sends you into migraine territory, we can help. We're not doctors (although co-author Bob LeVitus plays one in books and magazines), but we've each been wrangling with Macintosh files and folders for more than 14 years now, and we've learned a lot about what works and what doesn't — for us, that is. And while Mac OS X is very different from earlier versions of Mac OS, the fundamentals of organizing files and folders haven't changed that much. So this chapter spares you at least part of our 14-year learning curve.

Remember that we're talking about Mac OS here, and so, just like the Mac interface itself does, we encourage you to develop your own personal style. We don't preach (much) about the right way to organize your files. After you've read this chapter, you'll have all the ammunition you need to organize your files into a Mac environment designed by you, for you.

We won't pretend to be able to organize your Mac for you. Organizing your files is as personal as your taste in music. You develop your own style with the Mac. So in this chapter, we give you some food for thought: some ideas about how we do it, and some suggestions that should make organization easier for you, regardless of how you choose to do it yourself.

After we've discussed *your* files and folders, we'll offer more about the folders Mac OS X creates (and requires). In other words, by the end of this chapter, you'll not only know all about *your* files and folders, you'll also know about the files and folders Mac OS X creates when you install it, and what they do.

Working with Files and Folders

Before we go any further, you first need to understand a bit about files and folders: the difference between a file and a folder; how you can arrange and move files and folders around; and how to nest folders. Then you can concentrate on becoming a more savvy — and organized — Mac OS X user.

Files versus folders

When we speak of a *file*, we're talking about any icon except a folder or disk icon. A file can be a document, an application, an alias of a file or application, a dictionary, a font, or basically any other icon that *isn't* a folder or disk. The main distinction is that you can't put something *into* a file icon. Finally, disks are nothing more than big folders. A disk icon is, for all intents and purposes, the same as a folder icon.

First, we need to get some basic terminology out of the way. Specifically, understanding the concept of files and folders is crucial to comprehending the rest of this chapter.

When we talk about *folders*, we're talking about, well, folders. They look like folders and they can contain files or other folders (which we refer to as *subfolders*). You can put any icon — any file or folder — into a folder. Look in the margin to see a typical folder icon.

Here's an exception: If you put a disk icon into a folder, you get a copy of the disk (as we explain in Chapter 9). But don't forget that you can't put a disk icon into a folder on itself. In other words, you can only copy a disk icon to a different disk. Or, put another way, you can never copy a disk icon into a folder that resides on that disk.

File icons can look like practically anything. If the icon doesn't look like a folder or a disk, you can be pretty sure it's a file.

Creating new folders

So you think Apple has already given you enough folders? Can't imagine why you would need more? Think of creating new folders the same way you would think of labeling a new folder at work for a specific project. New folders help you keep your files organized, or enable you to reorganize them just the way you want.

Creating folders is really quite simple. To create a new folder, just follow these steps:

1. **Decide which window you want the new folder to appear in and then make sure that window is active; or, if you want to create a new folder right on the Desktop, make sure that the Desktop is active.**

   You can make a window active by clicking it, and you can make the Desktop active if you have windows onscreen by clicking the Desktop itself.

2. **Choose File⇨New Folder (or press ⌘+Shift+N).**

   A new, untitled folder appears in the active window with its name box already highlighted, ready for you to type a new name for it.

3. **Type in a name for your folder.**

   If you accidentally click anywhere before you type a name for the folder, the name box will no longer be highlighted. To highlight it again, select the icon (by single-clicking it), and then press Return once. Now you can type in its new name.

   Name your folders with relevant names. Folders with nebulous titles like sfdghb or Stuff — or worst of all, untitled folder — won't make it any easier to find something six months from now.

Navigating Nested Folders

Folders within other folders are often called *nested folders.* To get a feel for the way nested folders work in Mac OS X, check out Figure 10-1. You can see the following from the figure:

- ✔ Folder 1 is one level deep.

- ✔ Folder 2 is inside Folder 1, which is one level deeper than Folder 1, or two levels deep.

- ✔ Folder 3 is inside Folder 2 and is three levels deep.

- ✔ The files inside Folder 3 are four levels deep.

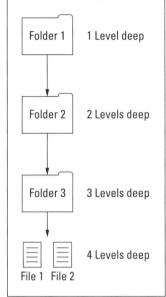

Figure 10-1:
Nested
folders,
going four
levels deep.

If the previous list makes sense to you, you're golden. What's important here is that you are able to visualize the path to Folder 3. That is, to get to files inside Folder 3, you open Folder 1 and then open Folder 2 to be able to open Folder 3. Understanding this concept is important to understanding the relationships between files and folders. Keep reviewing this section and eventually this concept will click — you'll slap yourself in the head and say, "Now I get it!"

Moving files and folders

You can move files and folders around within a window to your heart's content, as long as that window is set to Icon view (we discuss views in Chapter 7). Just click and drag any icon to its new location in the window.

Some people spend hours arranging icons in a window so that they're "just so." But because using Icon view wastes so much screen space, we avoid it like the plague.

You can't move icons around in a window that's viewed as a list or columns, which makes total sense when you think about it. See Chapter 7 for info on views.

Now say you move one file or folder into another folder. As you might expect from Apple, the king of Having Lots of Ways to Do Anything, you have choices. Use either of these two techniques to move any icon — folder, document, alias, or program icon — into folders or onto other disks.

✔ **Drag an icon onto a folder icon:** Drag the icon for one folder (or file) onto the icon for another folder (or disk icon) and then release the mouse button when the second folder is highlighted (see Figure 10-2). The first folder is now inside the second folder. Put another way, the first folder is now a subfolder of the second folder. This technique works regardless of whether or not the second folder's window is open.

Figure 10-2:
Dropping one folder into another.

✔ **Drag an icon into an open folder's window:** Drag an icon for one folder (or file) into the open window for a second folder (or disk), as shown in Figure 10-3.

Figure 10-3:
Dragging a folder into the open window of another folder.

If you try to move an item from one disk to another disk, it's only copied — not moved. Always. Without exception. If you want to *move* a file or folder from one disk to another, you have to trash the original manually after the copying is complete.

Copying files or folders

What if you want to *copy* an icon from one place to another, leaving the icon in its original location and creating an identical copy in the destination window? No problem — all it takes is pressing the Option key.

If you're wondering why anyone would ever want to copy a file or folder, trust us: someday you will. Suppose you have a file called `Long Letter to Mom` in a folder called `Old Correspondence`. You figure that Mom has forgotten that letter by now, and you want to send it again. But before you do, you want to change the date and delete the reference to Clarence, her pit bull, which passed away last year. So now you need to put a copy of `Long Letter to Mom` in your `Current Correspondence` folder.

Read about how to make a copy of a file using Save As in Chapter 8. That technique yields the same result as the methods we discuss in this section.

When you copy a file, it's wise to change the name of the copied file. Having more than one file on your hard drive with the same name is not a good idea, even if the files are in different folders. Trust us, having 10 files called `Expense Report` or 15 files named `Randall's Invoice` can be confusing, no matter how well-organized your folder structure is. Add distinguishing words or dates to file and folder names so that they're named something more explicit, such as `Expense Report 10-99` or `Randall's Invoice 10-30-99`.

You have three ways to copy a file or folder, as follows:

- ✔ **Drag an icon from one folder icon onto another folder icon while holding down the Option key (see Figure 10-2).** This technique works regardless of whether the second folder's window is open or not.

  When you copy something by dragging and dropping it with the Option key held down, the mouse pointer changes so that it includes a little plus sign (+) next to the arrow. Neat!

- ✔ **Drag an icon into an open window for another folder while holding down the Option key (see Figure 10-3).**

- ✔ **Choose File⇨Duplicate or Control+click the file or folder you wish to duplicate and select Duplicate from the contextual menu.** For more about the Duplicate command, check out Chapter 6.

You can have lots of files with the same name *on the same disk* (although, as we mention earlier, it's probably not a good idea). But your Mac won't let you have more than one file with the same name *in the same folder.*

Everything we've discussed so far in this chapter works at least as well for windows using the List view or Column view as it does for windows using Icon view. (You gotta love those disclosure triangles in the column view! We do.) In other words, we only used the Icon view in the previous examples because it's the best view to show you what's going on. For what it's worth, both authors find moving and copying files easiest in windows using either the List or Column views, not the Icon view we've been showing you. (For more sordid info on views, see Chapter 7.)

Opening files with drag and drop

Macintosh drag-and-drop is usually all about dragging text and graphics from one place to another. But there's another angle to drag-and-drop — one that has to do with files and icons. Here's the deal: You can open a document by dragging its icon onto the proper application. In other words, you can open a document you created with Microsoft Word by dragging the document icon onto the Microsoft Word application's icon. The Word icon will highlight, and the document will launch. Of course, it's usually easier to just double-click a document's icon to open it. The proper application opens automatically when you do. Or at least it does most of the time. This brings us to why we're explaining this drag and drop thing here.

If you try to open a file and Mac OS X can't find a program to open the file, Mac OS X prompts you with an error window, as shown in Figure 10-4. You can either click OK (and abort the attempt to open the file) or pick another application to open it.

Of course, you can click the Choose Application button and pick another program from a regular Open File dialog box (see Chapter 8 for details). If you click the Choose Application button, you see a dialog box (conveniently opened to your Applications folder, and shown in Figure 10-5). Applications that you can't use to open the file are dimmed. For a wider choice of applications, choose to view All Applications instead of Recommended Applications from the Show pop-up menu.

Figure 10-4: Oops! Mac helps you find the correct application.

There is no application available to open the document " TOC 2-7 ".

Choose Application...   OK

Figure 10-5:
Choosing an
application
to open
a file.

We know a better way: You can use drag-and-drop to open a file using a program other than the one that would ordinarily launch when you open the document. To do so, just drag the file onto the application's icon (or alias) and presto! the file opens in that application.

If the icon does not highlight and you release the mouse button anyway, the document will be dropped into the folder that contains the application (with the icon that didn't highlight).

You can't open every file with every program. For example, if you try to open an MP3 (music) file with Microsoft Excel (a spreadsheet), it just won't work — you'll either get an error message or a screen full of gibberish. Sometimes you just have to keep trying until you find the right program; other times, you won't have a program capable of opening the file.

Only applications that *may* be able to open the file will highlight when you drag the document on them. That doesn't mean the document will be usable, just that the application *can* open it.

Suffice it to say that Mac OS X is smart enough to figure out which applications on your hard drive can open which documents, and also to offer you a choice.

You're usually best off clicking the Choose Application button and sticking to the Recommended Applications choice in the Choose Application dialog box. But if that doesn't work for you, at least you now know another way — drag the file onto an application's icon and see what happens.

Organizing your stuff with subfolders

As we mention earlier in this chapter, you can put folders inside of other folders to organize your icons. A folder inside another folder is called a *subfolder*. Create subfolders based on a system that makes sense to you. Table 10-1 gives a few organizational topic ideas and naming examples for subfolders:

Table 10-1	Folder Organization Topics
Sort By Topic	*Sample Subfolder Topics*
By type of document	Word-Processing Documents, Spreadsheet Documents, Graphics Documents
By date	Documents May-June, Documents Spring '99
By content	Memos, Outgoing Letters, Expense Reports
By project	Project X, Project Y, Project Z

When you notice your folders swelling and starting to get messy (that is, becoming filled with tons of files), subdivide them again using a combination of these methods that makes sense to you. For example, suppose that you start by subdividing your Documents folder into multiple subfolders, as shown in Figure 10-6. Later, when those folders begin to get full, you might subdivide them even further, as shown in Figure 10-7.

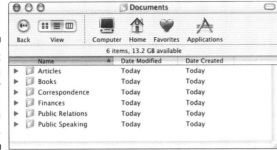

Figure 10-6: Organizing your Documents folder with subfolders.

Our point is: Allow your folder structure to be organic, growing as you need it to grow. Let it happen. Don't let any one folder get so full that it's a hassle to deal with. Create new subfolders when things start to get crowded. If you want to get a better feel for when to use subfolders, see the nearby sidebar.

Creating subfolders . . . or not

How full is too full? When should you begin creating subfolders in a folder? That's impossible to say, but having too many items in a folder can be a nightmare, as can having too many subfolders with just one or two files in them. Our guideline is this: If you find more than 15 or 20 files in a single folder, begin thinking about ways to subdivide it.

On the other hand, some of Bob's bigger subfolders contain things that he doesn't often access. For example, his `Bob's Correspondence 1992` folder contains more than 100 files. But because Bob wants to keep this folder on his hard drive just in case he does need to find something there — even though he doesn't use it very often — its overcrowded condition doesn't bother him. Your mileage may vary.

Here are some tips to help you decide whether to use subfolders or just leave well enough alone:

✔ **Don't create subfolders until you need them.** In other words, don't create a bunch of empty folders because you think that you might need them someday. Wait to create new folders until you need them; this prevents you from opening an empty folder when you're looking for something else — which is a complete waste of time.

✔ **Let your work style decide the file structure.** When you first start working with your Mac, you may want to save everything in your `Documents` folder for a week or two (or a month or two, depending on how many new documents that you save each day). After a decent-sized group of documents accumulates in the `Documents` folder, you may want to take a look at them and create logical subfolders for them.

If you want to monkey around with some subfolders yourself, a good place to start is the `Documents` folder — it's inside your home folder (that is, it's a *subfolder* of your home folder).

If you use a particular folder a great deal, make an alias of it and then move the alias from the `Documents` folder to the Dock, your home folder, or to your Desktop (for more info on aliases, see Chapter 4) to make the folder easier to access. For example, if you write a lot of letters, you could keep an alias to your `Correspondence` folder in your home folder, in the Dock, or on your Desktop for quick access. (By the way, there's no reason you can't have a folder appear in all three places if you like. That's what aliases are all about, aren't they?)

If you put the `Documents` folder in the Dock, you can press and hold on it to reveal its subfolders, as shown in Figure 10-8.

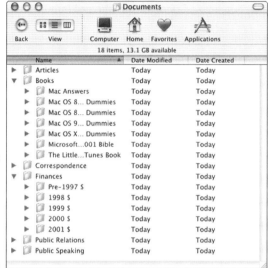

Figure 10-7:
Further
subdividing
a growing
Documents
folder.

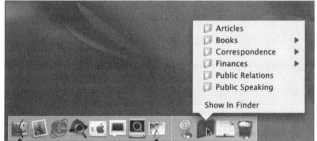

Figure 10-8:
It's super-
convenient
to have your
Documents
folder in the
Dock.

Getting Up to Speed with the Mac OS X Folder Structure

In addition to your personal files and folders, your Mac OS X system has its own folder structure. These folders contain the Mac operating system files, as well as folders that include system preferences, fonts, and other files that are used by everyone with access to this Mac. These shared files include applications, programs, utilities, and other software.

Also, each person who uses the Mac has his or her own set of folders that contain documents, preferences, and other information that's used by only that person.

If you're the sole person who accesses your Mac, you have only one user. Regardless, the folder structure that Mac OS X uses is the same, whether you have one user or ten.

We realize that a lot of people don't share their Macs with others. And if you're one of these folks, you might wonder why we keep mentioning sharing and multiple users and the like. Well, Mac OS X is based on the Unix operating system — a multi-user operating system that's used by high-end servers and workstations that are often shared by several people. Mac OS X has both the benefit of this arrangement and a bit of the confusion caused when a single user like you fires up a computer that could be set up for several people. That's why Mac OS X folders are organized the way that they are — with different hierarchies for each user, and for the computer as a whole.

All these files are stored in a nested folder structure that's a bit tricky to understand at first (we discuss nested folders in the previous section). This structure makes more sense after you spend a little time with it and learn some basic concepts.

In this section, we walk you through these different folder structures one by one, starting with the place where you'll spend most of your time — your home folder.

Getting inside your Computer (folder)

We'll start out with the Computer folder, which is the top level of the folder hierarchy. The Computer folder shows all the storage devices (hard drives, CD- or DVD-ROM, Zip disk, and so forth) that are currently connected to your Mac. Figure 10-9 shows two disks: Number 9 and X. You also see the Network icon, with which you can access servers or shared Macs on your network. (Don't quite know what file sharing's all about? Read Chapter 16 for the whole scoop on sharing files with other Macs and sharing your Mac with other users.)

Figure 10-9:
The contents of the Computer window.

To find the Computer folder, just press ⌘+Option+C, or click the Computer icon in the toolbar of any Finder window.

You may have more or fewer icons in your `Computer` folder than the three you see in Figure 10-9 (depending upon how many disks you have mounted), but we're going to drill down on the one that holds your Mac OS X stuff. In Figure 10-9, that hard drive is called *X* — of course, we have no idea what yours is called; if you haven't changed it, it's probably called *Macintosh HD*. Double-click that icon to open it.

Inside your boot disk icon (the one with OS X installed on it; the one called *X* in Figure 10-9) is everything on that disk. You should see five folders (unless you've added some). We'll go through each of them for you.

Applications

The `Applications` folder is located at the root level of your boot drive (the one with OS X installed on it), and is accessible with a click of the Application button on the toolbar, from the Go menu, or by pressing ⌘+Option+A. In this folder, you find all the applications that Apple includes with Mac OS X. All users of a given Mac have access to the items in the `Applications` folder. (Read more about the `Applications` folder in Chapter 13, and more about the toolbar in Chapter 6.)

Library

The `Library` folder at the root level of your Mac OS X hard drive is like a public library — it stores items that everyone with access to the Mac can use. You'll find two different `Library` folders on your hard drive — the one at root level of your OS X disk, and another in your home folder.

Okay, we weren't entirely truthful, but only for your own good: There's actually a third `Library` folder inside the `System` folder, which we'll discuss in a page or two. But for now, heed this warning: Leave this folder alone — don't move, remove, or rename it or anything within it. It's the nerve center of your Mac.

Think of the `Library` folder inside your home folder like a library in your own house (have you ever actually been in a house with its own library?). We talk more about these `Library` folders in upcoming sections.

You find a bunch of folders inside the `Library` folder at root level (the public `Library` folder). Most of them contain files you never need to open, move, or delete. (For what it's worth, just about all of them are preferences of one kind or another.) The only folder here that most users will ever work with is the `Fonts` folder, which houses all the fonts installed on the Mac. Fonts can either be available to everyone who uses the Mac (stored here) or only to a single user (stored in that user's `Library` folder, the one in their home folder). We discuss fonts more in Chapter 12.

Leave this `Library` folder pretty much alone unless you're using the `Fonts` folder. Don't remove, rename, or move any files or folders. Mac OS X uses these items and is very picky about where they're kept and how they're named.

System Folder

If you have Mac OS 9.1 installed on the same disk as OS X, this folder contains your Mac OS 9.1 System Folder (which the Classic environment requires). You can read more about Classic in Chapter 14.

System

The System folder includes the files that your Mac needs to start up and keep working. Leave this folder alone — don't move, remove, or rename it or anything within it. It's a part of the nerve center of your Mac.

If you've used any previous version of Mac OS, you should notice two things about the System folder:

✔ The folder doesn't include the same items, or the same arrangement of files and folders.

✔ The folder is now simply called System, rather than System folder.

Also gone are the System file and Finder file that have been around since the first Mac. Instead, a larger number of files make up the Mac OS X system (which is based on the Unix operating system).

Users

When you open the Users folder, you see a folder for each person who uses the Mac and the Shared folder.

The Shared folder that you see in the Users folder allows everyone who uses the Mac to use the files stored there. If you want other people who use your Mac to have access to a file or folder, this is the place to stash it.

In the next section, we drill down from the home folder bob1 to see what was inside. If user bob1 logs onto this Mac using his username, his home folder (bob1) opens when he clicks the Home button.

There's no place like home

Your home folder is the most important folder to you as a user — or at least the one where you will probably spend most of your time — but it's only part of Mac's higher-level folder structure. In this section, we walk you through this structure so that you understand where your home folder fits in, and so that you'll be able to find applications and other items shared among everyone who uses your Mac.

The new Mac folder structure takes getting used to, especially if you're an old-time Mac user who's used to arranging things pretty much the way you want. Take heart, though: After you get the hang of the new way of arranging things, it makes sense.

We strongly recommend that you store all the files that you create or work with in one of the folders of your home folder, whether in the Documents folder or in another folder that you create.

The advantage of using the Documents folder is that you can quickly locate the folder from the Go menu, or by pressing ⌘+Option+H (H for *home*, of course).

When you open your home folder, you see a Finder window with your username in the title bar. This username might be your first name, your first and last names, or your nickname — whatever you choose when setting up your Mac (we discuss your username in Chapter 16). Seeing your username in the Finder window's title bar tells you that you're in your home folder. Every user has a home folder named after their username in the Users folder. In Figure 10-10, you can see that Bob's home folder is named bobl — that's the nickname he used when he first set up his Mac.

Figure 10-10:
Bob's home
folder.

Your home folder has several folders inside it, created by Mac OS X. You can create more if you like — in fact, every folder that you *ever* create should be within your home folder. We explain this as we describe the other main folders on your hard drive in the following list.

Your home folder contains eight folders by default. The following four are the most important ones:

✔ **Documents:** This is the place to put all the documents (letters, spreadsheets, recipes, and novels) that you create. (For more on the Documents folder, check out Chapter 8.)

✔ **Library:** Preferences (files containing the settings that you create in System Preferences and other places) are stored in the Library folder, along with fonts (as described earlier in this chapter), links to your favorite items, Internet search sites, and other stuff used by you and only you.

✔ **Public:** If you share your Mac, you can't work inside other users' folders. But you can share files with others by storing them in this folder. (Read more about Public folders in Chapter 16).

✔ **Desktop:** If you store items (files, folders, applications, or aliases) on the Desktop, they appear there. The files themselves, however, are actually stored in this folder.

If you decide that you don't want an item on the Desktop anymore, you can delete it by dragging its icon from the Desktop folder to the Trash, or by dragging its icon from the Desktop itself to the Trash. Both techniques yield the same effect — the file is in the Trash, where it remains until you empty the Trash.

In previous versions of Mac OS, the Desktop folder resided at the root level of the Mac, and was invisible — items stored on the Desktop appeared on the Desktop and the folder containing them was hidden from view unless you were using File Sharing to connect to a remote Mac. In Mac OS X, each user has his or her own Desktop, and the items there are stored in the user's Library folder or within the Desktop folder.

✔ **Movies, Music, Pictures, and Sites:** All these folders except Sites are empty until you put something in them; Sites contains a few files that your Mac needs if you enable Web Sharing (in the Sharing System Preferences pane, which we describe in Chapter 15).

Your Library card

The Library subfolder of your home folder is the repository of everything that Mac OS X needs to customize your Mac to your tastes. You won't spend much time (if any) adding things to the Library folder, or moving them around within it, but it's a good idea for you to know what's in there. In the "Library" section earlier in this chapter, we discuss the Library folder that's used to specify preferences for the Mac as a whole. But *this* Library folder is all about you and your stuff.

Be cautious with the Library folder because Mac OS X is very persnickety about how its folders and files are organized. As we discuss in the "Library" section earlier in the chapter, you can add and remove items safely from most Library folders, but *leave the folders themselves alone.* If you remove or rename the wrong folder, you could render OS X inoperable. It's like the old joke about the guy who said to the doctor, "It hurts when I do that," and the doctor replies, "Then don't do that."

To find the Library folder, click the Home icon in the toolbar of any Finder window and then open the Library folder. You should see several folders there (the exact number of folders in the Library folder depends on the software that you install on your Mac — for example, if you have an e-mail account, you should see a folder called Addresses, but if not, it won't be there). Some of the more important standard folders in the Library folder include:

✔ **Assistants:** When you first set up your Mac or the Internet, an *assistant* helps you along. (See Chapter 13 and this book's Appendix for more on setting up your machine.) The actual files the assistant uses to do its thing are contained in this folder.

✔ **Favorites:** When you add an item to your list of Favorites, an alias of it goes here (scope out Chapter 4 for more about aliases). If you choose Favorites from the Go menu or click the Favorites button on the Finder window's toolbar, this is the folder you see.

If you decide that a particular item is no longer a favorite of yours, you can open this folder and drag the no-longer-loved item to the Trash.

✔ **Fonts:** This folder is empty unless you install your own fonts here. The fonts that come with Mac OS X are not stored here, but rather in the Library folder at the root level of your Mac OS X hard drive. We discuss that folder earlier in this chapter in the "Library" section.

If you want to install fonts that only you have access to, you put them here. To install a font, drag its icon to this folder. It will only be available when you're logged in; other users will not be able to use a font stored here. To install a font that's available to anyone who uses this Mac, drag it onto the "public" Library folder instead, the one you see when you open your hard disk's icon.

If your Mac is set up for multiple users, only users with *admin privileges* can put stuff into the "public" Library folder. (For more information on admin privileges, check out Chapter 16.)

✔ **Internet Search Sites:** The files in this folder are used by Sherlock to contact and search Internet sites. (Read through Chapter 11 for the basics on Sherlock.) Besides the big batch of Internet search sites that come with Mac OS X, you can use search engine files that you can download from the Internet. Store them here and use them with Sherlock.

✔ **Preferences:** The files in this folder hold the information about things that you customize in Mac OS X. Whenever you change a system or application preference, that info is saved to a file in the Preferences folder.

Don't mess with the Preferences folder! You should never need to open or use this folder unless something bad happens — like if you suspect that a particular preference file has become corrupted (that is, damaged). Our advice is to just forget about this folder and let it do its job.

Part III
Doing Stuff with Your Mac

The 5th Wave   By Rich Tennant

"IT'S NOT THAT IT DOESN'T WORK AS A COMPUTER,
IT JUST WORKS BETTER AS A PAPERWEIGHT."

In this part . . .

Moving right along, Part III comprises how to do stuff with your Mac. In this section, it's off to the Internet first — how to get it working and what to do with it after you do. Next, we help you decipher the myriad Print options to better help you become a modern-day Gutenberg. You'll also learn about the applications that come with Mac OS X, the Classic environment, and how to make Mac OS X look and feel the way you want it.

It's an excellent section if we do say so ourselves, and one you definitely don't want to miss.

Chapter 11

Internet-Working

● ●

In This Chapter

▶ Getting an overview of the Internet

▶ Presurfing with the Internet Setup Assistant

▶ Surfing the Web with Internet Explorer (IE)

▶ Searching with Sherlock

▶ E-mailing with Mail

● ●

Simply put, use the Internet to connect your Macintosh to a wealth of information residing on computers around the world. Lucky for you, Mac OS X has the best and most comprehensive Internet tools ever shipped with a Mac operating system. In this chapter, we cover the top two Internet tools: the *World Wide Web* (that's the *www* you see so often in Internet addresses) and *e-mail* (which stands for *electronic mail*).

This chapter covers only the barest minimum of stuff that you need to know to connect to the Internet. If you're interested in knowing more about Macs and the Internet, look for *The Internet For iMacs For Dummies* by Bob LeVitus and Natanya Pitts (published by Hungry Minds, Inc.) at fine bookstores everywhere. In all fairness, we have to admit that this book was written before OS X came along and doesn't have any OS X specific content. Still, it does cover the Internet in full and loving detail far beyond what we can provide in this chapter.

The Internet and Your Mac

The Internet, which is a giant conglomeration of connected computers sometimes referred to as the *Information Superhighway,* offers innumerable types of services. With an Internet connection, you can view text and graphics on your computer, even if the text and graphics are sitting on a computer in Tokyo and send and retrieve messages and computer files to and from almost anywhere in the world in milliseconds.

Other Internet services include live online chatting, bulletin board discussions called *newsgroups*, file transfer protocol (FTP), and video conferencing. After you have your connection set up (we discuss this process in the "Setting Up for Surfing" section later in this chapter), we urge you to check out these nifty features. Unfortunately, although these other features are pretty cool, going into much detail about them is also beyond the scope of this book.

The most interesting part of the Internet, at least in our humble opinion, is the Web. This is the part of the Internet in which you traverse (that is, *surf*) to Web sites and view them on your computer with software called a *Web browser*.

Mac OS X offers built-in Internet connectivity right out of the box. For example, your machine comes with

- ✔ Its own built-in Point-to-Point Protocol (PPP) client for making modem connections to the Internet. If you don't even know what a modem is, don't worry. Skip ahead to the next section and all will become clear.

- ✔ Microsoft's Internet Explorer (Web browser that enables you to browse the Web, download remote files via File Transfer Protocol [FTP], and more).

- ✔ The Mail application for e-mail.

Before we can talk about browsers and e-mail software, we first help you configure your Internet connection. Because most Mac users like things to be easy, Mac OS X includes a cool piece of software called *Internet Setup Assistant* to help you find and configure an account with an Internet service provider (ISP). After your Internet connection is up and running, you can use Internet Explorer, which is included with OS X, to cruise the Internet.

Setting Up for Surfing

Before you can surf the Internet, you need to do a few things first. We walk you through them in the following sections.

If you're a typical home user, you need three things to surf the Internet:

- ✔ A modem or other connection to the Internet, such as Integrated Services Digital Network (ISDN), Digital Subscriber Line (DSL), cable modem, or satellite Internet service (though at this writing we don't know of any of these last that are compatible with Macs).

  If you use any technology other than a regular (analog) modem to connect your computer to the Internet, your network administrator (the person who you run to at work when something goes wrong with your computer) or ISP will have to help you set up your Mac because setting up those other configurations is beyond the scope of this book.

✔ An account with an ISP (an Internet Service Provider such as EarthLink) or America Online. As we write this chapter, America Online has not released a version of their software that works with Mac OS X. While it may become available by the time you read this book, it didn't exist as of this writing.

✔ You need to have installed the Mac OS X default installation, which contains networking software your Mac needs to connect to the Internet (or any network for that matter).

It starts with the modem

A *modem* is a small, inexpensive device that turns data (that is, computer files) into sounds and then squirts those sounds across phone lines. At the other end, another modem receives these sounds and turns them back into data (that is, your files). All current Macs include an internal 56 Kbps modem.

To connect your modem, just plug a phone line into the modem. On Macs with internal modems, that simply means plugging one end of the phone cable into the phone-plug-shaped port on the side or back of your Mac and the other end into a live phone outlet. If you have an external modem, plug the phone cable into the modem and plug the modem cable into the modem port on the back of your Mac. The modem port is the one with the little phone icon next to it. Finally, plug the modem *into an AC power source.*

  The modem port on Macs with internal modems looks a lot like the Ethernet port. You could plug a phone cable into the Ethernet port, but it doesn't fit right and it wouldn't get you connected to the Internet. The modem port is the smaller of the two — look for the phone icon next to it. Conversely, the Ethernet port is the larger of the two. Look for an icon that looks something like this: <•••>. Both ports and their icons appear in the margin here (the Ethernet port is on the left).

High-speed connections

If you have a cable modem, digital subscriber line (DSL), or other high-speed Internet connection — or are thinking about getting one any of these — you can use them with your Mac. In most cases, you connect your Mac to the Internet via a cable plugged into the Ethernet port of your Mac and into an external box, which is either connected to a cable or phone outlet, depending on what kind of access you have to the Internet. Your cable or DSL installer-person should set everything up for you. If they don't, you'll have to call that service provider for help — troubleshooting your high-speed connection is, as we say, "beyond the purview of this book."

Your Internet service provider and you

After you make sure that you have a working modem, you need to select a company to provide you with access to the Internet. These companies are called *Internet service providers* (ISPs). Just like when choosing a long-distance company for your phone, the prices and services that ISPs offer vary, often from minute to minute. After you make your choice, you can launch and use Internet Explorer, Mail, or any other Internet application. Keep the following in mind when choosing an ISP:

- ✔ If you're using a cable modem, your ISP is your cable company. With DSL, your provider is either your local phone company or an ISP you've chosen to get your service connected. In that case, your ISP usually contacts the phone company and arranges for DSL installation and setup for you.

- ✔ If you subscribe to America Online (AOL), you don't need to do anything more than install the AOL software and log on to AOL. You can ignore the rest of this chapter except for the parts about surfing with Internet Explorer and the preferences section at the end. You don't need Mail (the e-mail program included with OS X) if you get your mail through AOL.

As we mention a few pages back, America Online has not released a version of its software that works with OS X. When one does become available, what we say above should be true.

In addition to America Online, check out dedicated Internet service companies such as EarthLink, Netcom, and AT&T. Also investigate what your local cable or phone company offers. In other words, it pays to shop around for the deal that works best for you.

- ✔ The going rate for unlimited access to the Internet, using a modem, is $10–$20 per month. If your service provider asks for considerably more than that, find out why. *Note:* If you have a cable modem, DSL, or other high-speed connection, you'll probably pay at least twice that much.

- ✔ When you installed OS X (assuming you did, and that it didn't come pre-installed on your Mac), the Installer program asked you a bunch of questions about your Internet connection, then set everything up for you. This process is detailed at the end of the book in the Appendix. If you didn't have an Internet connection (an ISP) at that time, you'll need to configure the Network System Preferences pane yourself. Although we cover Network System Preferences pane in depth in Chapter 15, how to configure it so your Mac will work with your ISP is beyond the scope of this book. If you have questions or problems, your ISP ought to be able to assist you. And if they can't, it's probably time to try a different ISP.

Browsing the Web with Internet Explorer

Apple includes Microsoft Internet Explorer with Mac OS X. You can use the other dominant Internet browser — Netscape 6 — but you have to download and install it first (you can find Netscape by poking around at www.netscape.com). In this chapter, we concentrate on Internet Explorer (IE) because it's installed and ready to go on your Mac by default. (And, because we both prefer it.) It's no problem to install and use more than one Web browser on your hard drive if you so desire.

If you don't like Netscape, check out OmniWeb, yet another Web browser. Unlike Netscape, OmniWeb was designed specifically for OS X. For more info visit www.omnigroup.com. Finally, the newest browser on the OS X scene is iCab. It was unfinished when we wrote this; you can check to see if a final version has been released at www.icab.de/. Frankly, all the browsers are pretty darned good; and if you're looking for an alternative to the included Internet Explorer browser, we recommend that you try each of the others to decide which you like best.

Getting up and running with IE

Before you can browse with IE, the first step is to open the program. No problem. As usual, there's more than one way. You can launch Internet Explorer by

✔ Clicking the Internet Explorer icon on the Dock (look for the big blue lowercase *e*)

✔ Double-clicking the Internet Explorer icon in the folder of the same name in your Applications folder

When you first launch IE, it automatically connects you to the Internet and displays an Apple Web page designed especially for new Net surfers (see Figure 11-1). We don't have room in this book to describe everything about IE, but we'll hit the highlights from the top of the IE window.

Click the Personalize Your Page! link at the top of the page to customize this startup page to display only the stuff you like.

"What's this button do?"

The buttons along the top of the window — Back, Forward, Stop, Refresh, Home, and so forth — do pretty much what their names imply. Play with them a bit, and you'll see what we mean.

Below the Address field are some more buttons that take you directly to pages that may interest you, such as the Apple.com Web site, the Apple tech Support Web site, and The Apple Store. Clicking any of them transports you instantly to that page.

Figure 11-1:
Apple's
Excite Web
page for
new users.

"Address me as Sir, rodent!"

Beneath the top row of buttons is the Address field. This is where you type Web addresses, or *URLs* (Uniform Resource Locators), that you want to visit. Just type one in and press Return to surf to that site.

Web addresses almost always begin with `http://www`. But Internet Explorer has a cool trick: If you just type a name, you usually get to the appropriate Web site that way without typing **http**, **//**, or **www**. For example, if you type **apple** in the Address field and then press Return, you go to `http://www.apple.com`. Or if you type **microsoft**, you're taken to `www.microsoft.com`. Try it; it's pretty slick.

"Get me a Tab, would you dahling?"

IE gives you five tabs down the left side of the browser window that let you look at two things at once. Just click a tab to open a pane on the left of your screen. To close the left window, just click the tab that corresponds to it.

Explore all the tabs if you want to get the most from Internet Explorer. Following is a brief description of each tab:

> ✔ **Favorites:** View a Web site in the main page on the right and the Web sites you like to visit most often are listed on the left. Otherwise known as *bookmarks*, this tab is where you save the addresses of your favorite Web sites. We briefly discuss in the "Playing Favorites" section later in the chapter.

- **History:** This tab holds links to all the Web sites you've visited recently.

- **Search:** Click this tab to hunt for sites and people on the Web.

- **Scrapbook:** Use this tab to save pages exactly as they are when you put them in the scrapbook. Because Web pages can change from day to day, this is convenient if you want to save a page for future reference, but you aren't sure that it'll still be the same later if you just bookmark it.

- **Page Holder:** With this tab, you can copy a page to browse its links without using the Back button. The linked pages come up in the main window on the right.

Change the size of the left tab's display window by clicking the vertical bar between it and the right pane and then dragging it to move the border.

Playing Favorites

Clicking the Favorites tab (top-left; next to the big red apple in Figures 11-1 and 11-2) shows your favorites on the left, while the page you're viewing remains on the right, as shown in Figure 11-2. You can open a Favorite by clicking it. To open a folder full of Favorites (they're the same favorites and folders on the IE Favorites menu), just click the disclosure triangle to the left of its heading.

Your copy of IE comes with some pointers — known in Web parlance as *favorites* (they're called *bookmarks* in Netscape) — that take you to other nifty Mac sites to check out.

Bookmarks are favorites, and *favorites* are bookmarks. Both words describe the same exact thing — shortcuts to Web sites. In this chapter, we use the words interchangeably. But be careful not to confuse Internet Explorer's favorites with Mac OS X's favorites. They serve a similar purpose: Both are shortcuts to something you use often, but they are not interchangeable. In other words, even though they're both called favorites, your OS X favorites are not used by IE, and your IE favorites are not used by OS X.

To manage your favorites, choose Favorites⇨Organize Favorites. A window listing your favorites and the folders containing them appears. You can move your favorites, create or remove folders, and otherwise treat favorites just like files in the Finder. To delete a favorite, just select it and then press Delete or Backspace.

Here you'll find favorites to Apple sites, hardware and software vendors, Mac publications, and more. Take a look at the list of great Web pages your pals at Apple have put together. Choosing any item from the Favorites menu takes you to that Web page. Be sure and explore the included Favorites when you have some time; most, if not all, are worth checking out.

Figure 11-2:
The too-fab
Favorites
tab in
action.

Searching with Sherlock

Looking for something on the Internet? Check out Sherlock, an application included with Mac OS X that can help you locate stuff on your computer, scour general-purpose Internet search engines with the options under the Internet button, or get more specific with one of the six other Internet buttons.

In this section, we show you how to find Sherlock, how to use it to search your hard drive or the Internet, and how to get help with it when all else fails.

Starting Sherlock

You have three ways to invoke Sherlock, you can

- Choose File⇨Find from the Finder menu bar.

- Press ⌘+F.

- Click the Sherlock icon on the Dock. (Read more about the Dock in Chapter 3).

A quick look at Sherlock's features

Whichever way you choose to start Sherlock, the Sherlock window appears when you do so, as shown in Figure 11-3.

Files button   Internet buttons   My Channel button   Find button

Figure 11-3:
Sherlock
finds stuff
on your
computer
and on the
Internet.

The top of the Sherlock window sports a series of buttons. From left to right they are: Files, Internet, People, Apple, Shopping, News, Reference, Entertainment, and My Channel. Click the button that best represents what you're searching for. If you're looking for a Web site, click Internet. If you want to search news sites, click News. If you want to search for products and prices, click Shopping. And so on.

Below the buttons is a text entry field. This is where you type the word or phrase you want to search for. When you've typed something, you click the magnifying glass icon to begin your search.

The bottom part of the Sherlock window changes depending on which button you've pushed (before a search). Then, it displays the results of your search (after you search, of course).

Actually searching with Sherlock

You use Sherlock to find things — on your hard drive and on the Internet. In this section, we'll first show you how to search with Sherlock. Then, after you've got the basics down, we'll talk more specifically about using Sherlock to finding stuff on your hard drive.

To use Sherlock, follow these steps:

While we use an Internet search in our example below, you follow the same steps to search your hard drive. After you know how to search with Sherlock, you know how to search both the Internet and your hard drive with Sherlock.

1. **Start Sherlock (we describe how in the "Starting Sherlock" section earlier in this chapter).**

2. **Click one of the seven Internet buttons to choose a channel (Figure 11-4 shows the News channel).**

   Yes, we know there are actually nine icons, but the leftmost icon represents your hard drive and the rightmost icon represents My Channel, where you can create your own channel to focus your Internet searches. The other seven buttons are for Internet searches.

   Space prohibits us from further coverage of the My Channel button. To learn more about it, open Sherlock Help (choose Help⇨Sherlock Help), type **My Channel** in the text entry field, and then click the Ask button. In seconds a detailed explanation fills your screen.

3. **In the text entry field beneath the Sherlock search buttons, type a word or a phrase you want to search for.**

   If you're doing a people search, type both the person's first and last name.

4. **(Optional) To limit your search to a specific site or sites, select (mark) the On check box next to the sites you want to search and deselect check boxes next to engines you don't want to search.**

   Sherlock will only search sites with a check mark to the left of their name. To use all available sites, make sure all the check boxes have check marks in them, as shown in Figure 11-4.

5. **To begin your search, press Return or click the magnifying glass button in the upper-right corner of the Sherlock window.**

   Sherlock passes your request along to the Web site(s) you select and then displays a list of search results, similar to Figure 11-5.

6. **Double-click any item in the results display list to launch your browser and display the Web page for that item.**

To start a new search, repeat Steps 2 through 6.

Unfortunately, in addition to whatever it is you're looking for, each Internet search also brings you a slew of intrusive advertising (at the bottom of the Sherlock window, as in Figure 11-5) that can't be turned off. Boo. Hiss.

Figure 11-4:
Choosing
an Internet
channel in
Sherlock.

Figure 11-5:
Sherlock
search
results for
Apple
Computer.

Searching for files on your hard drive

First make sure you click the hard drive button at the top of the window — the leftmost one. Then, in the text box just below it, type in the name of the file that you're looking for (novel in Figure 11-6), and then click the Find button (the magnifying glass icon) or press the Return key on the keyboard. In a flash, you see every file on the drive that you searched that matches the word you type in the text entry box.

As you see in Figure 11-6, several items on this hard drive contain the word *novel.*

Getting search results

When Sherlock concludes its search, select the folder or file that you want. At this point, you have three ways to open the folder or file. Choices, choices.

 ✔ Choose File➪Open Item.

 ✔ Press ⌘+O.

 ✔ Double-click the file in the middle or bottom part of the Sherlock window.

The bottom part of the Sherlock window shows you the path to any file you select in the middle of the window. In Figure 11-6, you can see that the Great American Novel folder is selected (it's highlighted). In the bottom part of the Sherlock window, you can see that item stored in the Documents folder. Furthermore, you can open any folder in the lower part of the Sherlock window (such as X, Users, bobl, Documents, Books, or Great American Novel in Figure 11-6) using any of the three techniques above.

Sometimes, when you find an item you want to look at other items in that same folder. If so, you can open the folder that contains the item, and — you guessed it — you have three ways to do that, too:

 ✔ Choose File➪Open Enclosing Folder.

 ✔ Press ⌘+E.

 ✔ Double-click the desired folder in the bottom part of the Sherlock window.

Finding stuff inside files

In addition to searching by file name and attributes, Sherlock also lets you search inside your files for a word or phrase. But before you can search by content you need to "index" your home folder, which we discuss in the next section.

Why do you have to index? Because without an index, it would take Sherlock hours to search every file on your disk. The index allows Sherlock to complete most finds by content searches in mere seconds.

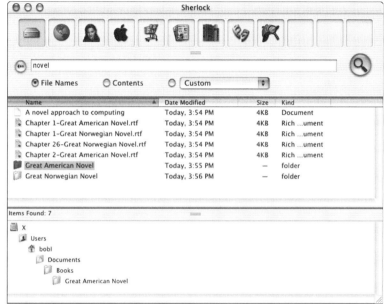

Figure 11-6:
Sherlock's
novel
search.

Indexing your home folder

Selecting the Contents radio button (beneath the text entry box) in the Sherlock window enables you to search for words within documents. So, for example, if you're looking for a letter that you wrote containing the phrase *You are a scumsucking dog*, you can search for the word *scumsucking* in every document in your home folder. But you do need to index your home folder before using this feature. Luckily, doing so is an easy (albeit sometimes slow) process.

To index your home folder, click Files button at the top of the Sherlock window, select your home folder in the middle part of the Sherlock window, and choose Find⇨Index Now.

If you want Sherlock to index your home folder automatically whenever Sherlock is opened, choose Sherlock⇨Preferences and select the `Automatically Index Items When Sherlock is Opened` check box. You can also select the `Automatically Index Folders When They're Added to the Files Channel` check box to do just that. We recommend selecting (marking) both boxes so that your indexes are kept up to date without any further intervention on your part.

Depending upon how many files you have and the speed of your Mac, indexing a home folder can take anywhere from a few minutes to many hours. But it's not a problem — because indexing occurs in the background, you can continue to work while Sherlock indexes. Nice touch, huh?

Users of Mac OS 8 and 9 will appreciate this feature. Under those versions indexing slowed your Mac to a crawl, making it nearly impossible to continue working in other applications. OS X's preemptive multitasking makes this a thing of the past — you won't even notice that Sherlock is indexing.

Narrowing your search options

If searching by name alone finds too many files, you can narrow your search by pulling down the Custom menu beneath the text entry field and choosing the last item, Edit. Or, you can choose Find⇨More Options. The More Search Options dialog box appears when you click the Edit button (see Figure 11-7). Customize your search by selecting one or more of the limiting criteria available within this dialog box.

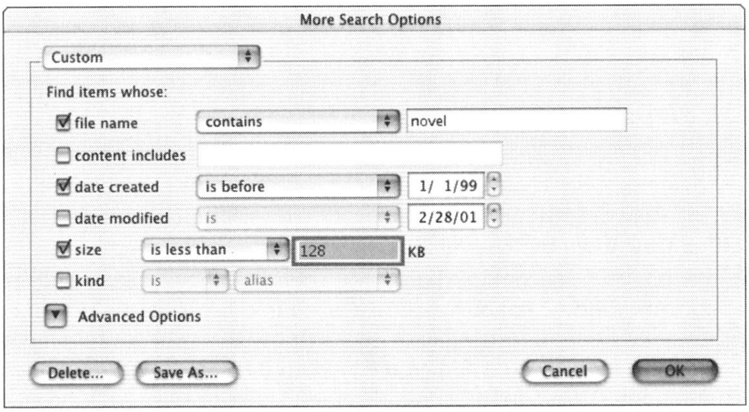

Figure 11-7:
A custom
search for
files that
contain
novel in
their names,
were
created
before
1/1/99, and
are smaller
than 128K.

> **More Search Options**
>
> Custom
>
> Find items whose:
> ☑ file name — contains — novel
> ☐ content includes —
> ☑ date created — is before — 1/ 1/99
> ☐ date modified — is — 2/28/01
> ☑ size — is less than — 128 — KB
> ☐ kind — is — alias
> ▼ Advanced Options
>
> Delete...   Save As...   Cancel   OK

Narrow your search by selecting or deselecting the following check boxes:

- ✔ **File name:** The name of the file.
- ✔ **Content Includes:** Finds words in documents. Requires indexing first (see next section).
- ✔ **Date Created:** The date the file was first saved.
- ✔ **Date Modified:** The last time the file was modified and saved.
- ✔ **Size:** The size of the file in kilobytes.

  A kilobyte (K) is a measure of how much space a file uses on your hard drive. There are 1,024K in a megabyte (MB); 1,024MB in a gigabyte (GB); 1,024GB in a terabyte (TB), and so on.

- ✔ **Kind:** Kind of file (application, alias, and so on).

For even more search options, click the Advanced Options arrow at the bottom of the window. You'll then see even more choices: File Type code; Creator Type code; Version (is or is not a particular number); Folder (is empty, shared, or mounted); Lock Attribute (file/folder is locked or is not); Icon Name (is locked or not); Custom Icon (has or doesn't have); and Visibility (is or isn't invisible).

Adding new search engines to Sherlock

You can add new search engines to Sherlock by downloading new plug-in files from these sites:

```
http://www.apple.com/sherlock/plugins.html
http://www.apple-donuts.com/sherlocksearch/index.html
```

After you download a new plug-in, it goes in `the Internet Search Sites` folder (which you'll find in the `Library` folder that's in your home folder). If you open this folder, you'll see a bunch of folders that correspond to the buttons at the top of the Sherlock window. Put the new plug-in into the appropriate folder.

Use aliases to make a single plug-in appear in more than one channel.

Checking out Help Center

We need to use another weasel-out here. We could write an entire chapter about using Sherlock, but one of the rules we *For Dummies* authors must follow is that our books can't run 1,000 pages long. So we're going to give you the next best thing: Open the Help Center (by choosing Help➪Sherlock Help from the Sherlock menu bar). A special Sherlock help window appears; you can search for any topic here.

Getting Your E-mail with Mail

Mail is a program that comes with Mac OS X that lets you send, receive, and organize your e-mail. You can also use Mail to create an address book that includes the e-mail addresses of your friends and family.

You can use other applications to read Internet mail. Netscape, for example, has a built-in mail reader, as does Microsoft Office 2001 (Entourage). But the easiest and best mail reader around (meaning, the best one on your hard drive by default) is probably Mail. And you can't beat the price; it's free!

Mail is fast and easy to use, too. Click the Mail icon on the Dock to send and receive mail; the Mail icon looks like a cancelled postage stamp. Mail's main window looks like Figure 11-8.

Composing a new message

Here's how to create a new e-mail message:

1. **Choose File⇨New Compose Window (or press ⌘+N).**

   A new window appears; this is where you compose your email message, as shown in Figure 11-9.

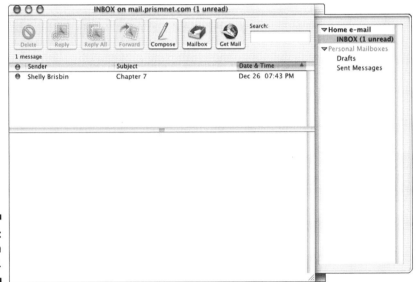

Figure 11-8:
Mail's main window.

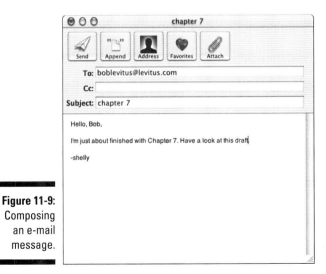

Figure 11-9:
Composing an e-mail message.

2. **Place your cursor in the To field and type someone's e-mail address.**

   Use the address that you see in Figure 11-9 (boblevitus@boblevitus.com) if you don't know anyone else to send mail to.

   After you finish addressing a mail message, you can add the recipient to your Mail address book. After you add an address to your Mail address book, all you have to do is type the first few letters of the recipient's name and Mail fills in the entire address for you. Neat, huh? (Choose Help⇨Mail Help to find out more about this feature.)

3. **Press the Tab key twice to move your cursor to the Subject text field, and then type a subject for this message.**

4. **Click in the main message portion of the window (refer to Figure 11-9 — it's the part with the text that begins, "Hello, Bob") and type your message there.**

5. **When you're finished writing your message, click the Send button to send the e-mail immediately or choose File⇨Save as Draft to save it in the Drafts folder so that you can work on it later.**

   If you do save your message to the Drafts folder (so you can write more later, perhaps), you can send it when you're ready by opening the Drafts folder, double-clicking the message, and then clicking the Send button.

Checking your mail

How do you check and open your mail? Easy. Just click the Get Mail button at the top of the main Mail window.

You can configure Mail to send and receive your mail every *x* minutes by choosing Mail⇨Preferences, and then clicking the Accounts icon at the top of the window. Pull down the Check Accounts for New Mail pop up menu and make a selection — every 1, 5, 15, 30, or 60 minutes — or choose Manually if you don't want Mail to check for mail automatically at all.

Adding an item to your address book

If you have any fair number of contacts — relatives, friends, or the odd enemy that you keep in touch with for self-punishment purposes — you may want to check out the nifty Address Book application that comes Mac OS X. You can enter new contacts in the Address Book application or while you're working in Mail.

Follow these steps to create a new entry in the Address Book:

1. **Launch the Address Book application by double-clicking its icon in the Applications folder.**

   The Address Book appears. The first time that you open Address Book, you see an empty address book.

2. **To create a new entry, click the New button at the top of the Address Book window.**

   An untitled address card appears. The First Name text field is initially selected (you can tell by the dark border it now has, as shown in Figure 11-10).

Figure 11-10: A completed address card in Address Book.

3. **Type the person's first name in the First Name text field.**

4. **Press Tab.**

   Your cursor should now be in the Last Name text field.

   You can always move from one field to the next by pressing Tab. And, in fact, this shortcut works in almost all Mac programs that have fields like these. Furthermore, you can move to the previous field by pressing Shift+Tab.

5. **Type the last name for the person into the Last Name text field.**

   Continue this process, filling in the rest of the fields shown in Figure 11-10.

6. **When you're done entering information, click the Save button.**

   The main Address Book window reappears displaying the info you just entered. A mockup contact for Bob appears in Figure 11-11.

To add more info about any Address Book entry, select it (as shown in Figure 11-11; you can tell it's selected when it's gray), click the Edit button at the top of the Address Book window, and then make your changes.

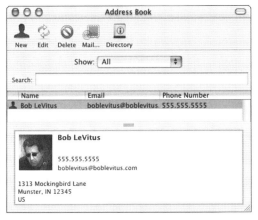

Figure 11-11: The new address card viewed in the main Address Book window.

You can do some pretty neat stuff with Address Book that we just don't have room to cover in this book. For example, you can organize your contacts into groups so that you can e-mail everyone in the group with one click. You can assign categories to your contacts so they're easy to find in bunches (use headings such as Soccer, Business, Family, or Friends). You can create a blank e-mail message to a contact by clicking the Mail button in the Address Book window. And much more.

A Quick Overview of iTools

iTools is a set of free Internet-based services provided by Apple. Although iTools isn't specifically a Mac OS X feature (they're available to Mac OS 9 users and have been for more than a year), we'd be remiss if we didn't at least mention them and give you some background so you can check them out. There are five iTools at this writing including:

 ✔ **Mac.com:** An e-mail service run by Apple that lets you have an e-mail address in the form of *yourname@mac.com*

 ✔ **iDisk:** Your own personal 20MB Internet-based virtual disk

 ✔ **HomePage:** The easiest way we know of to build your own home page

 ✔ **KidSafe:** A program that works with Mac OS to shield your kids from inappropriate material on the Internet

 ✔ **iCards:** Electronic greeting cards you can e-mail to your friends

The first two iTools — Mac.com and iDisk — are beautifully integrated with OS X. For example, the aforementioned Mail program is set up to work perfectly with a Mac.com e-mail account. All you have to do is supply your username and password. And iDisk is a choice in the Finder's Go menu, although you can't use it until you visit the Apple Web site and create your own (free) iTools account.

So what are you waiting for? To sign up, surf to `http://itools.mac.com`.

Chapter 12

Publish or Perish: The Fail-Safe Guide to Printing

*P*rinting is the process for getting what's on your screen onto paper. We know you probably know that, but our editor insisted we start this chapter by defining printing. And so we have.

Printing under OS X should be as simple as pressing ⌘+P and then pressing Return or Enter key. Happily, that's usually how easy printing something is. When it isn't, however, printing turns into a raging nightmare. If you configure your printer and printing software properly, printing is as easy as can be. And that's pretty darned easy.

In this chapter, we scare away the bogeymen to help you avoid any printing nightmares. We walk you through the entire process as if you just unpacked a new printer and plugged it in.

Even if you upgrade from an earlier version of Mac OS, you probably want to work through the steps in this chapter because things have changed significantly in Mac OS X.

Before Diving In . . .

Before we even start talking about hooking up printers, you ought to know a few things. So here's a little list that tells you just what those things are:

✔ **Read the documentation that came with your specific printer.** Hundreds of different printer makes and models are available for the Mac, so if we contradict something in your printer manual, follow your manual's instructions first. If that effort doesn't work, try it our way by using the techniques you'll be reading about in the rest of this chapter.

✔ **The Print and Page Setup sheets differ slightly from program to program.** Although the examples that we show you in this chapter are representational of what you will probably encounter, you may come across sheets that look a bit different. For example, the Print and Page Setup sheets for Microsoft Word include choices that we don't cover in this chapter, such as Even or Odd Pages Only, Print Hidden Text, and Print Selection Only. If you see commands in your Print or Page Setup sheet that we don't explain in this chapter, they're specific to that application; look within its documentation for explanation.

✔ **We use Apple's bare-bones word processor, TextEdit, for the examples in this chapter.** If you want to follow along, you'll find TextEdit in your `Applications` folder.

✔ **Don't forget Mac OS Help!** Many programs support this excellent Apple technology; it can be the fastest way to figure out a feature that has you stumped. So don't forget to check the Help menu before you panic. (We cover the Help menu in Chapter 6.)

So, with those things in mind, get ready, set, print!

Ready: Connecting and Adding Your Printer

Before you can even think about printing something, you'll have to connect a printer to your Mac, and then tell OS X that the printer exists. Here's how.

Connecting your printer

We must stress that there are thousands of printer models you could connect to your Mac, and each one is a little different from the next. In other words, if what you're about to read doesn't track with the printer you're trying to connect, we again implore you to RTFM (that's "Read The Fine Manual," in case you're wondering.)

That said, here are some very general steps to connecting a printer:

1. **Connect the printer to your Mac with the cable snugly attached at both ends (printer and computer).**

For your printer to work, you've got to somehow connect it to a data source. (Think of your phone — you can't receive calls without some sort of connector between the caller and the callee.)

You need to plug the printer cable into the appropriate port on the back of your Mac. Therein lies the rub. Mac technology has changed dramatically since the previous editions of this book, when we used to say, "Begin by connecting the printer to the Printer port on the back of your Mac (with both the Mac and the printer turned off, of course — but you knew that, didn't you?)." Now we tell you, "You need to plug the printer cable into the appropriate port. . . ." Why are we being so vague? Because we have to. You see, these days, printers don't always connect to the same port. Some printers connect to the Ethernet port or to an Ethernet hub. Others connect through the Universal Serial Bus (USB) port. We've even seen a few that connect via the FireWire port. So read the instructions that came with your printer and plug your printer into the appropriate hole (port) for your Mac.

Typically, your printer connects to your machine with a USB, Ethernet, or FireWire cable. Don't confuse this with your printer's AC power cord (the kind you find on everyday appliances). If your printer didn't come with a cable that fits into one of the ports on your Mac, contact your printer manufacturer and ask for one; it's cheesy not to provide the proper cable with a printer.

3. **Plug the AC power cord printer cord into a power outlet (yup, the regular kind in the wall).**

   Note: Some printers require you to plug one end of the AC power cord into the printer; others have the AC power cord attached permanently. The point is that your printer won't work if it's not connected to a power source.

4. **Turn on your printer (check your manual if you can't find the switch).**

5. **If your printer came with software, install it on your hard drive, following the instructions that came with the printer.**

6. **Restart your Mac.**

   That's it!

Setting up a printer for the first time

After you connect your computer and printer with a compatible cable, provide a power source for your printer, and install the software for your printer, you need to configure your Mac so that it and your printer can talk to each other.

The Print Center application, which we are about to discuss, is the tool that you use to tell your Mac what printers are available. Note that many of the steps involving Print Center require that your printer is turned on and warmed up (that is, run through its diagnostics and start-up cycle).

Follow these steps to set up a printer for the first time:

1. **Launch Print Center by clicking the** Applications **button in the tool-bar of any Finder window, opening the** Utilities **folder, and double-clicking Print Center.**

2. **Click the Add button at the bottom right of the Print Center window.**

   The Printer List window appears; this is where you choose the kind of connection you have to your printer. Most printers are either connected directly to your Mac via a USB port, or over a network, using AppleTalk.

3. **In the Add Printer window, click the Directory Services pop-up menu and choose the type of printer connection that you have so that you can find the printer that you want to use.**

   In Figure 12-1, we choose AppleTalk because the printer we'll be working with is on a network, connected to the Mac via an Ethernet cable on an AppleTalk network.

   After you choose your printer connection type, you see the names and kinds of available printers in the Printer List window. In Figure 12-1, our AppleTalk printer, named *LaserWriter*, appears.

AppleTalk and USB are by far the most common kinds of printer connections for Macs. Another option available in the Add Printer window is LPR. If your printer is on a TCP/IP network, you need to configure the printer using its network address. LPR printers are almost always found on large corporate networks. Fortunately, you can almost always find network administrators available for such larger networks. Your administrator should be able to help you set up an LPR printer.

If you encounter trouble setting up a printer for Mac OS X (or even if you don't have any trouble), you may want to contact your printer's manufacturer about getting the latest, greatest driver. Many printer manufacturers are offering new drivers with enhanced functionality. You may find new drivers for your printer on the Web. Your printer manufacturer likely has the driver you need available for (free) download on its home page.

Figure 12-1:
Available
printers
with the
specified
connection
type appear
here.

4. **Click to select the name of the printer that you want from the list and then click the Add button.**

This window closes and the Printer List window appears, containing the printer you just added. If you've added printers before, they appear here, too. Now you can print your first document! Make sure, though, that you have the document set to look how you want it to print. Read through the "Set: Setting Up Your Document with Page Setup" section later in this chapter for more info.

Telling your Mac about your printer

Even if a printer is connected to your Mac or is available via a network, your Mac doesn't know it exists until you explicitly use the Add Printer command to create access to it. Adding a printer enables you to identify the kind of direct or network connection you have, and to customize any settings you want before you try to print your first document.

Checking for AppleTalk if you don't see your printer

If you have an AppleTalk printer but don't see it on the list when you click the AppleTalk option from the pop-up menu (shown in Figure 12-1), check in System Preferences to see whether AppleTalk is active. (We cover System Preferences in Chapter 15, but here's how you check this.)

1. **Choose System Preferences from the Apple (🍎) menu.**

   The System Preferences window opens.

2. **Open the Network Preferences pane by clicking the Network icon in the System Preferences window.**

   The System Preferences window turns into the Network window.

3. **Choose Built-in Ethernet from the Configure pop-up menu.**

   The tabs across the top pane change to reflect Ethernet settings.

4. **Click the AppleTalk tab of the Network pane, and check to see whether the Make AppleTalk Active check box is selected.**

5. **If the Make AppleTalk Active check box is not checked, check (select) it.**

6. **After you make AppleTalk active, quit System Preferences and go back to the Print Center application (click its icon on the Dock; or, if you quit or restarted, launch it — it's in the** Utilities **folder inside your** Applications **folder) and add your AppleTalk printer. (See the section "Setting up a printer for the first time" where we detail adding your printer.)**

7. **When you've added and configured a printer, you may quit Print Center.**

To tell your Mac about your printer, follow these steps:

1. **If your printer is not turned on, turn it on (if you don't know how to turn on your printer, consult its manual).**

2. **Open Print Center (we show you how in the previous section).**

   If you've previously used Print Center to configure a printer for your Mac, the name of that printer appears in the Printer List window. If you've never walked through this process before, you see a dialog box that lets you know that you have no printers available (shown in Figure 12-2), asking whether you would like to add a printer. We tell you how to do that earlier in this chapter.

Figure 12-2:
No printers available — yet!

You have no printers available.

Would you like to add to your list of printers now?

Cancel   Add...

Set: Setting Up Your Document with Page Setup

After you set up your printer, the hard part is over. You should be able to print a document quickly and easily — right? Not so fast, Buck-o. Read here how the features in the Page Setup sheet can help you solve most basic printing problems. With this sheet, you can also choose paper size, page orientation, and scaling percent (see Figure 12-3).

Become familiar with Page Setup — you may not need to use it right this second, but it's a good friend to know. Almost every program that can print a document has a Page Setup command on its File menu.

Note that some programs use the name *Page Setup*, and others use *Print Setup*. (Print Setup is the quaint, old-fashioned term, more popular in the System 6 era than today.)

Users of inkjet printers or non-PostScript printers may see slightly different versions of the Print and Page Setup sheet. The differences should be minor enough not to matter.

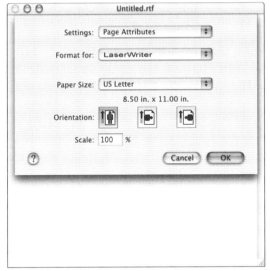

Figure 12-3:
The Page
Setup sheet
in TextEdit.

Click the little question mark in the lower-left corner at any time for help with the Page Setup sheet. Page Setup help will open immediately in the Help Viewer if you do.

The options within the Page Setup sheet are as follows:

✔ **Settings:** When the default Page Attributes displays in this pop-up menu, you see what configuration options are available, as you see in Figure 12-3. In that same pop-up menu, you can also choose Summary to get a list of the options that apply to the current document, based on what you've set up in the Page Setup sheet.

✔ **Format For:** In this pop-up menu (in the middle of the Page Setup sheet), you find the name of the active printer. If you have several printers configured, you can choose any of them from this list. As you see in Figure 12-3, our LaserWriter printer is on the menu.

✔ **Paper Size:** Use options in this pop-up menu to choose the type of paper currently in the paper tray of your printer, or to choose the size of the paper that you want to feed manually. The dimensions of the paper you choose appear below its name.

Page Setup sheet settings remain in effect until you change them. If you print an envelope, don't forget to change back to Letter before trying to print on letter-sized paper.

- ✔ **Orientation:** Choose from options in Orientation to tell your printer whether the page you want to print should be a portrait-oriented page (like a letter, longer than it is wide) or landscape-oriented (sideways; that is, wider than it is long) page. Click one of the icons with the little person on it, which are, from left to right: Portrait, Landscape facing left, and Landscape facing right. You can see them in Figure 12-3 next to the word Orientation.

- ✔ **Scale:** Use the Scale control percentages to enlarge or reduce your image for printing. Just type a new value into the Scale text entry box, replacing the default number 100.

Most programs also offer additional Page Setup choices. If your program offers them, they'll usually appear in a pop-up menu in the Page Setup sheet. Adobe Photoshop and Microsoft Word have them; TextEdit doesn't.

Go: Printing with the Print Sheet

After you connect and configure your printer, and set up how you want your document to print, you come to the final steps before that joyous moment when your printed page pops out of the printer. Navigating the Print sheet is the last thing standing between you and your output. In the sections that follow, we'll talk about some print options you'll probably need someday.

Although most of the Print sheets that you see look like the figures we show in this chapter, others may differ slightly. The features in the Print sheet are strictly a function of the program with which you're printing. Many programs choose to use the standard-issue Apple sheet as shown in this chapter, but not all do. If we don't explain a certain feature in this chapter, chances are good that it's a feature that's specific to the application you're using and is explained in that program's documentation.

Printing a document

If everything has gone well so far, the actual act of printing a document is pretty simple. Just follow the steps below and in a few minutes, pages should start popping out of your printer like magic.

1. **Open a document that you want to print.**

2. **Choose File⇨Print (or press ⌘+P).**

   You see the basic Print sheet, as shown in Figure 12-4.

3. **Wait a few minutes; then walk over to your printer and get your document.**

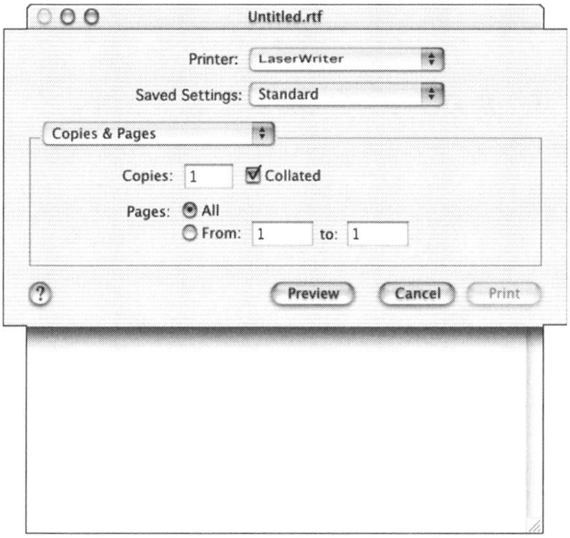

Figure 12-4:
Your basic
Print sheet.

Choosing from different printers

Just as you can in the Page Setup sheet, you can choose which printer you want to use from the Printer pop-up menu of the Print sheet. Remember that you can only choose from the printers that you have added using Print Center, as we discuss in the "Setting up a printer for the first time" section earlier in this chapter.

Choosing custom settings

If you've created a custom group of settings previously, you can choose from them in the Saved Settings pop-up menu of the Print sheet. We touch more on this feature in the "Save Custom Settings" section later in this chapter.

The Print sheet also features another pop-up menu — the one labeled Copies & Pages in Figure 12-4 — that offers additional options. In addition to Copies & Pages, you can choose

- Layout
- Output Options
- Summary
- Save Custom Setting

We go through these options and their suboptions one at a time in the following sections.

Dictating perfection . . . sort of

The Print command appears in the File menu in the vast majority of the Mac programs that you'll use. Every so often you may come across a program that doesn't follow these conventions, but we would say at least 95 percent of commercial Mac programs put the Print command in the File menu and use ⌘+P for its keyboard shortcut.

One of the best things about the Mac is that Apple has published a set of guidelines that all Mac programs should use. Consistency among programs is one of the Mac's finest features. Notice how 95 percent of all programs house the Open, Close, Save, Save As, Page Setup, and Print commands in their File menus and the Undo, Cut, Copy, and Paste commands in their Edit menus? That's the kind of convenience and consistency that the Macintosh Human Interface Guidelines recommend.

Macintosh Human Interface Guidelines also recommend that the keyboard shortcut ⌘+P should be reserved for the command "plain text" (just like how the keyboard shortcuts ⌘+B and ⌘+I are usually used to format bold and italic text, respectively). Fortunately, software developers listened to Apple about the second item and ignored Apple about the first, so ⌘+P is almost always the shortcut for the Print command in the File menu.

Note: The ⌘+P keyboard shortcut *won't* work for you if any one of the following is true with the software you're using:

✓ The Print command is on a different menu.

✓ There *is* no Print command.

✓ The Print keyboard shortcut is anything but ⌘+P.

If any of the above is true for a program you're using, you just have to wing it. Look in all the menus, and check out the product's documentation to try and get a handle on the Print command for that program. You can also write the software company a brief note mentioning that it could make things easier on everyone by putting the Print command in the proper place and using the generally agreed-upon keyboard shortcut.

Copies & Pages

When Copies & Pages is selected in the pop-up menu, you can choose how many copies to print and the page range you want to print.

Click in one of the fields in the sheet, and then press the Tab key. Your cursor jumps to each of the text fields in the sheet in rotation. Pressing Shift+Tab makes the active field jump backward.

✓ **Copies:** In this text field, set how many copies you want to print. The Print sheet defaults to one copy (1) in most applications, so you'll probably see the numeral 1 in the Copies field when the Print sheet appears. Assuming that's the case, don't do anything if you want to print only one copy. If you want to print more than one copy of your document, highlight the 1 that appears in the Copies field and type the new number of copies that you want.

✔ **Pages:** Here you find two radio buttons to choose from: All or From. If you want to print your entire document, select the All option. If you want to print only a specific page or range of pages, select From and then type the desired page numbers in the From and To text entry boxes. For example, suppose that you have a 10-page document. You print the whole thing and then notice a typo on page 2. After you correct your error, you don't have to reprint the whole document — only the one with the correction. Reprint only page 2 by typing a **2** in both the From and To fields. You can type any valid range of pages (you can't print out page 20 if your document is only 15 pages long) in the From and To fields.

Layout

Choose Layout from the pop-up menu to set the number of pages per printed sheet, the layout direction, and whether you prefer a border. (See Figure 12-5.)

✔ **Pages per Sheet:** Choose from preset numbers here in this pop-up menu to set the number of pages you want to print on each sheet. (Note that the pages will appear smaller than full-size if you use this option.)

✔ **Layout Direction:** Choose from one of four buttons that govern the way the small pages are laid out on the printed page.

Click one of these buttons, the proxy (the rectangle on the left that's displaying the numbers 1–16 in sequential order in Figure 12-5) will change to show you the effect of your choice.

✔ **Border:** Your choices from this pop-up menu are single hairline, single thin line, double hairline, and double thin line.

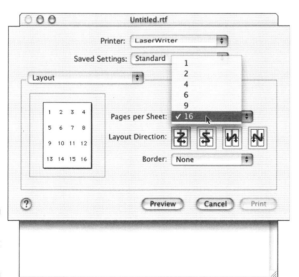

Figure 12-5:
The Layout dialog box.

Output Options

Choose Output Options from the pop-up menu to save your file as a PDF. *PDF* stands for *Portable Document Format,* the file format made famous by Adobe and its Acrobat program. Almost anyone with a computer can open and view PDF documents using Acrobat Reader or the OS X Preview application, which you'll find in the `Applications` folder.

Unless the program you're using added something, PDF is the only choice on this screen. So why the heck is it called Output Options? We think it should be singular and say something more descriptive, such as "Save as PDF."

If you're preparing a file for someone else to use on another computer, PDF is often the best format to use because it preserves both text and graphics exactly as they appear on-screen.

Summary

When you select Summary in the pop-up menu, you can see the printing details for your document, as shown in Figure 12-6. Look here to verify your print job settings: how many copies you want, whether you want them collated, the page range of your print job, your layout choice(s), and whether to save a file as a PDF.

Save Custom Settings

After you finalize the printer settings for Copies & Pages, Layout, and Output Options, you can choose Save Custom Settings from this same pop-up menu. From now on, a Custom setting appears as an option in the Saved Settings pop-up menu. Just choose your saved set before you print any document with which you want to use it.

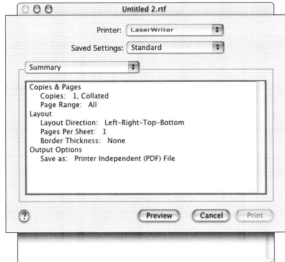

Figure 12-6:
Summary
for the to-
be-printed
document.

Previewing Your Documents

When you click the Preview button on a Print sheet, you see a version of the page or pages you're about to print, displayed by the Preview utility at a size small enough to allow you to see the whole page at once (see Figure 12-7).

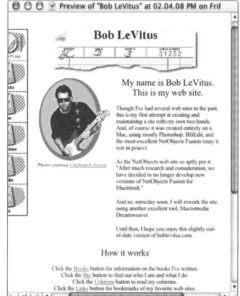

Figure 12-7:
A Print
Preview of
an Internet
Explorer
document.

If you have any doubt about the way that a document will look when you print it, check out Preview first. When you're happy with the document preview, just choose Print from the File menu (or press ⌘+P). Preview works with the Preview application that Apple includes with Mac OS X. With the Preview feature, you do cool things like

- ✔ See all the pages in your document one by one.
- ✔ Zoom in or out to get a different perspective on what you're about to send to the printer (pretty cool!).
- ✔ Spot errors before you commit to printing something. A little upfront inspection can save you a lot of paper and frustration.

✓ Many applications include, or allow you to include, header or footer fields to fill in. *Headers* include information or page numbers that run at the top of each page, like this book uses. *Footers* — you guessed it — are the same thing, but they display at the bottom of a page. Sometimes they aren't visible while you're working on a document, but will appear on the printed version (if you set them to). Use Preview to get a look at the header or footer before you print a document. Just zoom in on that area of the page to take a closer look and make any changes you want to within the application that created the file.

Check out the Preview program's Display menu. Here you can zoom in or out, rotate your document, move forward or backward (through multi-page documents), and other stuff. We urge you to pull down the Display menu and check it out.

Font Mania

Jazz up your documents — or make them a little more serious — with different fonts. To a computer user, *font* means typeface — what the characters look like. Although professional typographers will scream at our generalization, we'll go with that definition for now.

Tens of thousands of different fonts are available for the Macintosh. You don't want to use the same font you'd use for a garage sale flyer that you would for a resume, right? Lucky for you, Mac OS X comes with a bunch of fonts, as shown in Figure 12-8. Some are pretty predictable, such as Times New Roman (it's the font of this paragraph), but OS X gives you some artsy ones, too, such as Brush Script. If you get really get into fonts, you can buy single fonts and font collections anywhere you can buy software. Plenty of shareware and public domain fonts are also available from online services and user groups.

Installing new fonts

To install any new font, drag its icon into one of the two Fonts folders you have access to, as follows:

✓ If you want other users to be able to access the new font, drag the font's icon to the Fonts folder with universal access inside the Library folder at the root level of your hard drive. (The two Library folders are covered in Chapter 10.)

✓ If you only want yourself to have access to the new font, drag the font's icon to the Fonts folder located in the Library folder inside your home folder. No other users will be able to access fonts in this folder.

Figure 12-8:
Mac OS X
includes
these fonts.

Types of fonts

There are many font formats with names like OpenType, Mac TrueType, Windows TrueType, PostScript Type 1, bitmap, and dfont. No problem — Mac OS X supports them all. In fact, the only font format we know of that OS X doesn't support is PostScript Type 3.

That said, the two most common formats for Macs are TrueType and PostScript Type 1. Following are descriptions of both of these two main font types.

- ✔ **TrueType fonts:** These Apple standard-issue fonts come with Mac OS X. In common use on Macs, as well as on Windows machines, these fonts are scaleable. *Scaleable fonts* use only a single outline for the font, and your Mac makes these fonts bigger or smaller when you choose a bigger or smaller font size in a program.

- ✔ **Type 1 fonts:** These fonts are often referred to as PostScript Type 1 fonts, and they are the standard for desktop publishing on the Mac. Tens of thousands of Type 1 fonts are available. (Not nearly as many TrueType fonts exist.)

  Type 1 fonts come in two pieces: a bitmap font suitcase; and a second piece, called a printer font. Some Type 1 fonts come with two, three, or four printer fonts, which usually have related names. Just toss all the parts in the appropriate library folder and you'll have those fonts available in every program you use.

Chapter 13

Applying Yourself to the Applications Folder

. . . .

In This Chapter

▶ Checking out applications included with Mac OS X

▶ Tips for getting the most out of some of them

▶ A folder chock-full of useful utilities

. . . .

Mac OS X comes with a whole folder full of applications — software that you can use to do everything from surfing the Internet to playing QuickTime movies to checking the time. In this chapter, we give you a thumbnail view of each program in the Applications and Utilities folders, at least the ones we don't cover in other chapters — and tell you a bit about working with applications in Mac OS X.

Software developers often get ideas for cool shareware and commercial applications from what they find in the Mac OS Applications or Utilities folders. They look at what Apple has provided for free and say, "Hey, I can add some cool features to that!" The next thing you know, you have new and improved versions of Mail, Terminal, Grab, TextEdit, and others. If you use an Apple-supplied application but find it lacking, check your favorite shareware archive (www.versiontracker.com, www.macdownload.com, www.software.com, and www.tucows.com are a few good ones) for a better mousetrap.

Folder Full of Apps

The applications that you get with Mac OS X are all stored in (where else?) the Applications folder. Hang with us as we run 'em down!

First, though, you need to open the `Applications` folder, the contents of which you can see in Figure 13-1. You can get there by using any of the following three easy ways:

- ✔ Click the Applications button on the toolbar in any Finder window
- ✔ Choose Go➪Applications
- ✔ Press ⌘+Option+A

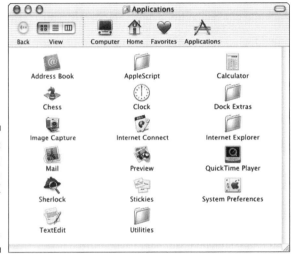

Figure 13-1:
Checking out the Mac OS X `Applica-tions` folder.

Address Book – c.H. 11

 Just like it sounds, the Address Book is the place to store contact information for your family, friends, and anyone else who you want to keep track of. It works with the Mail application, enabling you to quickly look up e-mail addresses when you're ready to send a message. We talk some more about the Address Book in Chapter 11.

AppleScript

AppleScript is like a tape recorder for your Mac. It can record and play back things that you do, such as opening an application or clicking a button. The following sections should give you some indication how much — or how little — you care about AppleScript.

Discovering whether you give a hoot about AppleScript

Describing AppleScript to a Mac beginner is a bit like three blind men describing an elephant. One man might describe it as the Macintosh's built-in automation tool. Another might describe it as an interesting, but often over-looked, piece of enabling technology. The third might liken it to a cassette recorder, recording and playing back your actions at the keyboard. A fourth (if there were a fourth in the story) would assure you that it looked like computer code written in a high-level language.

They would all be correct. AppleScript is the Mac's built-in automation tool. It's a little known (at least up to now) enabling technology. It is like a cassette recorder for programs that support AppleScript recording. And scripts *do* look like computer programs, which could be because they *are* computer programs.

If you're the kind of person who likes to automate as many things as possible, you may love AppleScript. It's a simple programming language that you can use to create programs that give instructions to your Mac. For example, you might create an AppleScript that launches Mail, checks for new messages, and then quits Mail. The script could even transfer your mail to a folder of your choice.

We call AppleScript a time and effort enhancer. AppleScript, if you just spend the time and effort it takes to understand it, will save you oodles of time and effort.

Therein lies the rub. This stuff is far from simple. And it's far beyond the purview of a *For Dummies* book. Still, it's worth learning about if you'd like to script repetitive actions for future use.

You can put frequently used AppleScripts on the Dock or on your Desktop for easy access.

Checking out AppleScript

The `Applications` folder contains an `AppleScript` folder, which, in turn, contains the Script Editor and Script Runner programs, plus a folder full of sample AppleScripts.

Script Editor is the application that you use to view and edit AppleScripts. Although more information on Script Editor is beyond the scope of this book, it's a lot of fun. And the cool thing is that you can create many AppleScripts without knowing a thing about programming. Just record a series of actions that you want to repeat and use Script Editor to save them as a script. After you save a script, activate it with a double-click.

If the concept of scripting intrigues you, we suggest that you open the `Example Scripts` folder and rummage through it. When you find a script that looks interesting, double click it to launch the Script Editor program where you can examine it more closely.

Calculator

Need to do some quick math? The Calculator application gives you a simple calculator, with all the basic number-crunching functions that your pocket calculator has. To use it, you can either click the keys with the mouse or you can use your numeric keypad (on your keyboard) to type numbers and operators (math symbols such as +, –, and =). Check out the Calculator in Figure 13-2.

Figure 13-2:
The
Calculator.

We find it interesting that the only thing that's changed about the Calculator since the Mac was invented is the interface. In other words, no functionality has been added or removed in almost 20 years. How many computer programs can say that? (For the curious: Calculator was a Desk Accessory in early versions of the Mac OS and an Apple Menu item in versions 8 and 9.)

Chess

Chess is a computerized chess game that's not half bad, as shown in Figure 13-3 (notice in the figure that the Dock is hovering over the window; you can autohide the toolbar by checking the Automatically Hide and Show the Dock check box in the Dock pane in System Preferences). To play a game, launch Chess and then choose Game⇨New. If you're playing the computer, you play as white, so click a white piece and move it. The computer responds by moving a black piece. When it's your turn, move again. The computer will move again. And so on until the game is finished. Obviously, this is *Mac OS X For Dummies* and not *Chess For Dummies,* so we don't tell you how to bolster your chess game here.

Figure 13-3:
The super-
snazzy Mac
OS X 3-D
Chess
game.

There are a couple of preferences you may want to tinker with in the Chess program. If you want to make the computer a more formidable opponent, choose Chess⇨Preferences and drag the Level slider to the right (towards the word "Hard"). You can also choose to play human versus human, and change the name the computer uses (the default name is the highly unimaginative "Computer" until you change it). The last option in the Preferences dialog box lets you turn Voice Recognition on or off (by default it's on; you can see the voice recognition thingy at the right side of the Chess window in Figure 13-3). If you choose to use it, you can speak your moves ("Knight G1 to F3," and so on) as long as you have an appropriate microphone connected to your Mac.

If you need a hint (as Bob often does), choose Move⇨Hint or press ⌘+Shift+H. The computer shows you the move *it considers to be* your best choice. The chess piece it suggests you move and the square it thinks you should move it to both blink. You don't have to take the computer's advice. If you don't like the move it suggests, just move another piece instead.

Clock

Frankly, given the fact that you've got a clock in the menu bar, this program is of little use. You don't need to use the Clock application unless you need to make changes to the time display on your Mac.

When it's running, Clock is easily visible on the Dock; its icon displays the current time in analog or digital format, for your viewing pleasure.

All you can do in the Clock application (choose Clock⇨Preferences) is choose whether the clock appears in a floating window or on the Dock, and whether it shows an analog or digital display.

To set your Mac's date and time, change the settings in the Date & Time pane of System Preferences, not the Clock application. You also use this System Preference to set menu bar clock options, including whether or not to display the menu bar clock.

Dock Extras

Dock Extras is a folder that contains little files that enhance your Dock. After you install a Dock Extra, you just click and hold on its icon, as shown in Figure 13-4, to choose from a pop-up menu.

If you used an earlier version of Mac OS, Dock Extras in the Dock are a lot like Control Strip items in the Control Strip.

To install a Dock Extra, merely drag it onto the Dock. The Dock Extras you can check out are

- ✔ **Displays.dock:** This one is pre-installed when you install Mac OS X; it provides instant access to different screen resolutions and numbers of colors displayed on screen, as shown in Figure 13-3.

- ✔ **Battery Monitor.dock:** Drag this item onto the Dock to see how much battery time you have remaining. (Obviously, this one is only useful for PowerBook or iBook users.)

- ✔ **Signal Strength.dock:** Drag this item onto the Dock to see how much Airport signal your Mac is receiving. (Obviously, this one is only useful if you have a wireless Airport network and your Mac is on it.)

Figure 13-4:
A Dock
Extra in
action.

Why do all these things end with a .dock suffix? So you know they're Dock Extras.

Image Capture

Use this program to transfer images from your USB digital camera. If you don't have a digital camera, don't worry about it. If you do have one and the software that came with it doesn't work with OS X, try Image Capture.

Internet Connect

This program replaces the old PPP application in earlier versions of Mac OS.

Internet Explorer

Internet Explorer (IE) is Microsoft's Web browser for the Mac, and (lucky you!) it ships with OS X. Read our discussion of IE in Chapter 11. There's an Internet Explorer folder here in the Applications folder, and within that is the Internet Explorer icon from which you can start IE. But the quickest way to open IE is still to click its icon on the Dock; it looks like an *e*.

Mail

Mail is the free e-mail program that comes with OS X. We cover Mail in Chapter 11.

Preview

You use Preview to open, view, and print portable document files (PDFs), as well as most graphics files (TIFF, JPEG, PICT, and so on). *PDF files* are formatted documents that include text and images. User manuals, books, and the like are often distributed as PDF files. You can't edit a PDF file with Preview, but you can leaf through its pages or print it. It's also the application that pops open when you click the Preview button in the Print dialog box, as you discover in Chapter 12.

Many OS X programs offer PDF as a file format you can save your own documents in.

Adobe's Acrobat Reader application has many more features than Preview does. You can search for words in Reader, for example, but you can't in Preview. However, Preview is a good way to quickly check out or print a PDF file. You can download Acrobat Reader from Adobe at www.adobe.com.

QuickTime Player

 Use the QuickTime Player to view QuickTime movies or streaming audio and video. The quickest way to launch it is by clicking its icon on the Dock. It also opens automatically when you open any QuickTime movie document file.

Sherlock

 We discuss Sherlock — the cool search tool that you can use to find files, Web sites, people software, stuff to buy, and lots more — in Chapter 11. To quickly open Sherlock, click its icon on the Dock (it looks like Sherlock Holmes' hat with a magnifying glass. Alternatively, you can type the keyboard shortcut ⌘+F from the Desktop.

Stickies

 Stickies are electronic Post-it Notes for your Mac. They're a convenient place to jot notes or phone numbers. We show you some Stickies in Figure 13-5.

Stickies are supremely flexible. Move them around on-screen (just drag 'em by their title bar) and change their text to any font and color you desire using the Note menu. Make your Stickies any color you like using the Color menu. You can collapse a Stickie by Option+Clicking its grow box in the top-right corner of the title bar. Also, you can print them and import and export text files from them.

Anything that you type on a Stickie is automatically saved as long as you keep that note open. But when you close a note (by clicking its close box, choosing File➪Close, or pressing ⌘+W), you lose its contents forever. Fortunately, Stickies give you a warning and a second chance to save the note in a separate file on your hard drive. You can also export Stickies (File➪Export Text) and save Stickies as Plain Text, RTF (rich text format) files, or as RTFD (rich text format with attachments) files. The last two formats support fonts and other formatting that plain text format does not.

 Stickies have grown up in Mac OS X. They work pretty much as they always have, but now you have more options available, such as a spell checker. You can also import pre-Mac OS X Stickies, in addition to plain text files. The old Stickies application supported colors, but not fonts, as Mac OS X Stickies do.

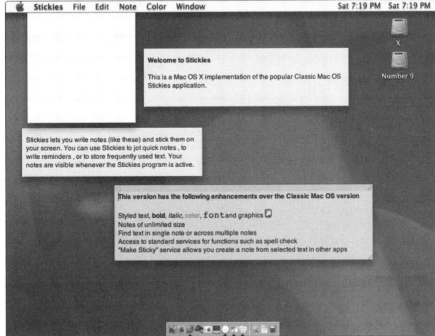

Figure 13-5:
Stickies —
Post-it
Notes for
your Mac.

System Preferences

We mention System Preferences throughout this book. For complete details, though, check out Chapter 15.

You can open the System Preferences application three ways:

- Double-click its icon in the `Applications` folder.
- Click its icon on the Dock.
- Choose System Preferences from the Apple (🍎) menu.

TextEdit

TextEdit is a word processor/text editor that you can use to write letters, scribble notes, or open Read Me files. Although it's not as sophisticated as AppleWorks or Microsoft Word, you can use it for some text formatting and to check your spelling.

TextEdit supports images, too. (Just copy an image in another program and paste it into a TextEdit document. Or, you can use drag-and-drop to drop an image into a TextEdit document from many applications.)

Here's a neat (but mostly useless) trick: Drag any icon from the Finder into a TextEdit document and drop it there. The icon then appears in the document. (It's not a real icon. You can't open it or anything — it's just a picture.)

Utilities

Here's another folder full of stuff. Most of the items in the Utilities folder work with other applications to do some useful thing. You may never open a lot of these applications. The Utilities folder appears in Figure 13-6; stick with us for a brief tour of each application you find there.

Aladdin

Aladdin is the company that makes the ubiquitous StuffIt program. StuffIt is a compression format — a way of making files smaller before you transfer them over the Internet or copy them onto a Zip or other removable-media disk. StuffIt Expander from Aladdin can open StuffIt (.sit) files, PC Zip files (.zip), BinHex files (.hqx), and several others. Double-click these kinds of files to open them with StuffIt Expander, or drag them onto the StuffIt Expander application or an alias of it.

Apple System Profiler

Apple System Profiler is a little program that gives you information about your Mac. What a concept! If you're curious about things such as what processor your Mac has or what devices are currently connected to it, give the Profiler a try. Poke around the Commands menu and check it out; this little puppy is benign and won't hurt anything.

Figure 13-6:
The
Utilities
folder.

If you ever have occasion to call for technical support for your Mac, software, or peripherals, you're probably going to be asked to provide information from Apple System Profiler. So don't get rid of it just because you don't care about this kind of stuff.

Applet Launcher

Applet Launcher is a program that runs Java applets. With this program, you can run a Java applet without launching a Web browser. We expand a bit on Applet Launcher in Chapter 22.

Battery Monitor

If you have an iBook or PowerBook, this application enables you to keep track of how much battery life remains.

ColorSync Utility

This is a single-purpose program that verifies the contents of ICC profiles installed on your Mac. If you don't use ColorSync (Apple's color matching technology to ensure what you see on screen is the same as what you print on any device), don't worry about it. We talk a bit about ColorSync in Chapter 22, though, in case you're interested.

Console

Console displays system messages that may help you troubleshoot problems with Mac OS X — assuming you know how to interpret them. Don't let it scare you — most folks will never need Console. Mac OS X is based on *Unix,* a powerful operating system with lots of incredibly geeky features that most Mac users don't really want to know about, and that Apple hides from you unless you want to work with them. But for those who want to find out what's going on under the hood of Mac OS X, or even to tinker around with the "engine," the Console application provides a window into the deep, dark world of Unix. (We talk more about Console in Chapter 22.)

CPU Monitor

Check here to see how your Mac's CPU (its processor; CPU stands for *central processing unit*, by the way) is performing.

DigitalColor Meter

This is a little program that displays what's on your screen as RGB (red-green-blue) or CIE (the acronym for a chromaticity coordinate system developed by the Commission Internationale de l'Eclairage, the international commission on illumination) values. If you're not a graphic artist or otherwise involved in high-end color document production, you'll almost certainly never need it.

Directory Setup

This little program is meant for system administrators on large networks. If your computer is connected to a campus or corporate network, talk to your network administrator about these settings. If you're a home user, just ignore it.

Disk Copy

In most cases, you install new software on your Mac from a CD-ROM or by downloading it from the Internet. Software vendors typically use an installer program that decompresses and copies files to their proper places on your hard drive. After a restart, you're back in business.

Apple has a variation on this theme called the *disk image*. When mounted on your Desktop — *mounting* meaning visible to the operating system — a disk image looks and acts just like a real disk. You can open it and see its contents in a Finder window; you can copy files from its window to another disk; and you can drag it to the Trash to remove it from your Desktop. To make a disk image appear on your Desktop you double-click the image file. At that point, the Disk Copy application takes over and puts an icon that for all intents and purposes looks like a disk on your Desktop.

Because disk images can be transferred via the Internet, and because they act just like disks, they're a great substitute for a CD-ROM or other disc-based software installers. A software maker can create both a CD version of an installer and a disc image that can be downloaded.

Disk Copy pretty much does its job — mounts images when you double-click them. You shouldn't need to spend any time working with it, although a couple of preference settings enable you to verify that the image file is not corrupted, allowing you to keep a log of its activities.

If you're a Mac OS 9 user, Disk Copy is pretty much the same. The difference is that this version is optimized for use with OS X and sports the new, improved OS X interface.

Disk Utility

If you're having problems with your hard drive or need to make changes to it, Disk Utility is a good place to start. This application has two components: First Aid and Drive Setup.

Both Drive Setup and First Aid are pretty much the same as before but optimized for use with OS X and sporting the new Aqua interface.

First Aid

If you suspect that something's not quite right with your Mac, the First Aid portion of Disk Utility should be among your first stops. Use First Aid to verify and, if necessary, repair an ailing drive. We show you how to use First Aid in Chapter 18. To use it, click the First Aid button on the left side of the Disk Utility window. Then, click on a volume's icon and click Verify. You get information about any problems the software finds. If First Aid doesn't find any problems, you can go on your merry way, secure in the knowledge that your Mac is A-okay. If verification turns up trouble, click Repair to have the problem fixed.

You can't use Disk Utility First Aid to fix a CD-ROM or DVD-ROM disc. These discs are read-only and can't be altered. Nor can you use it to repair the active boot disc (the disc with your copy of OS X on it). To do that you must reboot from the Mac OS X CD and run the copy of Disk Utility on it. You *can* fix Zip disks, SuperDisks, DVD-RAM discs, or any other writeable media that can be mounted by your Mac.

Drive Setup

Use Drive Setup to format (that is, *completely erase*) a disk and to create disk partitions. We discuss Drive Setup in Chapter 18. You can't do either of these things on the startup disc — the one with Mac OS X on it.

When you format a disk, you erase all information on it, permanently. Formatting cannot be undone and shouldn't be attempted unless you are absolutely sure this is what you want to do. Unless you don't want or need whatever's currently on the disk, you need a complete backup of the disk before formatting. If the data is critical, you should have at least two (or even three) "known-to-be-valid" back-up copies of it before you reformat.

Display Calibrator

Use this little program to calibrate your display — that is, adjust the way it displays white and colors. It's easy and kind of fun. Give it a try — just launch it and follow the simple instructions you see in the Display Calibrator Assistant window, as shown in Figure 13-7. We suggest you give it a try; it will probably make what you see on your screen look better.

Of partitions and volumes

Partitioning a drive lets you create multiple volumes. A *volume* looks and acts just like a hard drive, but if it's a partition, it's not a drive at all. Rather, it's a section of the drive that's completely separate from all others. You can create any number of partitions, but it's a good idea to limit yourself to no more than a small handful. Lots of people, including your authors, use one partition for Mac OS X and another for Mac OS 9.

You can only create drive partitions on a newly formatted drive. So, to partition a drive, first format it in Drive Setup and then create partitions. Before you do, give some thought as to how large of a partition you want to create. You won't be able to change your mind later.

We think that partitions should be no smaller than 2GB. You can get away with 1GB if you have a 4GB or smaller drive, but you don't need to create a lot of little partitions just to store your stuff. Instead, use folders: They work just great for organizing things the way you like. The one exception to this rule is if you burn a lot of CDs with your CD-RW drive. In that case, a 650MB partition lets you "prototype" your CDs before you burn them, and see just how much stuff will fit on a single 650MB disc.

By the same token, we think you should keep down the limit the number of partitions that you create. A PowerMac G4 with a 20GB drive does just fine with two (or maybe three) partitions.

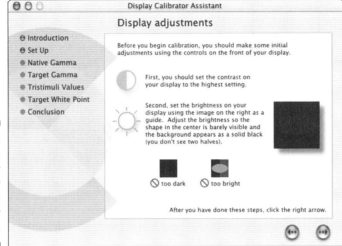

Figure 13-7:
Use the
Display
Calibrator
Assistant to
adjust your
monitor.

Grab

Want to take a picture of your screen? We do this a lot so that we can bring you the screen shots (what you see in the figures) in this book. You can use Grab to take a picture of all or part of the screen and then to save the file for printing or sending around to everyone you think might like to see your Desktop pattern, or how you've organized your windows.

Grab's best feature is the ability to do a timed screen capture. Like those cameras that let you start the timer and then run to get into the shot, Grab gives you ten seconds to bring the window that you want to the front, pull down a menu, get the cursor out of the way, or whatever you need to do to get the screen just right.

Grab's default behavior is to display no cursor. If you want to show a cursor in your screen shots, choose Grab⇨Preferences, and then select a pointer from the ten choices in the Preference dialog box by clicking on it. Or, to have no cursor, click the topmost, leftmost item, which is an empty box (that indicates "no cursor.")

Installer

Here's another application you'll never need to open yourself. But don't get rid of it, because software developers, including Apple, write installer scripts that automate the process of putting software on your Mac. These scripts know where everything should go, and in what order. But, in order to run, those installer scripts need to find this little program. So just leave it alone and everything will be hunky-dory.

Key Caps

Ever wonder what keys to use to make a trademark symbol (™), a bullet (•) or a Greek beta (ß) character? Use Key Caps to discover how. You can also use Key Caps to see what characters are available in the Symbol font, which is a special typeface with characters that aren't letters and numbers but dingbats (special printing symbols).

Take a look at the keyboard display in Key Caps; it looks like your standard Mac keyboard. Now hold down the Option key and look again. All the keys show the characters produced when you use them in combination with the Option key held down (see Figure 13-8).

You can see different characters by pressing different combinations of modifier keys. In Figure 13-8, you can see a standard keyboard when you press Shift (top), what the standard keyboard looks like when you press the Option key (middle), and what the keyboard looks like when you press the Option and Shift keys together (bottom).

The Font menu of Key Caps lists all the fonts installed on your Mac. When you select one and then type a character or characters into the Key Caps text field, you can see how the font will look, and also what, if any, special characters that font has. Choose Symbol or Zapf Dingbats to get a look at the non-text characters you can choose when using these fonts.

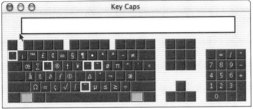

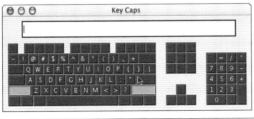

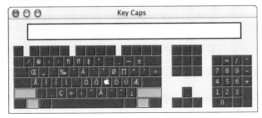

Figure 13-8:
Key Caps
displays the
characters
that appear
when you
press a
modifier
key.

Copy and Paste work in the Key Caps program. If you type something in Key Caps, you can select (highlight) it, copy it (to the Clipboard), and then paste it into another document. You can also select what you type and then drag it to an open document and drop it there.

Keychain Access

A Keychain is a way to consolidate all your passwords — the one you use to log into your Mac, your e-mail password, and passwords required by any Web sites. Here's how it works: You use a single password to unlock your Keychain (which holds your various passwords) and then you don't have to remember all your other passwords. Rest assured — your passwords are secure because only a user who has your Keychain password could reach the other password-protected applications.

To add passwords to the Keychain, you must first create a Keychain and a password. Then you can add passwords to the chain. To create a new Keychain, choose File➪New Keychain.

After you set up a Keychain, just open Mail or another application that supports the Keychain and change your password. Respond *Yes* when prompted whether you want to add the password to the Keychain.

How do you know which programs support the Keychain? You don't until you're prompted to save your password in a Keychain in their Open dialog, connect window, and so forth. If they support the Keychain, a program offers a check box for it in the user-id/password dialog box or window.

The Keychain is particularly cool if you have multiple e-mail accounts that each have a different password. Just add them all to the Keychain and you can get all your mail at once with one password.

To add a Web site password to a Keychain, open the Keychain Access application and click the Add button. The New Password Item window opens. Type the URL of the site in the Name text field, type your username in the Account text field, and then type your password in the Password text field, as shown in Figure 13-9.

To use the new URL password, double-click the URL in the Keychain Access window. A small Get Info window will pop up. Click the Go There button to launch your browser (if it isn't already running) — you're taken and logged in to the Web site you choose.

NetInfo Manager

Here's another little program for system administrators on large networks. If you're a home user, just ignore it.

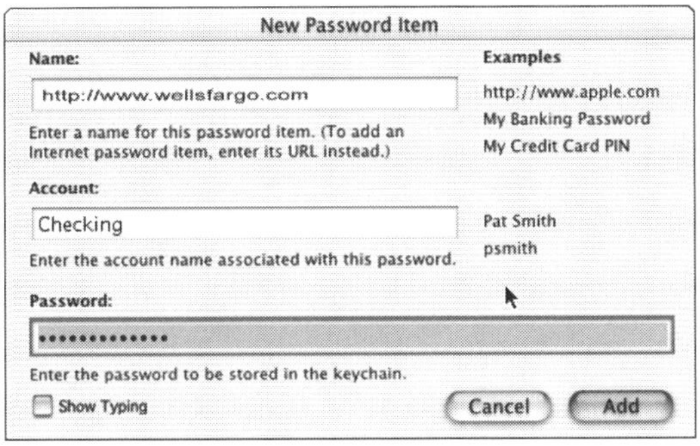

New Password Item

Name:

http://www.wellsfargo.com

Enter a name for this password item. (To add an Internet password item, enter its URL instead.)

Examples

http://www.apple.com
My Banking Password
My Credit Card PIN

Account:

Checking

Enter the account name associated with this password.

Pat Smith
psmith

Password:

••••••••••••

Enter the password to be stored in the keychain.

☐ Show Typing   (Cancel) (Add)

Figure 13-9:
Add a URL
to the
Keychain in
Keychain
Access.

Network Utility

And here is yet another little program for system administrators on large networks, But unlike the others — the ones we've told you to ignore if you're a home user — this one may come in handy if you're a veteran Internet user. It offers common Internet utility functions such as `ping`, `traceroute`, `whois`, `finger`, and such. If you don't know what any of this means, don't worry. Just ignore this program and you'll be fine.

Print Center

Print Center is the program you use to configure your Mac to use printers, and to manage print jobs. We discuss Print Center in Chapter 12.

ProcessViewer

Here's another behind-the-scenes tool. In Unix (the operating system behind Mac OS X), applications and other things going on are called *processes*. Each application (and the operating system itself) may run a number of processes at once. In Figure 13-10, you see 41 processes running. Interestingly, only three applications are open (the Finder, Grab, and ProcessViewer itself).

Geeks and troubleshooters can use ProcessViewer to identify what processes are running, which user "owns" the process, and how much of the CPU and memory the process is using. You can even stop a process if you think it may be causing problems for you.

Messing around in ProcessViewer is not a good idea for most users. If you're having problems with an application, or with Mac OS X, try quitting open applications, force-quitting applications (⌘+Option+Esc), or logging out and then logging back in again, before you start mucking around with processes.

SetupAssistant

Setup Assistant runs the first time after you install OS X. After that, attempting to run it tells you that it is a one-time shot and to use Network tools in System Preferences to establish your setup.

Terminal

Mac OS X is based on Unix. If you need proof, or if you actually want to operate your Mac as the Unix machine it is, Terminal is the place to start.

Because Unix is a command-line based operating system, you need to use Terminal to type commands. You can issue commands that show a directory listing, copy and move files, search for file names or contents, or establish or change passwords. In short, if you know what you're doing, you can do everything on the command line that you can in the Aqua Interface of Mac OS X. For most folks, that's not a desirable alternative to the windows and icons of the Finder window. But take our word for it, true geeks who are also Mac lovers get all misty-eyed about the combination of a command line and a graphical user interface.

If you do decide to tinker with Terminal and the Unix-y innards of Mac OS X, please take some time to bone up on Unix itself. Everything you learn about Unix will work on Mac OS X. A good book on the subject is *Learning the UNIX Operating System (Nutshell Handbook)* by Jerry Peek, Grace Todino, and John Strang. Or try *UNIX Visual QuickStart Guide* by Deborah S. Ray and Eric J. Ray, which is the Unix book Bob keeps on his desk, just in case.

Figure 13-10: The Process Listing window of Process Viewer.

	Process Listing				
Find:		Show: All Processes			
Name	User	Status	% CPU	% Memory	
init	root	Running	0.0	0.1	
mach_init	root	Running	0.0	0.1	
ntpd	root	Running	0.0	0.1	
Window Manager	bobl	Running	13.2	17.4	
loginwindow	bobl	Running	0.0	1.3	
slpd	root	Running	0.0	0.2	
DisplayServices	bobl	Running	0.0	1.1	
SecurityAgent	bobl	Running	0.0	2.7	
pbs	bobl	Running	0.0	0.9	
slpdLoad	root	Zombie	0.0	0.0	
Dock	bobl	Running	0.0	1.8	
nfsiod	root	Running	0.0	0.0	
ATSServer	bobl	Running	0.0	1.3	
inetd	root	Running	0.0	0.0	
AppleFileServer	root	Running	0.0	0.9	
LAServer	bobl	Running	0.0	0.3	
autodiskmount	root	Running	0.0	0.1	
open	bobl	Zombie	0.0	0.0	
syslogd	root	Running	0.0	0.1	

41 processes.　　Sample every [20] seconds

▷ More Info

Chapter 14

Kickin' It Old School: A Look at the Classic Environment

In This Chapter

▶ Defining Classic

▶ Finding out how Classic works

▶ Launching Classic

▶ Booting from Mac OS 9.1 instead of using Classic

*W*hen you install Mac OS X on your Mac, you actually get two operating systems. Mac OS X, of course, runs your machine, but Mac OS 9.1 — the Mac OS version just before Mac OS X — is available too, if you need it.

Why would Apple give you two operating systems, and what in the world do you do with more than one? We explain this in the following section, and later we explain how two operating systems on one computer work together, how you can use them, and why you would want to.

Mac OS X requires version 9.1 of Mac OS, commonly referred to as Mac OS 9.1, to provide the Classic environment. But most (if not all) programs don't distinguish between Mac OS 9, 9.0.1, 9.0.2, 9.0.3, 9.0.4, and 9.1. Apple calls them *Classic applications,* but we mostly call them *Mac OS 9 programs* to avoid confusion. In other words, when we talk about stuff that works with (or appears in) all versions of Mac OS 9 (9.0, 9.0.1, 9.0.2, 9.0.3, 9.0.4, and 9.1), we say "Classic application," or, more often, "Mac OS 9 program." When we're talking about the Classic environment itself, or another feature or program that *requires* Mac OS 9.1, we are careful to say "Mac OS 9.1."

You Can Call It Classic

Mac OS X is the software that controls your Mac; as we describe in Chapter 1, it's the magic that starts your computer, displays the Desktop, and gives you access to all the tools that you use every day to work with your files and applications.

Mac OS 9.1, which is called *Classic* when running under Mac OS X, actually runs inside an *operating system emulator* — software that does most of, but not all of, what an *operating* system does by pretending to be one (see the nearby sidebar for more on emulators). When you launch an older application, it's as if you've booted a computer within your computer; that is, Classic first emulates the startup process, loading all the stuff that it needs to mimic Mac OS 9.1 and run the application.

Classic is an application, just like AppleWorks, Internet Explorer, or TextEdit. With the Classic application running, you can use Mac OS 9.1's Apple () menu and you can open Mac OS 9.1 applications. You also have access (by switching to another window) to your Mac OS X Desktop and applications. Finally, you can switch to another program (from a Classic program) by choosing it from the Application menu on the far right of the Mac OS 9.1 (Classic) toolbar.

What's so great about Classic?

If you're a Mac newbie, or don't have applications or other tools that work with Mac OS 9, you might wonder why Apple would go to the trouble of including Classic in Mac OS X, and why you would want to use it. Well, we think Classic makes OS X a lot better by making available a panoply of older programs that would otherwise be relegated to the slag heap. And long-time Mac users love Classic because it provides access to programs that haven't been updated for Mac OS X (the following section discusses this reason in much greater detail).

When emulation *isn't* the sincerest form of flattery

Emulators aren't just for Classic. Some, like Classic, do everything that an operating system does except boot up the computer. Some bridge the PC/Mac gap: With Windows 2000 emulators (such as Virtual PC) for Mac OS, for example, you run Windows software on your Mac in a window that looks like, well, Windows. Other kinds of emulators, such as those used in companies in which a Mac or PC needs to connect to a mainframe or other big computer, run the mainframe's software in a window on your desktop computer. Most emulators, including Classic, enable you to use the keyboard shortcuts and commands that the emulated system (Mac OS 9, in the case of Classic) uses.

Doin' the Classic dance and liking it

If you're a former Mac OS 9 user, you probably have lots of applications and documents that ran under Mac OS 9. For example, say you have Microsoft's Word 2001. You don't have a Mac OS X version of Word (at the time this book was printed, Word for OS X doesn't exist yet), but you still have your copy of Word that worked great with Mac OS 9 to use while you wait for Microsoft to ship the new Mac OS X version of Word. Are you with us? Old software, old files, new operating system.

Although you certainly will want programs written for OS X — often called "Built for Mac OS X" or *OS X native* applications — rather than programs that run as Classic applications, sometimes you have no choice: The program you want either runs under Classic or not at all.

To make software work with Mac OS X, the folks who write it — *developers* — have to rewrite — or, *port* — OS 9 programs for Mac OS X. Or, they have to create them from scratch using special programming tools designed to create native OS X applications. Not all developers have done this yet because lots of people still use older Macs with older versions of Mac OS and because rewriting programs costs money and takes time. As time passes, we expect to see more and more native OS X apps and fewer and fewer OS 9 (Classic) apps.

Working with Classic

Frankly, there's not much to working with Classic. If you launch an old program, it launches itself and just works. But, in the inimitable *For Dummies* tradition, we're going to tell you all about it anyway. First we'll talk about launching Classic. Then we'll talk about opening Classic applications. Last but not least, we'll show you how to boot up with OS 9.1, for those occasions where Classic just won't do.

Launching Classic (Or letting it launch itself)

You don't really launch Classic. It launches itself whenever you open any Mac OS 9 application (or a document that belongs to that application). When you do, your Mac figures out that the program or document is a "classic," and the Classic environment launches automatically.

That's not exactly true. While you can't launch Classic in the traditional sense (by opening its icon), you can make it launch using the Classic System Preferences pane. In the upcoming "Setting Classic Preferences" section, we'll show you how.

The first time that you launch Classic, a dialog box appears and asks you to allow Mac OS X to install some files in the Mac OS 9.1 system folder — the folder that runs the Mac OS 9.1 environment you'll be working with. These files are needed to bridge the gap between Mac OS X and Mac OS 9.1, so click the OK button when you see the dialog box.

After you launch Classic, you first see a small status window with a progress bar and a Stop button, just in case you change your mind and don't want Classic to launch.

After you start Classic, you can watch the emulator load by clicking the right-pointing triangle in the bottom left of the Classic status window. Clicking this triangle expands the window to show you the progress of the startup process (as shown in Figure 14-1). If you're a Mac OS 9 user, you'll recognize the Welcome screen.

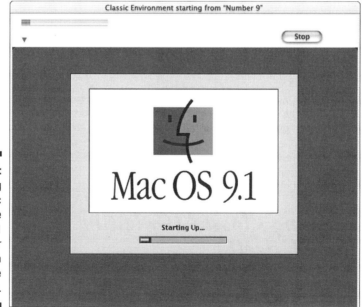

Figure 14-1:
Opening Classic launches the Mac OS 9.1 emulator with a Welcome screen.

If you don't choose to view the startup process by expanding the Classic window, just wait a bit and watch the progress bar inch its way along until Mac OS 9.1 launches and is ready to use. At that point, the Classic window disappears, your Classic application becomes active, and you see the Mac OS 9.1 menu bar. Check it all out in Figure 14-2.

Opening a Classic app

With Classic active, you can launch a pre-Mac OS X application by double-clicking its icon. If Classic isn't already running, double-clicking a Classic application automatically launches both Classic and the application. When you double-click a Word file, for example, the Classic application launches and so does Word.

You can tell when you're using a Classic program because when it's active (front-most on your screen), you see the old OS 9.1 menu bar, complete with a multicolored menu.

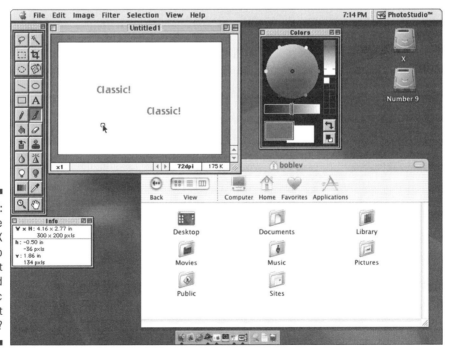

Figure 14-2:
See the Mac OS X Desktop peeking out from behind the Mac OS 9.1 paint program?

"Toto, we're not in OS X, anymore . . ."

Classic is a strange bird, combining things that are familiar from each of the
two operating systems on your Mac. In the following sections, we walk you
through what to expect when Classic is active.

Menu bar

The menu bar that you see when working in a Classic application is the Mac
OS 9.1 version. You'll know it by the multihued logo in the top-left corner
(Mac OS X has a solid blue menu).

The OS X icon will look gray instead of blue if you select the Graphite
Appearance (instead of the default blue) in the General System Preferences
pane. In any event, it's always a solid color in the OS X menu bar, and always
rainbow-colored in Classic menu bar.

The Mac OS 9.1 menu bar appears when you have a Mac OS 9 application
open and active. If Classic has been launched but no Classic application is
running, you'll see the Mac OS X menu bar.

Because space here won't allow us to go over all of the features you can
access from the Classic menu bar, we'll point out a few and encourage you to
explore them on your own. Although most of the menus on the menu bar
belong to the Classic application that's open, a couple — sometimes more —
are part of Mac OS 9.1.

The first feature of the Mac OS 9.1 menu bar is the menu (topped by that
rainbow logo, as shown in Figure 14-3). The old customizable Apple menu
is among the coolest of all Mac OS 9 features, and one that lots of Mac OS X
users miss. This menu contains all sorts of things: It houses tools for working
with parts of Mac OS 9 (control panels, the calculator, and so forth), as well
as aliases to folders (or files, if you've put them there). The beauty of the
menu is that it's available in all Classic Mac applications.

Another menu that we want to tell you about is the Application menu, located
at the far-right corner of the OS 9.1 menu bar. You'll know it by the application's name and icon. The Application menu includes commands that are
very much like some of those on the Mac OS X menu. In addition, you find
items that let you select any application that's currently running, including
both Classic and Mac OS X applications.

Figure 14-3:
Access the
original menu when
a Classic
application
is open.

Dock and icons

Just like in Mac OS X, the Finder's Desktop and windows are visible when
you're working in the Classic environment. That includes the Dock and any
icons you have on the Desktop. The Dock is pretty smart about Classic: When
you open a Classic application, the application's icon appears on the Dock;
the icon disappears when you quit the application. In Figure 14-4, you can see
the Dock with two Classic and a bunch of Mac OS X applications running.
Telling them apart is tricky — the Classic application icons are, well, uglier
than the Mac OS X ones. Where OS X icons have clean lines, OS 9 icons are
jaggy and . . . well . . . ugly. That's because they're old, lower-resolution icons.
Check out Figure 14-4 to see for yourself.

Finder windows

Whether a Classic application or the Mac OS X Finder is active, you may see
Mac OS X Finder windows (assuming any are open and your Classic application isn't blocking your view of them). You can use them to open or move
files as you normally would with Mac OS X alone. If you double-click a file
that belongs to a Mac OS 9 application, that program opens when you launch
the Classic application.

Classic icons

Figure 14-4:
Pretty and
not-so-
pretty icons
on the Dock.

Getting back to OS X

To get out of Classic and back to OS X, just click the Desktop, any Mac OS X icon in the Dock, any OS X application in the Application menu, or any Finder window, and you're back to good ol' OS X quick as a bunny.

Setting Classic preferences

In Chapter 15, we talk about System Preferences panes, but because the preferences for Classic are important to this discussion, we'll cover them here and now.

If you have multiple hard drives or partitions with Mac OS 9.1 installed on them, you can choose which one to use as the operating system for the Classic environment. You make that choice in the Classic pane of System Preferences. (See Chapter 15 for more on System Preferences in general.) Just select the drive or partition (ours is labeled Number 9 in Figure 14-5), and the next time that you launch Classic, it uses that volume's copy of Mac OS 9.1. Volumes that don't include Mac OS 9.1 (such as the disk X in Figure 14-5) appear dimmed in the preferences window.

By selecting the Start up Classic on Login to This Computer check box, you tell Mac OS X to do just that. The advantage is that you won't have to wait a minute or two for Classic to launch the first time that you launch a Classic application. The disadvantage is that it takes your Mac a minute or two longer to boot, and uses RAM and other system resources.

We think it affects performance to keep Classic running when you don't need it, so we prefer to keep this feature disabled.

Note the three buttons at the bottom of the System Preferences Classic pane's Start/Stop tab (the last two are used mostly when the Classic environment crashes, freezes, or otherwise acts improperly):

✓ **Start:** Launches Classic without first launching a Classic program. (If Classic is already running, this button reads Stop.)

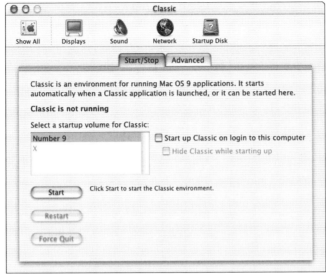

Figure 14-5:
Classic
System
Preferences.

- ↙ **Restart:** Restarts Classic (big surprise), which is like rebooting OS 9.1 without having to reboot Mac OS X.

- ↙ **Force Quit:** Forces the Classic environment to quit, even if it's crashed or frozen.

Getting more info on Classic

To get the most from Classic, take a look at the version of this book that was written especially for Mac OS 9: *Mac OS 9 For Dummies* (well, duh!). Bob (co-author of this book) is very proud of it. You'll discover a lot more about the wonders available to you in the Classic environment.

Booting from Mac OS 9.1

As we mention earlier in the chapter, some programs — mostly games — just won't work when you try to run them in the Classic environment under OS X. When that happens (and if you want to use that program), you'll have to start up your Mac with OS 9.1.

No problem; it's a snap. Here's how to boot your Mac so it runs OS 9.1 instead of OS X:

1. **Open System Preferences by clicking its icon in the Dock or choosing System Preferences from the Mac OS X menu.**

2. **Click the Startup Disk icon to open the Startup Disk pane.**

3. **Click the Mac OS 9.1 icon to select it, as shown in Figure 14-6.**

4. **Restart your Mac by choosing Restart from the menu.**

    That's all there is to it. When your Mac comes back to life, you'll be running Mac OS 9.1.

We're referring above to the Mac OS X menu, not the Classic rainbow menu. If you have Classic or a Classic application open, click the Desktop once to make sure it's the Mac OS X menu you see.

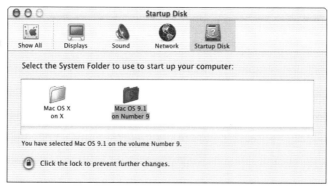

Figure 14-6:
Choose
Mac OS 9.1
to start up
your Mac
(while
running
Mac OS X).

If you have both OS 9.1 and OS X on the same volume or disk, be careful not rename any of OS X's folders or throw any of OS X's folders in the Trash (while you're running OS 9.1). The results could be catastrophic — you could easily render OS X inoperable.

When your Mac runs OS 9.1 and you want to run OS X again, you can't open the Startup Disk System Preferences pane because it's part of Mac OS X and it isn't available while running OS 9.1. Now what?

Again, no problem. You do it the old fashioned way — by using the Startup Disk control panel.

1. **Open the Startup Disk control panel by choosing Control Panels⇨Startup Disk from the OS 9.1 menu.**

2. **Click the Mac OS X icon, as shown in Figure 14-7.**

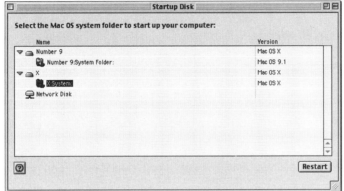

Figure 14-7:
Choose
Mac OS X to
start up your
Mac (while
running
Mac OS 9.1).

3. **Click the Restart button in the Startup Disk window.**

   That's it. In a few moments, you'll be back up and running with Mac OS X.

Chapter 15

What Your Mac Prefers

- -

- -

*E*veryone works a bit differently, and we all like to use our Macintoshes in a certain way. System Preferences is the place in Mac OS X where you can set options that are just right for you. You can set everything from the appearance of your screen to the kind of network or Internet connection you have — and a whole lot more. In this chapter, we take you on a tour of all the Mac OS X System Preferences panes. Hang on; it's gonna be a long, but informative, ride.

Introducing System Preferences

Choose System Preferences from the Apple () menu to get a gander at all the options we'll be looking at in this chapter. Check out all the features you can change from the System Preferences window, as shown in Figure 15-1.

We call the thing you see in Figure 15-1 the System Preferences window. But when you click any of the icons, the bottom part of the window changes to reflect the options for the icon you click. When this happens, we call the bottom part of the window a *pane*. So, for example, when you click the Date and Time icon in the System Preferences window, the bottom part of the window becomes the Date and Time System Preference pane.

System preferences is Apple's new name for Control Panels — a set of tools that's been around since the earliest versions of Mac OS. Note a few differences between system preferences and control panels, though. For one thing, third-party software vendors could use control panels to give you a way to configure options for their applications. In Mac OS X, system preferences are an Apple-only affair.

Some system preferences relate to topics we cover in other chapters. The most notable of these are the Network and Internet preferences, which we discuss in Chapter 11. We let you know in this chapter any time that we skip a preference that you can read about in another chapter.

Take a look at the System Preferences window in Figure 15-1. By default, the main system preferences icons — Monitors, Sound, Network, and Startup Disk — appear in the toolbar. Apple kindly put them up top so that you can find them more easily and because these are probably the ones you'll use most frequently. Also on the toolbar (far left) is the Show All button. We tell you more about this in the next section.

Figure 15-1:
The System
Preferences
window:
Change
your world.

Who is Apple to decide which system preferences you'll be using most? If you want to change this configuration, add your own favorites to the toolbar by simply dragging any icon you like from the bottom of the window onto the toolbar. Your new custom design is waiting for you each time that you open System Preferences. To remove an item, just drag it off the toolbar — it'll disappear with a "poof."

Using System Preferences

Before we examine the items in the System Preferences window, we need to explain a couple of things about using them. This info applies to all system preferences, so listen up.

To use a system preference, just click it once to open its pane. You can double-click if that habit is engrained in your mouse finger, but there's no need.

Okay, so you've finished working with a preference's pane, but you want to open another one. You could simply close the one you've been working on, or you could cut to the chase by clicking the Show All button, which is located at the far left of the top row of icons on the preferences window (as shown in Figure 15-1). Clicking the Show All button returns the icons for all available preferences to view on the screen.

Here's an even more convenient way: Choose the system preferences you want from the Pane menu in the menu bar. All the icons that you see in Figure 15-1 also have an entry on this menu; choose one, and its system preference pane appears immediately.

Unlocking a preference

Many system preferences need to be unlocked before you can use them because Mac OS X creates preferences for each person who has a user account on the Mac. Also, each time that you want to change options for yourself, you must unlock the system preference you want to work with. See Figure 15-2 to see what a locked preference looks like. You don't have to unlock all system preferences to change them, just some of them. When we come to a system preference that must be unlocked before you can use it, we let you know up front. Deal? Good.

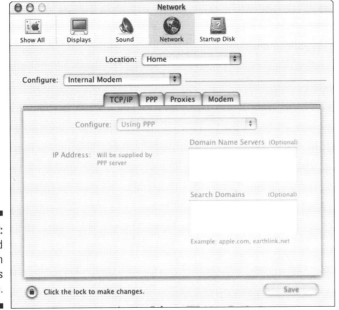

Figure 15-2:
A locked system preferences pane.

Only users with administrator privileges can unlock system preferences. See Chapter 16 for more info on administrators and permissions.

To unlock a preference

1. **Click the lock icon in the lower-left corner of the system preferences pane (shown in the margin).**

   Mac OS X responds with a dialog box in which you enter your name and password.

2. **Enter this user information and click OK.**

   Mac OS X unlocks the system preference you're working with.

In Figure 15-3, you see the Network System Preferences pane after being unlocked. Notice that you can now make changes to it; in Figure 15-2, before you unlocked it, all the options were grayed out and impossible to change.

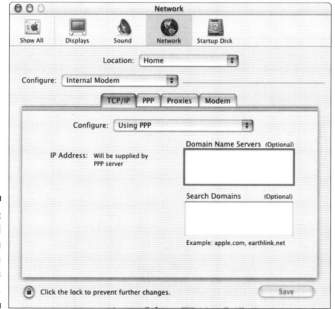

Figure 15-3:
An unlocked system preference displays its options.

Locking a preference

To relock a system preference's pane (after you unlock it), merely click the lock icon again. It will lock itself instantly.

Setting Preferences

Ready to dig into each of the system preferences? Great. We start on the first row of the System Preferences window (refer to Figure 15-1) and work our way through each icon in alphabetical order, one by one.

Classic

Open the Classic pane to choose the drive or drive partition that contains a Mac OS 9.1 System Folder to use when working in the Classic environment. (We dig deep into the Classic environment in Chapter 14.) Suffice it to say that if you have Mac OS 9 applications, or are nostalgic for the way things were in Mac OS 9, you need to use the Classic pane.

ColorSync

The ColorSync pane offers you color-matching technology that ensures color consistency between screen representation and color output. We talk a bit more about ColorSync in Chapter 22.

Don't mess with this preference unless you know what you're doing and you know you have to. This preference's settings are irrelevant to the average user: Nothing good whatsoever will happen if you change them. Unless you are also using the ColorSync color-matching system on your printing devices and scanners, this preference is of no importance.

Date & Time

Within the Date & Time System Preferences pane, you can configure your Mac's internal clock, which many programs use, and configure the clock you see in the menu bar. Four tabs appear — Date & Time, Time Zone, Network Time, and Menu Bar Clock — which you use to set all things timely.

Setting the date

Set the correct date on your Mac from the Date & Time tab of the Date & Time pane. First, set the options beneath the Today's Date heading. Either click a day in the current month's calendar, or use the navigational arrows to choose a month or year in the past (left) or in the future (right). Then click the calendar day you want. You can see the Date and Time tab (of the Date and Time System Preferences pane, if you want to be fussy about it) in Figure 15-4.

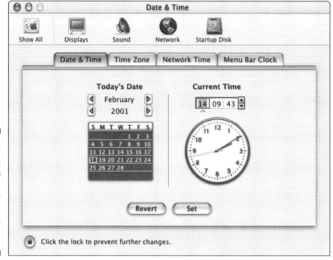

Figure 15-4:
The Date & Time tab of the Date & Time System Preferences pane.

You won't be able to set the date or time if you have already set up your Mac to receive the correct time from a network time server. (We discuss time servers in the "Setting Network Time" section later in this chapter.) If you don't see the arrows, you can use to change the month, year, or time, click the Network Time tab (on the far right) and click the Stop button to disable automatic time checks. Return to the Date & Time tab, and you're able to make the changes you want.

Setting the time

You can also set your machine's time from the Date & Time tab. In the Current Time field that appears above the clock face, click the number that you want to change. That number should be highlighted, a pair of up and down arrows appears to the right of this field, and there will also be a little gray arrowhead below the field subject to change. Increase the selected number by clicking the up arrow; decrease it by clicking the down arrow. You can also use the arrow keys on the keyboard to increase or decrease the number. Or you can type a new number right over the selected number.

When you've got the time how you want it, click the Set button. Or, if you mess up, click the Revert button to return to the way it was before you began.

Use the Tab key to move from number to number. The settings for the hour, minute, and second are selected in sequence when you press the Tab key. If you want to move backward through the sequence, press Shift+Tab. As long as you hold the Shift key down, you cycle through the numbers in reverse order when you press Tab.

Note that the time expressed runs on a 24-hour (military) clock. The Date & Time System Preferences doesn't include any a.m. or p.m. options.

Setting the time zone

Click the Time Zone tab to set your machine according to what time zone you're in. Click your part of the world on the map that appears, or choose a time zone from the pop-up menu. The map is updated to show your time zone when you do.

Setting Network Time

Network time servers are very cool, enabling you to synchronize your Mac's clock to a super-accurate time server on the Internet. To use a time server, however, you must be connected to the Internet when your Mac checks the time.

Follow these steps to set up access to a time server:

1. **Click the Network Time tab of the Date & Time System Preferences pane (shown in Figure 15-5).**

2. **Beneath the Network Time Server section and next to the Configure heading, select the Manually radio button and then type** time.apple.com **in the NTP Server text field.**

time.apple.com is Apple's network time server. You're allowed to use it, of course.

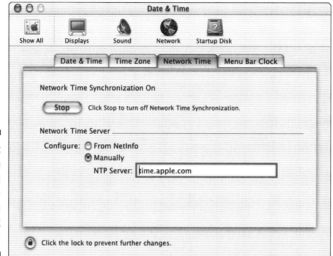

Figure 15-5:
Set up
automatic
synchroniza-
tion with a
network
time server.

We love this new-ish feature (it was added in OS 9). We're both anal about this type of thing and love having our clocks 100 percent accurate. We used to use SetClock (freeware for modems) or Vremya (freeware for TCP/IP connections) to do the same thing, but now we don't have to, thanks to Apple's foresight.

If you have trouble with the network time server feature, Apple posts a technical note that lists dozens of alternative network time servers. You can find this tech note (and several other tech notes you may find useful) by going to the Apple Tech Info Library (http://til.info.apple.com/) and searching for *network time server*. Search for article number 24753, issued 07/12/2000.

The Menu Bar Clock tab

This tab controls the display of the clock in the right corner of your menu bar. The five options in this tab are accompanied by a check box to turn each on or off. Those options are

- ✔ **Show the Clock in the Menu Bar.** As you might expect, if you select this check box, you'll see a clock on the right side of the menu bar. Left unselected, you don't.

- ✔ **Display the Time with Seconds.** Select this check box to display the time with seconds (04:20:*45*).

✔ **Append AM/PM to the Time.** If you select this check box, you see AM or PM after the time (4:20 *PM*).

✔ **See the Day of the Week.** See the day of the week before the time (*Monday* 4:20 PM) when you select this check box. If this check box is not marked, all you see is the time (4:20 PM).

✔ **Flash the Time Separators.** Select this check box to have the separating colons (:) between the hours and minutes (and seconds if you select the Display the Time with Seconds check box) blink on and off. If you deselect this check box, you still see the colons but they don't blink.

Displays

 Click the Displays icon in the System Preferences window for options to set up your Mac's monitor. When you open this window, you see the Mac's current monitor settings on the Display tab (see Figure 15-6).

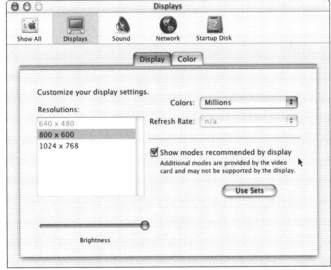

Figure 15-6:
The Display tab shows the Mac's current display settings.

To change the monitor's settings, select the number of colors that you want your monitor to use from the Colors pop-up menu. Most monitors and video cards support multiple resolutions, and some also allow you to choose a refresh rate.

By default, OS X selects the Show Modes Recommended by Display check box, enabling you to pick only those options that OS X thinks are best for your video card and display. If you deselect this check box, you have more choices, but they aren't necessarily the best ones.

Most monitors have settings to adjust their brightness and some also enable you to adjust their gamma settings. If your monitor supports these features, you see the Brightness and Gamma Control slide bars at the bottom of the Display preferences windows. If you have these features, adjust them the way that looks best to your eyes.

The Use Sets button enables you to save sets of display settings — colors, resolution, brightness, and gamma (if your monitor supports gamma).

Finally, from the Color tab you can choose a preconfigured profile for your monitor (if it's an Apple brand monitor), or calibrate your display yourself. To do this, click the Calibrate button and an assistant will walk you through the process.

Dock

We cover the Dock and its preferences in great detail in Chapter 3. Rather than waste any more trees, we'll just move along to. . . .

Energy Saver

All recent Mac models are Energy Star compliant — you can preset your machine to turn itself off at a specific time or after a specified idle period. Here's how:

1. **Click the Energy Saver icon in the System Preferences window.**

   In the top part of the dialog box that appears, you can choose to have your computer go to sleep (a low-power mode) automatically after so many minutes of idle time (kind of like a killer screen saver).

2. **To turn this feature on, move the slider beneath the heading labeled** Put System to Sleep Whenever It's Inactive For **until the desired time appears beneath it.**

   You can choose as little as 30 minutes, or go to the other extreme and turn it off by moving the slider to Never. Check it out in Figure 15-7.

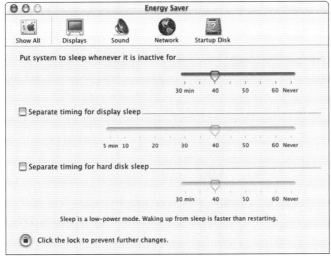

Figure 15-7:
Move the
top slider to
the number
of minutes
your Mac
waits before
taking a
snooze.

You can also set sleep times for your Mac's display and/or hard drive. Setting the display to sleep might come in handy if you want your Mac to keep doing what it's doing and you don't need to use the monitor. The hard drive sleep option is less useful unless you've got a PowerBook. Set the hard drive to sleep after a few minutes of inactivity while you're using a battery, for example (to save your power reserves). However, give the computer as a whole a bit more time, in case you've just gone out for a coffee break and you'd like to keep the computer awake until you get back.

To activate display or hard drive sleep, select the check box next to the headings Separate Timing for Display Sleep or Separate Timing for Hard Disk Sleep, respectively, and drag the slider to the idle time you want.

To wake up your Mac from its sleep, merely move your mouse or press any key on the keyboard.

Drag the slider to 30 or 45 minutes for sleep; then remember to turn off your Mac manually when you're not going to need it for a day or more.

General

General Systems Preferences give you control over the color scheme you see in Mac OS X as well as what happens when you click a scroll bar (see Figure 15-8).

Don't get too excited. It only controls two color settings: the color that text becomes highlighted when you select it; and what color that buttons pulsate (throb) to get your attention.

Throbbing buttons are always the default button. If you press Return, the default button is pressed. In earlier versions of Mac OS, the default button had a thick border to indicate that it was the default. So throbbing buttons in OS X are the same as buttons with a thick border in Mac OS 9 (and earlier).

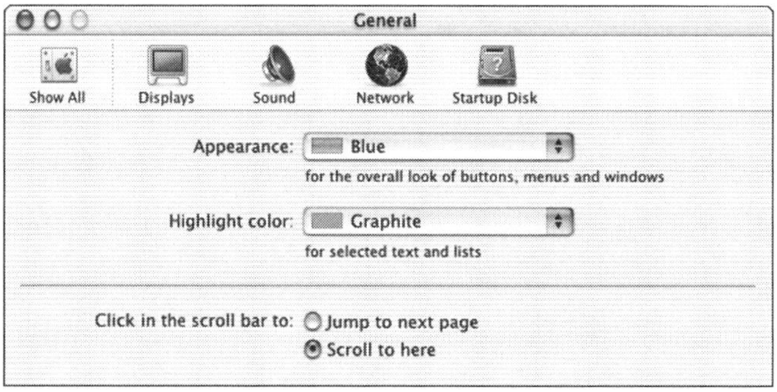

Figure 15-8:
The General
System
Preferences
pane.

Appearance options

In the General System Preferences pane you can choose specific aspects of how your Mac looks and feels.

- ✓ **Appearance pop-up menu:** Use choices from this menu to choose from different appearances, changing the overall look of buttons and window controls (such as the gumdrops in the scroll bars). Apple, however, in its infinite wisdom, provides only two choices — Blue and Graphite. Other appearances may be available (try the Internet) but thus far are not sanctioned by Apple.

- ✓ **Highlight Color pop-up menu:** From here you can choose the color that text becomes when you select it in a document or in an icon's name in the Finder window. This time Apple isn't so restrictive — you have seven highlight colors to choose from.

Scroll bar behavior

Select from two radio buttons next to the Click in the Scroll Bar To heading in the General System Preferences pane to choose whether clicking in a scroll bar area either above or below a scroll bar moves your view of a window up or down by a page (the default behavior for OS 9), or to the point in the document roughly proportionate to where you click in the scroll bar.

Select the Scroll to Here radio button if you often work with long (multipage) documents. You'll find it quite handy for navigating long documents. And don't forget — the Page Down key on your keyboard does the same thing as selecting the Jump to Next Page choice, so you'll lose nothing by selecting Scroll to Here.

International

If you're in the U.S., you may assume that you don't need to set anything in the International System Preferences pane. After all, you chose to see your Mac's menus and commands in U.S. English when you first installed Mac OS X. But wait — the International preferences has more in it than just a choice of language. Here's where you can set date and time formats — probably the most useful feature for U.S. folks — and yes, you can choose a new language here, too.

The International System Preferences pane has five tabs: Language, Date, Time, Numbers, and Keyboard Menu. We describe each in the following sections.

Language

Here you find options that you can choose to set your Mac's order of preference for languages used in applications. Make your choices in the top half of this screen; to organize your choices, drag an entry up or down in the list. If an application uses the first language that you indicate in this list, then you see the application's commands and menus in that chosen language. If your first language choice isn't available, the next option is used, and so on.

The lower portion of the Language tab lets you select a script to attach to the language you chose in the top part of this pane. The script you choose affects sort order, case conversion, and word definitions.

Date

Set the format for date and time display in applications on the second tab (Date) of the International System Preferences pane. These settings are accessible by applications for formatting purposes, as are those for Time, below. This is where you specify setting — such as a 24-versus a 12-hour clock, and month-day-year ordering — so that all your applications can format the values appropriately, both those from the clock and those you enter from the keyboard or programmatically.

Note that when you change an option in the Date tab, you can see the results displayed at the bottom of this tab. Change the look of your date settings from the choices in the Region pop-up menu, located near the top of the Date tab window. Take a look at Figure 15-9 to see how the default U.S. date settings appear.

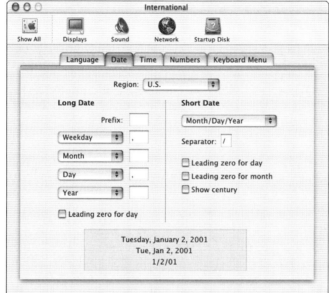

Figure 15-9: Change the display of date info in the Date tab.

You can also choose non-U.S. date settings from the Region pop-up menu. If you change other settings in the Date tab, Custom appears in the Region pop-up menu, indicating that you've fiddled with its preset date options — you wild thing, you!

Under the Long Date heading (on the left side of this window), you can choose four items to display: Weekday, Month, Day, and Year. Each has its own pop-up menu. Each time that you make a change, the results appear at the bottom of this window, as we mention earlier in this section. Use these menus to change the order of display, which is a lot of what the regional settings are about. In Europe, for example, the day of the month typically appears before the name of the month (8 May 2000), while U.S. folks usually like their months to show up first (May 8, 2000).

You can also add a text prefix (any text you want) to appear before the long date. Just type it in the Prefix text box.

Finally, if you select the Leading Zero for Day check box, dates before the 10th of the month (the 1st through the 9th) appear with a zero before them (01, 02, and so on).

Check out the options under the Short Date heading you find on the right side of the Date tab window. Options you can set here include a pop-up menu to set Month/Day/Year format and what type of separator symbol you want to use, such as a front slash (/) or a dash (-). From the three check boxes beneath Short Date, you can also choose to use a leading zero in your dates for a day (*01*-12) or a month (11-*01*), and whether to show the century in your date format (12-12-*00*).

Time

The Time tab is the third (middle) tab of the International System Preferences pane (as shown in Figure 15-10). Like what you find on the Date tab, the Time tab offers you options from the Region pop-up menu. Choices within this menu (located at the top of the Time tab window) correspond with the way time is written in various parts of the world. Use the radio buttons on the left side of the window to choose whether to use a 12- or 24-hour clock and whether to set noon and midnight as 0:00 or 12:00. You can also set how you want to set time before and after noon (AM or p.m., for example), what type of separating punctuation to use between hour and minute (such as the colon in 12:13 p.m.), and a check box for setting the use of a leading zero for the hour (4:56 or 04:56). Again, like the Date tab, when you change an option in the Time tab, you can see the results displayed at the bottom of this tab.

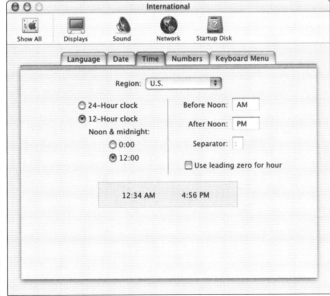

Figure 15-10: Choose the items and order to display in the Time tab.

Numbers

Set options on the Numbers tab of the International System Preferences pane to choose which characters to use when displaying decimal numbers, as well as which separators to use to set off thousands (1,000 or 1.000, for example). Like what you find on the Date and Time tabs, the Numbers tab offers you options from the Region pop-up menu. You can also pick a currency symbol, such as $ or £.

Keyboard Menu

Here you can select from a variety of check boxes here to choose a new keyboard mapping — from a variety of countries. When you do, a new menu appears in the Finder's menu bar, as shown in Figure 15-11.

Or, if you're so inclined, choose a Dvorak map: That's the one with keys mapped in an alternative layout that places the most commonly used keys on the home row. You can choose this from the Keyboard list.

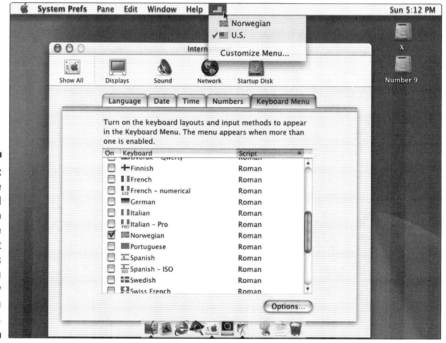

Figure 15-11:
The Keyboard Menu tab and the menu that appears when you check any item in the list.

Do not under any circumstances click the Options button on the Keyboard Menu tab unless you have good reason to use foreign keyboard layouts on occasion. The ⌘+Option+Spacebar keyboard shortcut, when turned on, can cause unpredictable behavior if you later forget that you turned it on. Use this thingy with caution, especially if you use Photoshop (which uses ⌘+Option+Spacebar as the shortcut for Zoom Out).

Internet

The Internet System Preferences pane is where you configure Mac OS X for Internet access — your home page, preferred search engine, default Web browser, and so on.

There are four tabs in this pane; here's what they do:

- ✓ **iTools:** If you have an iTools account, you can type your name and password here so that you don't have to type them every time you use an iTool. (See Chapter 11's section on iTools if you want to know what they're are all about.) Click the Free Sign Up button and your Web browser will open and take you to the Apple iTools Sign Up page.

- ✓ **Email:** On this tab you specify your chosen Email reader — Mail is pre-selected, but if you use another program, this is where to select it. Here are also fields for your e-mail address, incoming mail server, account type, account ID, password, and mail server.

    If you're not sure what goes in these fields, ask your Internet Service Provider (ISP).

    If you use Mac.com (one of the iTools) as your e-mail provider, you can select the Use iTools Email Account check box. When you do, many of the fields are filled out (correctly) for you.

- ✓ **Web:** This tab is where you choose your default Web browser program. Internet Explorer is pre-selected, but if you prefer a different browser, select it from the Default Web Browser pop-up menu.

    Under the Default Web Browser pop-up menu are fields where you can specify your home page, default search engine, and the folder you want downloaded files to go into.

    The default folder for downloaded items is your Desktop, which we think is pretty convenient. You'll never have to hunt for that file you just downloaded; it'll be right there on the Desktop where you can easily find it. That said, you can then move it to any folder you have access to if you so desire.

✔ **News:** This tab is where you choose your default News Reader program, provide the Internet address of your news server, choose whether to read news as a member or a guest, and type your user account ID and password.

Internet *newsgroups* are online discussions you can read and participate in. Tens of thousands of them are going on at any given time, on a wide variety of topics. The particulars of newsgroups and how to set up your Mac for their use is beyond the purview of this book, but if newsgroups sound interesting to you, talk to your ISP for the scoop on signing up.

Keyboard

Open the Keyboard System Preferences pane for options to modify how your keyboard responds to your keystrokes; take a gander at your choices in Figure 15-12.

Figure 15-12: Governing how your keyboard responds to your touch.

Adjust the Delay Until Repeat slide bar to set how long you have to hold down a key before it starts repeating.

Drag the Key Repeat Rate slider to set how fast a key repeats when you hold it down. This feature comes into play, for example, when you hold down the dash (-) key to make a line or the asterisk (*) key to make a divider.

You can type in the box at the bottom of the window to test your settings before closing this panel.

Login

When you start up your Mac, or if you use it after someone else has, you must log in before you can get to your files and begin working. You also need to enter your name and password to get to some options, as we describe in the "Using System Preferences" section earlier in this chapter.

The Login System Preferences pane enables you to choose programs that you'd like to launch automatically when you log in (such as the OS X equivalent of Startup Items in OS 9.1), and here you can also disable the log-in requirement.

After you click the Login preference icon, two tabs appear: Login Items and Login Window, both of which we discuss in the following sections.

Login Items

In the Login Items tab (as shown in Figure 15-13), you can pick applications or documents that you want to start up each time you log in to your Mac. Choose from — or add to — a list of options beneath the heading These Items Will Open Automatically When You Log In.

To add a new log-in item, click the Add button at the bottom of this window and then locate the program you want. (For help on how to locate a file, read through Chapter 8.) When you find the program that you want and click the Open button, it appears in the Login Items tab as shown in Figure 15-13. If you want the program's windows hidden (but still want the program running), select the Hide checkbox to the left of its name.

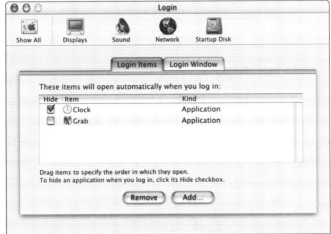

Figure 15-13:
Adding
applications
to login
items.

To remove an application, just click it to select it, and then click the Remove button at the bottom of this window.

Login Window

If you want to avoid the log-in process and you don't have any reason to worry about someone else logging on and making mischief (or if you don't share your Mac), you may decide to disable the log-in requirement.

When you disable logging in, you also affect the preferences set by anyone else who shares your Mac. So, if your Desktop pattern, keyboard settings, and so forth are different from those of someone else who uses your machine, those preferences won't be properly reflected if each of you don't have your own log-in account. Even if you're not worried about security, consider keeping logging in enabled if any other users have accounts on this machine.

To disable the logging in requirement, you may first need to unlock the Login System Preference. Click the Login Window tab of Login preferences, and then unlock it. (For more on unlocking a preference, see the "Using System Preferences" section earlier in this chapter.) To disable log in, select the Automatically Log In check box. Next, enter your username and password. Click the Save button to save your changes.

Note that only one account is allowed to use auto-login. If another user wants to use this Mac, you need to choose Log Out from the menu or press ⌘+Shift+Q.

Mouse

Adjust the settings in the Mouse System Preferences pane, as shown in Figure 15-14, to set your mouse speed and double-click delays. Move the Tracking Speed slider to change the relationship between hand movement of the mouse and cursor movement on the screen. A faster tracking speed settings (moving the slider to the right) sends your cursor squirting across the screen with a mere flick of the wrist; slower mouse speed settings (moving the slider to the left) make the cursor crawl across in seemingly slow motion, even when your hand is flying. Set this setting as fast as you can stand it — we like the fastest speed. Try it: You might like it.

If you have a portable Mac with a trackpad, such as a PowerBook or iBook, you'll see an additional tab — Trackpad — where you can set the tracking speed and double-clicking behavior of your trackpad.

Figure 15-14:
Setting how fast your mouse moves and double-clicks.

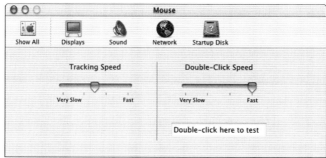

The Double-Click Speed setting determines how close together two clicks must be for the Mac to interpret them as a double-click and not as two separate clicks. Move the slider arrow to the leftmost setting (Very Slow) for the slowest. With this setting, you can double-click at an almost leisurely pace. The rightmost position (Fast) is the fastest setting, which we prefer. The middle area of the slider represents a double-click speed somewhere in the middle.

Changes in the Mouse System Preferences pane take place immediately, so you should definitely play around a little and see what settings feel best for you. You can test the effect of your changes to the Double-Click Speed setting in the Double-Click Here to Test text box at the bottom of the window before you close this preference pane.

Network

Set options in the Network System Preferences pane to connect your Mac to the Internet or to a network. While we talk a little about this pane in Chapter 11, we promised you more detail here. So here's some detail.

If you're part of a large office network, check with your system administrator before you change anything in this pane. If you ignore this advice, you run the risk of losing your network connection completely.

At the top of this pane is the Location pop-up menu. If you use your Mac in more than one place, you can set up a separate configuration for each location, and then choose it from this menu. A *location*, in this context, consists of all the settings in all the tabs in the Network System Preferences pane. After you've got this entire pane configured the way you like, pull down this menu and choose New Location. Type in a name for the new location and click OK. Then you can change all the settings in this pane at once by choosing that location from the pop-up menu.

If your Mac has a single network or Internet connection, like most home users have, just choose Automatic from the Location menu and be done with it.

Below the Location menu is the Configure pop-up menu. Here you choose your Internet connection. If you use a modem to connect to the Internet, choose Internal Modem. If you have another type of Internet access, such as ISDN, cable modem, or DSL, choose Ethernet.

Below this menu you see some tabs. Unfortunately, you'll need to talk to your ISP or network administrator to find out how to configure them; we can't tell you how in this book. We will, though, give you a brief rundown on what each one does:

✔ **TCP/IP:** TCP/IP is the language of the Internet. On this tab you specify things such as your IP Address, Domain Name Server, and Search Domains.

✔ **AppleTalk:** AppleTalk is a homegrown network protocol invented by Apple. Some (but not all) printers require it to be turned on for them to function. For more information about AppleTalk in general, this tab in particular, and printers, see Chapter 12.

✔ **Proxies:** If you're on a large network or your Mac is behind a firewall, you may need to specify one or more proxy servers. If so, your network administrator can help you with this tab's settings. If you are a home user, you'll probably never need to touch this tab. Finally, some ISPs require you to specify proxy servers; if you need to do this, ask your ISP what to do.

✔ **PPPoE** or **Modem**: If you chose Ethernet from the Configure menu, you see the PPPoE tab (which stands for Point-To-Point Protocol Over Ethernet). Your ISP will tell you if you need to do anything with this tab. If you chose Modem from the Configure menu, instead of PPPoE you see the Modem tab, where you can choose your modem from the pop-up Modem menu. You can also turn the modem's speaker on or off, and choose Tone or Pulse dialing.

QuickTime

QuickTime is Apple's multimedia technology for both Mac and Windows. When you watch a movie on your Mac (unless you're watching a DVD, of course), chances are good that it's a QuickTime file.

QuickTime is probably already configured properly. When you click the QuickTime preference icon, you see five tabs: Plug-In, Connection, Music, Media Keys, and Update. Just check to make sure that QuickTime is set as follows, and then leave this preference alone.

The Plug-In tab (see Figure 15-15) deals with the way your Internet browser handles multimedia files.

✔ Select the Play Movies Automatically check box if it's not already checked.

✔ You can leave the Save Movies in Disk Cache check box deselected unless you want to use your Internet browser's disk cache to hold QuickTime movies as they are downloaded.

✔ Select the Enable Kiosk Mode check box to hide QuickTime settings within your browser.

✔ The MIME settings button at the bottom of this pane offers advanced options for the way the QuickTime Plug-In handles various multimedia file formats. We suggest you leave it alone unless you're instructed to change it by someone knowledgeable, such as your ISP or a software manufacturer.

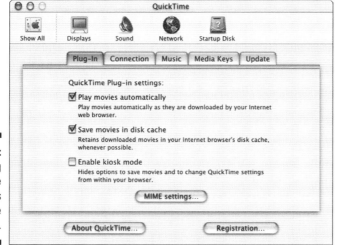

Figure 15-15:
Setting
QuickTime
options
on the
Plug-In tab.

✔ Click the Connection tab and select the speed of your Internet connection by choosing the appropriate option from the Connection Speed pop-up menu.

If you're not sure what your connection speed is, ask your ISP (Internet Service Provider). If you're not sure what an ISP is, we suggest that you read Chapter 11.

✔ The Transport Setup button at the bottom of this pane offers advanced options for receiving files over the Internet. We suggest you leave it alone unless you're instructed to change it by someone knowledgeable, such as your ISP.

Ignore the Music and Media Keys tabs. We still haven't figured out what they're for, even though they've been in QuickTime for years. If you want to use a music synthesizer other than the built-in QuickTime Music Synthesizer, or if someone sends you a secured media file (or you download one), you'll have to figure it out then. So far neither of us has ever had to touch these two settings.

✔ Change settings in the Update tab to update your QuickTime software automatically (if you have an Internet connection). Because each successive version of QuickTime has added cool and useful features, we suggest that you select the Check for Updates Automatically check box. After you do, your Mac will check for new versions of QuickTime whenever you connect to the Internet. As Martha Stewart says, "It's a good thing."

Screen Saver

 Most computer experts will tell you that you don't really need a screen saver to protect your monitor from screen burn-in these days. But if you really want a screen saver — some folks like to see pictures floating around the screen when they're not working — you can use the Screen Saver preference to set one. Mac OS X comes with several screen saver modules; to see what the selected module looks like in action, click the Test button. Press any key to end the test.

To set up the screen saver, first choose a Screen Saver from the list in the Screen Saver tab of the Screen Saver preference pane. Next, click the Activation tab and drag the Time until screen saver starts slider to the number of minutes you want the Mac to wait before activating the screen saver. You can also choose to require a password to wake up the screen saver in this tab.

 Click the Hot Corners tab to choose which corner(s) of your screen activates the screen saver and which deactivates it. Now, when you move your mouse to a selected corner, you activate or deactivate the screen saver.

Sharing

 This is another option that you'll use when networking your Mac. There are two facets of Sharing — sharing a single Mac with other users, and sharing files via an office network or the Internet. Read all the gory details in Chapter 16. (We also discuss Web sharing in Chapter 22.)

Software Update

Occasionally, Apple releases a new version of some of the software that's part of a Mac system. Such releases may be a patch for the system software, a bug fix for a utility program, or even a new version of Internet Explorer. You can set Software Update (see Figure 15-16) to check for new software, as well as to notify you of changes and download the fresh, hot files to your Mac. Note that you must have an Internet connection to use this feature.

You can choose to update your software automatically or manually by selecting the appropriate radio button in this preference pane. Select Automatically (look for the Update Software heading) and you can choose how often your

Mac checks for updates. (Make your choice from the Check For Updates pop-up menu.) Click the Update Now button at the bottom of the window to manually check for update any time you like, even if you've selected the Automatically radio button.

Figure 15-16:
You can use
Software
Update to
check for
new system
software.

Sound

 Use options in the Sound System Preferences pane (shown in Figure 15-17) to control the way your Mac plays and records sound.

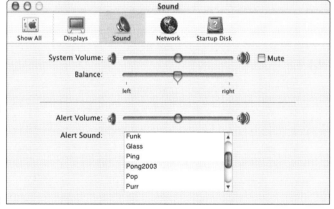

Figure 15-17:
The Sound
System
Preferences
pane.

If you don't have external speakers attached to your Mac, adjust the System Volume slider to change the volume of your Mac's built-in speaker. Selecting the Mute check box turns off your Mac's internal speaker. Use the Balance slider to make one stereo speaker louder than the other.

In the lower portion of this window, you can set Alert Sound and Alert Volume options. Here you can choose your Mac's Alert Sound, also known as its *beep sound*. The Alert Volume slider controls alert (that is, beep) volume.

You can find new sounds on the Internet at your favorite shareware archive (www.versiontracker.com, www.macdownload.com, www.software.com, and www.tucows.com are a few that we like and recommend.)

To install new sounds, move them into the Sounds folder inside the Library folder at root level on your hard drive if you want them to be available to all users of this Mac. Or put them in the Sounds folder inside the Library folder in your home folder if you want to be the only one that can use them. (See Chapter 10 for more info on these two Library folders.)

Speech

Choose your desired Speech settings from the Speech System Preferences pane. Click the Text-to-Speech tab to set the voice your Mac uses to communicate with you. Check out the list you find on the left side of the Speech Systems Preferences pane (as shown in Figure 15-18) to select the voice your Mac uses for text-to-speech applications. After you make a selection, you hear a sample of the voice you chose. You can also read the defining characteristics (the language, gender, age, and description) of each voice as you move through this list of voices. Use the Rate slider (bottom right of the window) to speed up or slow down the voice. Then click the Play button to hear this voice at its new speed. We like Fred, who says, "I sure like being inside this fancy computer."

Click the Speech Recognition tab to set up speech recognition — the ability to talk to your Mac and have it understand you. Alas, we're going to have to use another weasel-out here — we just don't have a chapter's worth of space left to explain it.

You'll need a decent microphone to use this feature. Unfortunately, Macs don't come with one, and the mike that's built into iMacs isn't quite good enough. Even worse, many new Mac models, including the G4 PowerBooks, don't even have a microphone port, so you have to use a microphone that connects via your USB port. Luckily, both USB microphones and converters for connecting standard microphone connectors to USB are fairly common these days.

Dr. Bott is a great little Mac-only company that specializes in little items like USB microphones and analog-to-USB converters. Its Web address is www.drbott.com, or you can call 877-611-2688. Eric Prentice is the CEO; tell him Bob sent you.

Figure 15-18:
The Speech
System
Preferences
pane's
Text-to-
Speech tab.

You can't use this feature to dictate text to your Mac — you'll need IBM's ViaVoice or MacSpeech's iListen to do that. But you can use it to launch programs ("Computer, open Microsoft Word") and other stuff, like emptying the Trash, when you say to. Frankly, neither of us has used it for more than a few minutes — it just doesn't work well enough yet. Still, it's kind of neat and worth playing with if you've got the time and a decent Mac microphone.

Startup Disk

From choices within the Startup Disk System Preferences pane, you select which hard drive, server volume, or hard drive volume (if you've partitioned your hard drive) should act as the startup disk when more than one drive with system software is connected to the Mac. To use it, first unlock the Startup Disk preference if you have to (for more on unlocking a preference, see the "Using System Preferences" section earlier in this chapter) and then click the icon for the drive you want to start up the Mac next time you restart.

This feature is very useful if you have both a Mac OS X start-up disk and a start-up disk with another version of Mac OS on it, such as Mac OS 9 or Mac OS 8.6. If you want to start up with the older operating system, just click that disk's icon in the Startup Disk System Preferences pane and restart your Mac; it now starts up with OS 9.

To restart your Mac under OS X, choose Restart from the menu. To restart your Mac under OS 9, choose Special⇨Restart.

If you have OS 9.1 installed on the same volume as OS X, you can set this preference to choose which OS you boot from. You see two System Folder icons at the top of the pane — one with OS 9.1, and the other with OS X. Click the one you want to boot from, and then restart.

For more information on using the Startup Disk System Preference pane, skip to the end of our discussion of the Classic environment in Chapter 14.

Part IV
U 2 Can B a Guru

The 5th Wave   By Rich Tennant

"WE SHOULD HAVE FIXED THIS IN VERSION 9."

In this part . . .

Here we get into the nitty-gritty underbelly of Mac OS X. In this part, we cover semi-advanced topics including sharing (files, that is), and backing up your files, followed by the all-important troubleshooting chapter, which takes you on a quick tour of Dr. Mac's (okay, Dr. Bob's) top trouble-shooting tips for those times when good software goes bad.

Chapter 16

"Mine! Miiiiine!" Sharing Your Mac and Liking It

*H*ave you ever wanted to grab a file from your Macintosh while you were halfway around the world, or even around the corner? If so, we've got good news for you — it's not difficult with Mac OS X, believe it or not, even though computer networking in general has a well-deserved reputation for being complicated and nerve-wracking. The truth is, you won't encounter anything scary or complicated about sharing files, folders, and disks (and printers, for that matter) among computers — as long as the computers are Macs. Your Mac includes everything you need to share files and printers. Everything, that is, except the printers and the cables.

Mac OS X is a multi-user operating system. After you create a user account for someone to share your Mac, that user can log on to your Mac two different ways with the same username and password. They can log *on* while sitting at your Mac or they can log *into* your Mac from a remote location via the Internet or a local area network.

The first sections of this chapter provide an overview of sharing and tell you every-thing you need to know to set up new user accounts and share files successfully. We don't show you how to actually share a file, folder, or disk in the "Consummating the Act of Sharing" section later in this chapter. Trust us, there's a method to our madness. If you try to share files without doing all the required prep work, the whole mess becomes confusing and complicated — kind of like networking a pair of PC clones.

One last thing: If you're the only one who uses your Mac and you don't intend to share it or its files with anyone else, you can safely skip this whole chapter if you like.

Introducing File Sharing

File sharing enables you to use files, folders, and disks from other Macs on a network — any network including the Internet — as easily as if they were on your own local hard drive. If you have more than one computer, file sharing is a must. It's fun, it's easy, and it's way better than SneakerNet. (According to the unpublished epic, "The Dr. Macintosh Unabridged Dictionary," *SneakerNet* is the moving of files from one computer to another via floppy disk or other media, such as Zip, Jaz, Orb, CD-R, CD-RW, DVD-RAM, and so on.)

Before diving in and actually sharing, first check out a few necessary terms:

- ✔ **Network:** For our purposes, a *network* is two or more Macs connected by Ethernet cables or AirPort wireless networking.

- ✔ **Ethernet:** A network protocol and cabling scheme that lets you connect two or more computers so they can share files, disks, printers, or whatever.

- ✔ **Ethernet ports:** The Ethernet port is where you plug an Ethernet cable into your Mac.

Be careful. On your Mac and printer, the Ethernet ports look a lot like phone jacks, and the connectors on each end of an Ethernet cable look a lot like phone cable connectors. But they aren't the same. Ethernet cables are typically thicker, and the connectors (called RJ-45 connectors) are a bit larger than the RJ-11 connectors that you use with telephones (see examples of both types of connector ends in the margin). When you connect an Ethernet cable to your Mac, you won't be able to put it into your RJ-11-friendly modem port (and you shouldn't try). Standard phone cables fit into Ethernet ports, but you shouldn't try that either. It's unlikely that either mistake will cause any permanent damage, but it won't work and will certainly frustrate you to no end.

✔ **Local devices:** Devices that are connected directly to your computers, such as hard drives or CD-ROM drives, are *local*. Your internal hard drive, for example, is a local device.

✔ **Remote devices:** Devices that you access (share) over the network are *remote*. The hard disk of a computer in the next room, for example, is a remote device.

✔ **Protocols:** When you read or hear about networks, you're likely to hear the words AppleTalk, Ethernet, and TCP/IP bandied about with great regularity. These are all *protocols,* or kinds of languages that networks speak. Macs can speak several different protocols, but every device (Mac or printer) on a network needs to speak the same protocol at the same time in order to communicate.

Support for the AppleTalk protocol is built into every Mac. Your Mac includes all the software that you need to set up an AppleTalk network; the hardware that you need to provide is Ethernet cables, and a hub (unless you use cross-over cables) or AirPort base station.

Although you can use TCP/IP to do a lot of the same things you can with AppleTalk, we concentrate on Apple's protocol, AppleTalk. By learning how to activate and use it, you'll master the basics that you need to dig into the language of the Internet.

AppleTalk is particularly useful when you have all Macs on your network. It's the easiest to configure and doesn't require additional information such as IP addresses. If you want to use the Internet to connect to another computer (or have it connect to yours), however, you need to use TCP/IP.

Portrait of a home office network

A typical Mac home office network consists of two Macs, an Ethernet hub, and a network laser printer. Check out Figure 16-1 to see the configuration of a simple network. In the figure, the black lines between the devices are Ethernet cables and below those is a hub (we tell you more about cables and hubs in the "Three ways to build a network" section later in this chapter). With the setup you see in Figure 16-1, either Mac can use the other Mac's files, and both Macs can print to the same printer. You need enough Ethernet cable to run between all your devices.

A network can and often does have, dozens or hundreds of users. Regardless of whether your network has 2 nodes (machines) or 2,000, the principles and techniques in this chapter apply.

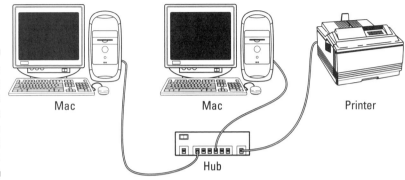

Mac   Mac   Printer

Hub

Three ways to build a network

Back when you could connect a whole bunch of Macs and printers by simply running cables between them, most small Mac networks were pretty much the same. You attached a small device (a LocalTalk connector) to the first Mac, and then ran plain old telephone cable to the next Mac, which also had a LocalTalk connector. By stringing more phone cable and more LocalTalk connectors, you had yourself a little network.

Today, building a Mac network is a little more complicated. Most Macs that support Mac OS X don't include LocalTalk ports, and Ethernet and wireless networks require a little more setup.

In this chapter, we assume that you're working on a small network, the kind typically found in a home or small business. If you're part of a mega-monstrous corporate network and you have questions about your particular network, talk to the PIC (*person in charge,* also known as your *network administrator*). If you're trying to build one of these mega-networks, you'll need a book a lot thicker than this one.

The following list gives you three common ways to build a modern network.

  ✔ **AirPort:** If all your Macs are equipped with AirPort wireless cards and if you have the AirPort base station, you don't need cables at all. Just plug in the base station, and Macs with AirPort cards can communicate with each other. If you use an Ethernet printer (connected to your Mac by Ethernet cable), you need to connect it to the base station before you can print from your wireless Macs. Both the base station and printer have Ethernet ports, so you can use a cross-over cable to make the connection.

While this setup is more expensive than Ethernet cables and a hub, it's also more flexible — you can move your devices anywhere (well, almost anywhere; you're limited to 150 feet per AirPort).

For more information about wireless networking, check out the Apple AirPort Web page at `www.apple.com/airport/`.

✔ **Small Ethernet:** If you have only two devices to network (two Macs, or a Mac and an Ethernet printer, in most cases), you can use an Ethernet cross-over cable to connect them directly to one another via the Ethernet ports. You can purchase a cross-over cable (which looks just like a standard Ethernet cable) at your local electronics store. *Note:* Be sure to ask for a cross-over cable, or your network won't work. Plug one end of the cross-over cable into one of your two devices, and the other end into the other.

An Ethernet cross-over cable won't work with a hub; a regular Ethernet cable won't work without one. Therefore, it makes sense to label your cross-over cable(s) as such; they look exactly like regular Ethernet cables, and it's easy to become confused if you have a bunch of similar-looking cables.

✔ **Traditional Ethernet:** All modern Macs have an Ethernet port. To connect your Mac to a network, you need Ethernet cables for each Mac, and a little device called a *hub.* (It's like the middle of a wagon wheel, with spokes representing the wires coming out of it.) An Ethernet hub includes two to eight Ethernet ports. You plug the hub into a wall outlet, and then connect Ethernet cables from each of your Macs and printers (from their Ethernet ports) to the hub. Voila! — instant network. Hubs are pretty cheap, starting at about $75; cables start at a few bucks, increasing in price as the length of the cable increases.

If you have a cable modem or DSL as your Internet connection, you may need a router instead of a hub. A router is nothing more than an intelligent hub. A router is used the same way as a hub, but costs a bit more. Your ISP can tell you if you're going to need one. For what it's worth, Bob has a cable modem, but his works fine with a cheap hub; he didn't need a more expensive router.

Setting Up File Sharing

Before we get into the nitty-gritty of sharing files, you must complete a few housekeeping tasks, such as turning on file sharing, turning on AppleTalk (if you want to share files with an AppleTalk-enabled file server or print to an AppleTalk printer), and enabling sharing over TCP/IP (that is, over the Internet).

Turning on file sharing

Before you can share files, you have to turn on Mac OS X's built-in file sharing feature. Follow these steps to do so:

1. **From the Apple (🍎) menu on the Finder menu bar, choose System Preferences (or click the System Preferences icon on the Dock), and then click the Sharing icon.**

   The System Preferences Sharing pane appears.

2. **In the bottom of the Sharing pane, type a name in the Computer Name text field if you haven't already done so.**

   In Figure 16-2, you can see that Bob names his bob1. You can name yours anything you like.

3. **While still in this pane, click the Start button (beneath the heading File Sharing Off) to activate file sharing (see Figure 16-2).**

   Why does the text above this button read File Sharing Off? Because it *is* off. After you click the Start button, the button name changes from *Start* to *Stop,* and the text above the button changes to File Sharing On, indicating that file sharing is on.

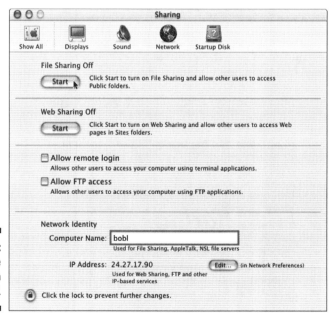

Figure 16-2:
Turning file
sharing on
and off.

Starting AppleTalk

If you want to share files with an Apple file server or print to a networked printer that requires AppleTalk, as many do, you have to enable AppleTalk. (See the "Introducing File Sharing" section earlier in this chapter for a definition of AppleTalk.)

To turn AppleTalk on, stare at your computer and say, "I love you, AppleTalk!" Just kidding. Here's how to turn it on for real:

Follow these steps to activate AppleTalk:

1. **From the menu on the Finder menu bar, choose System Preferences (or click the System Preferences icon on the Dock).**

   The System Preferences window appears.

2. **In the System Preferences window, click the Network icon (located in the toolbar and also in the main part of the window).**

   The Network System Preferences pane appears.

3. **If the pane is locked, click the lock icon (bottom-left corner) to unlock the Network System Preference; if it's not, don't.**

   If your Mac is set up for multiple users, only users with administrative privileges (the first user, created when you installed Mac OS X, and any other user you've given administrative privileges to in the Users System Preference pane, which we discuss in the "Access and Privileges" section later in this chapter) can unlock these locks.

4. **Type your name and password into the little window that appears and click OK.**

   Now you see the AppleTalk tab of the Network System Preferences pane in all its glory — on-screen and in Figure 16-3.

4. **Choose Built-in Ethernet from the Configure pop-up menu (if it isn't already chosen) and click the AppleTalk tab.**

   The AppleTalk tab of the Network System Preferences pane appears.

5. **Select the Make AppleTalk Active check box (so that it's got a check mark in it).**

6. **Click the Save button in the lower-right corner of the AppleTalk tab to confirm your action.**

   That's it. You can quit the System Preferences application now.

Figure 16-3:
The AppleTalk tab of the Network pane.

Sharing with TCP/IP

TCP/IP is the network protocol used on the Internet. It's also the protocol used by Mac OS X for sharing files. It enables Macs, PCs, and other computers communicate with each other (sometimes, but not always, via the Internet), even if they're running different operating systems. TCP/IP is always "on" so you don't have to do anything further about it.

If you want remote users to be able to use an FTP client program (instead of using file sharing on another Mac) to upload and download files to and from this computer, select the Allow FTP Access check box in the Sharing pane in System Preferences. If you want to enable Windows, Linux, or users of other operating systems to share files with you, this check box needs to be checked. (We talk more about FTP and FTP clients in Chapter 22.)

Mac users could use an FTP client to access your Mac, but they'll probably want to use file sharing instead, as it's easier.

Computers connect to one another using a number-based addressing system (known as an *IP address*) that's standard all over the world. You can (and most big companies do) use this system to communicate in offices and over the Internet. If you need to know more about using TCP/IP to connect to computers on your network than we've told you here, talk to the system administrator or the network geek in charge of these things where you work.

We touch more on TCP/IP in the "Connecting to a shared disk or folder" section later in this chapter, where we tell you how to use it to connect to a Mac or other server that's running it.

Access and Privileges (Who Can Do What)

Before you can share your Mac with other users or share files over a network, you need to tell your Mac who is allowed to do what. Lucky for you, this process just happens to be what we cover in this section.

Users and groups and guests (Oh my!)

Mac file sharing (and indeed, Mac OS X as well) is based on the concept of users. Shared items — drives or folders — can be shared with no users, one user, or many users, depending on your needs.

- **Users:** People who share folders and drives (or your Mac) are defined as *users*. A user's access to items on your local hard drive is entirely at your discretion. You can configure your Mac so that only you can access its folders and drives, or so that only one other person (or everyone) can share its folders and drives.

  When you first set up your Mac, you created your first user. This user automatically has administrative powers, such as adding more users, changing preferences, and having the clearance to see all of the folders on the hard drive.

  For the purposes of this book, we assume that some users for whom you create identities won't be folks who actually sit at your Mac, but rather those who only connect to it from a remote location when they need to give or get files. But they *could* use the same name and password to log on while sitting at your desk.

  For all intents and purposes, a remote user and a local user are the same. In other words, after you create an account for a user, that user can log on to this Mac while sitting in your chair in your office or log on to this Mac from a remote location via AppleTalk/Ethernet or the Internet.

- **Administrative users:** While a compete discussion of the special privileges a user with administrator privileges has on a Mac running OS X is far beyond the scope of this book, it's important to note two things:

- The first user created (usually when you install Mac OS X for the first time) is automatically granted administrator powers.

- Only an administrator can create new users, delete some (but not all) files from folders that aren't in his or her home folder, lock and unlock system preference panes, and a bunch of other stuff. If you try something and it doesn't work, make sure you're logged in as a user with admin privileges.

As long as you have administrator privileges, you can give any user administrator privileges by selecting the Allow user to administer this machine check box. You'll find this check box when you create a new user or edit an existing user in the Users pane of System Preferences.

✔ **Groups:** Groups are Unix-level designations for privilege consolidation. For example, there are groups named `staff` and `wheel` (as well as a bunch of others). Your main account is, for example, is in the `wheel` group.

If you're wondering whether you can create your own groups, as you could under OS 9 and earlier Mac operating systems. The answer is "yes," and "no." If you know Unix enough to do it yourself, then "yes," but if you don't, then the answer is "no, please don't." Unix-related tasks such as this are far beyond the scope of this book.

✔ **Guests:** Anyone who accesses public folders on your Mac via file sharing is called a *guest.* They don't need a username or password. If they're on your network, they can see and use your public folder(s). If they're on the Internet and know your IP address, they can see and use your public folder(s). All guests can access public folders, luckily.

Creating users

Before users can share folders and drives (or share your computer for that matter), you need to create user identities for them. You perform this little task in the Users pane of System Preferences.

Guests can use public folder(s) — but no other folders — without having a user account.

To create users for the purposes of file sharing, you need to add the user as a user of your computer, too. In other words, giving a user access to certain folders on your system means that the user also has folders of his or her own on the Mac. When you add (create) a User, you need to tell your Mac who this person is. This is also the time to set passwords and administrative powers of this new user. Here's the drill:

1. **From the menu on the Finder menu bar, choose System Preferences (or click the System Preferences icon on the Dock) and click the Users icon.**

The Users pane appears. In this pane (shown in Figure 16-4) you can see the name of the first user (look under the Name heading) and the administrative control this user had (look under the Kind heading).

As we mentioned previously, the first user created (usually at the same time you installed Mac OS X) always has administrator privileges.

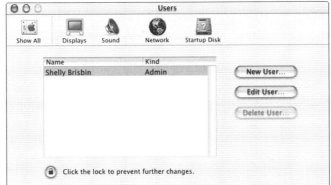

Figure 16-4:
The Users pane shows who can use this Mac.

2. **In the Users pane, click the aptly named New User button (upper-right).**

   A New User window opens.

3. **In the Name text box, type the full name of a user who you want to add.**

   In the Short Name text box, your Mac inserts a suggested abbreviated name (or *short name,* as it's called). Check out Figure 16-5 to see both.

   In Figure 16-5, we added Bob LeVitus as a user, typing his full name in the Name field. You don't really need to type the user's full name, but we do so in this example to show you the difference between a name and a short name.

   The name of each user's folder (in the Users folder) is taken from the short name that you enter when you create a user.

4. **Press the Tab key to move to the next field.**

   Mac OS X suggests an abbreviated version of the name in the Short Name field (as shown in Figure 16-5). Because we have only one Bob around here, we'll change the suggested *boblevit* to just plain *bobl,* which is the short name he prefers. (In other words, we type **bobl** into the Short Name field, replacing the suggested *boblevit.*)

Figure 16-5:
Name the
new user;
your Mac
suggests a
short name.

New User:Bob LeVitus

Name: Bob LeVitus
Example: Mary Jones

Short Name: boblevit
Example: mjones (8 characters or fewer,
lowercase, no spaces). Used for FTP, etc.

Password:
Must be at least 4 characters

Verify:
Retype password

Password Hint:
(optional)

A hint should not easily reveal your password
to others.

☐ Allow user to administer this machine

Cancel   Save

A short name can't be longer than eight characters and can't contain
spaces.

Users can connect to your Mac (or log on to their own Macs, for that
matter) using the short name, rather than having to type their full
names. The short name is also used in environments in which user
names can't have spaces, and are limited to eight or fewer characters. If
a user who you create will be logging into this Mac via Telnet or FTP, he
or she will need to use a short name because these Internet standard
protocols don't support spaces or long names like the Mac does.

5. **Press the Tab key to move to the next field.**

   The cursor moves to the Password text box.

6. **In the Password text box of the New User window, type a password for
   this user and then press the Tab key on your keyboard to move your
   cursor to the Verify text field.**

7. **In the Verify text box of the New User window, type the password
   again to verify it.**

8. **(Optional) To help remember a password, type something to jog the
   user's memory in the Password Hint text box.**

   If a user forgets his or her password and asks for a hint, the text you
   type in the Password Hint field will pop up, hopefully causing the user to
   exclaim, "Oh yeah . . . now I remember!" A password hint should be
   something simple enough to jog the user's memory, but not so simple
   that an unauthorized person might guess. "Your first name" is not a very
   secure hint. Perhaps "Your first teddy bear's name backwards" would be
   a better hint.

9. **If you want this user to administer the Mac (that is, have access to
   preferences, be able to create users, and so forth), select the Allow
   User to Administer This Machine check box.**

If you don't want to give the user this power, just click the Save button in the lower-right corner of the New User window without checking the check box.

The new user now appears in the Users pane.

Changing a user

Circumstances may dictate that you need to change a user's identity, password, or accessibility. Follow these steps to change a user's name, password, or administration privileges:

1. **From the menu on the Finder menu bar, choose System Preferences (or click the System Preferences icon on the Dock).**

   The System Preferences window appears.

2. **In the System Preferences window, click the Users icon.**

   The Users System Preferences pane appears.

3. **Double-click the user's name or click it once to select it and then click the Edit User button.**

   The User Window for that person appears.

4. **Make your changes by selecting the existing username, short name, and/or password and replacing it with new text.**

   In order to change a user, you must be logged in using an account that has administrator privileges.

5. **Click the Save button.**

Removing a user

To delete a user — in effect, to deny that user access to your Mac — select the user (from the Users pane in System Preferences) who you want to delete and click the Delete User button. You will be asked to confirm that you really want to delete the user. Click OK.

To remove a user from your Mac, you must be logged in using an account that has administrator privileges, which we discuss later in this chapter.

Mac OS X knows best: Folders shared by default

When you add users in the Users pane of System Preferences (as we describe earlier in this chapter), Mac OS X automatically does two things behind the scenes to facilitate file sharing: it creates a set of folders, and it makes some of them available for sharing.

When you add a user, Mac OS X creates a folder hierarchy for each user on the Mac, as we describe in Chapter 10. The user can create more folders if necessary, and can add, remove, or move anything inside of these folders. Even if you open a user account solely to allow him or her to exchange files with you, your Mac automatically creates a folder for that user. Unless you, as the owner of your Mac, give permission, the user can't see or use folders outside the home folder (which has the user's name) except for the Shared folder in the Users folder and the Public folder in each user's folder (as well as subfolders of those folders), as described below.

✔ **Public:** A Public folder is located inside each user's folder. That folder is set up to be accessible (or *shared*) by any user who can log onto the Mac. Furthermore, any user can log on (as a guest) and put things into or copy things out of this folder, as long as they know your Mac's IP address, even if they don't have an account on this Mac at all. Files put into the Public folder can be opened or copied.

Inside each user's Public folder is a Drop Box folder. Just like the name implies, this folder is where others can drop a file or folder for you. Only that user can open the Drop Box to see what's inside or to move or copy the files that are in it. Imagine a street-corner mailbox — after you drop your letter in, it's gone, and you can't get it back out.

✔ **Shared:** In addition to a Public folder for each user, Mac OS X creates a Shared folder for all users of this Mac. The Shared folder *isn't* available to guests, but it's available to every person who has an account on this machine. You find the Shared folder within the Users folder (the same folder where you find folders for each user). The Shared folder is the place to put stuff that everyone with an account might want to use. In Figure 16-6, you can see the Users folder for Bob's Mac, where Bob (bob1), Shelly (shelly), and Bob's wife Lisa (lisa) each have user folders (you can also see the Shared folder that all three of them use).

Figure 16-6:
Each user can open or copy items from the Shared folder.

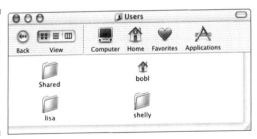

Here's an example of how all this works. If Bob has a user account called `Bob` on Shelly's Mac, he can log in and work with any item in his user directory: the `bob1` directory. He can also put files in his `Public` folder that he wants to share with others users who have accounts on Shelly's Mac. Or he can put them in the `Shared` folder if he wants them available to guests logged on remotely as well. If Bob wants to share a file with just Shelly, he can put it in the `Public` folder under *her* user account; or, if he wants to be sure that no one but Shelly sees it, he can put it into the `Drop Box` folder that's located inside her `Public` folder. The privileges to do all of this are set up when the user account is created — you don't have to lift a finger.

Sharing a folder or disk by setting privileges

As you might expect, access privileges control who can use a given folder, or any disk (or partition) other than the active startup disk (that is, the one you booted Mac OS X from).

Why can't you share the Mac OS X hard drive that you booted from? Mac OS X won't let you. Why not? Because it contains the operating system (which is running if you booted from this drive) and other stuff nobody else should have access to.

Throughout the rest of this chapter, whenever we talk about sharing a folder, we also mean disks and disk partitions other than your startup disk (which, when you think of it, are nothing more than big folders anyway). Why are we telling you this? Because it's awkward to keep typing "a folder or any disk (or partition) other than your active Mac OS X hard drive." So anything we say about sharing a folder also applies to sharing any disk (or partition) other than your active Mac OS X hard drive. Got it?

You can set access privileges for the folder's owner, for all of the people who have accounts on the Mac (a group), or for everyone who has the Mac's address, whether they have an account or not (guests). To help you better understand, we'll talk a little first about owners and groups.

Contemplating different kinds of users

When you consider who can use which folders, there are three distinct kinds of users on the network. We describe each of them in this section. Then, in the "Useful settings for access privileges" section later in this chapter, we show you how to share folders with each of them.

✔ **Owner:** The owner of a folder or drive can change the access privileges to that folder or drive at any time. The name that the first user types in when logging on to your Mac — or the name of your home folder — is the default owner of shared folders and drives on that machine. Ownership may be given away (more on that in the "Useful settings for access privileges" section later in this chapter). Even if you own the Mac, you can't change access privileges for a folder on it that belongs to another user. The owner must be logged in to change privileges on his or her folders.

Some folders are owned by system, which really means Mac OS X owns them. If you select one of these and look at its privileges, you'll see the designation (Figure 16-7) above the second drop-down list of the Info window. Folders that aren't in the User directories belong to system. You can't change those access privileges.

Figure 16-7:
Mac OS X
(system)
owns this
folder, and
you can't
change its
access
privileges.

Info: Library

Library

Show: Privileges

Owner "system" can:
　Read & Write

Members of group "admin" can:
　Read & Write

Everybody else can:
　Read only

Copy these privileges to all enclosed folders
Copy

✔ **Group:** The group that includes everyone who has an account with administrator privileges on your Mac is called admin. Everyone in the admin group has access to shared and public folders over the network, as well as any folder that the admin group has been granted access to by a folder's owner.

Mac OS X users who have used Mac OS 9 may wonder what's happened to the Users and Groups feature, which enabled you to create any number of user groups on a Mac. Because Mac OS X is based on the Unix operating system, which deals very differently with permissions and access privileges than older versions of Mac OS did, it can't support old-style users and groups. If you're brave or knowledgeable enough to dig into Unix, you can make your own groups in Mac OS X. Creating a Unix group confers identical access privileges and powers on its members. Although creating a group is beyond the scope of this book, the process basically involves gaining root access to the Unix system and working at the command line, or tinkering with the groups directory using NetInfo Manager.

If you feel adventurous and know a little Unix, try this: Open the Terminal program (in the Utilities folder inside the Applications folder), type **man group**, and press Return. Terminal displays the "manual pages" for the "group topic." Press Return as many times as needed to scroll through the entire document. It probably won't help you create a group, but reading it won't hurt anything.

The admin group includes every user of a given Mac that has administrative privileges. So giving any user administrative privileges automatically makes them a member of the admin group. While the admin group is not as good as the old Users and Groups feature (in Mac OS 9 and earlier), it's a little better than no groups at all.

✔ **Everyone:** This category is an easy way to set access privileges for everyone with an account on your Mac at once. Unlike the wheel group, which includes only users with administrative privileges, everyone includes, well, everyone (everyone with an account on this Mac, that is).

If you want people who do not have an account on this Mac to have access to a file or folder, it needs to go in your Public folder, where they can log on as a guest.

Sharing a folder

Say that you have a folder that you want to share, but with slightly different rules than those set up for the Public folder, the Drop Box folder within, or for your personal folders. These rules are called *privileges,* and they tell you how much access someone has to your stuff.

Actually, the rules governing Shared and Public folders are privileges, too, but they're set up for you when Mac OS X is installed.

We suggest that you only share folders that are located within your home folder, or a folder within it. Because of the way Unix works, the Unix permissions of the enclosing folder can prevent access to a folder for which you *do* have permissions. Trust us, if you only share folders in your home folder, you'll never go wrong. If you don't take this advice, you could wind up having folders that other users can't access, even though you gave them the appropriate permission.

You can set access privileges for folders within your Public folder (like the Drop Box folder) that are different from those for the rest of the folder.

We said it before but it bears repeating: Whenever we talk about sharing a folder, we also mean disks and disk partitions other than your active Mac OS X hard drive (which you just can't share, period). So don't forget that anything we say about sharing a folder also applies to sharing any disk (or partition) other than your active Mac OS X hard drive.

To share a folder with another user, follow these steps:

1. **Select (single-click) the folder or drive icon, and choose File⇨Show Info (or press ⌘+I).**

   The Info window for the selected item opens.

2. **Choose Show⇨Privileges from the pop-up menu at the top of the window.**

   The sharing options appear, as you see in Figure 16-8.

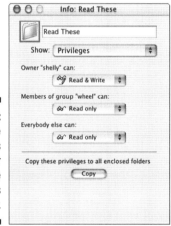

Figure 16-8:
The privileges for a folder inside Shelly's User folder.

3. **Set access privileges for this folder by using the access privileges pop-up menus to control how much access each type of user has to the shared folder or drive.**

   When you click one of these pop-up menus, you see the privilege description that corresponds to the icon.

   You can choose from four types of access for each user or group. (Each type of access has a distinctive icon next to its name in the pop-up menu, as shown in Table 16-1.)

Table 16-1	Access Privileges	
Access Privilege	*Icon*	*What It Allows*
Read & Write	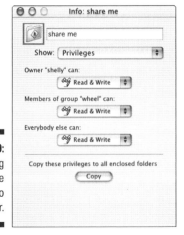	A user can see, add, delete, move, and edit files just as if they were stored on his or her own computer.
Read only		A user can see and use files that are stored in a shared folder, but can't add, delete, move, or edit them.
Write only (Drop Box)		A user can drop files into your shared folder or drive.
None		A user can neither see nor use your shared folders or drives.

Useful settings for access privileges

The following sections show you some of the more common ways that you can combine access privileges for a folder. You'll probably find one option that fits best with the way you work and the people you want to share with.

Allow everyone access

In Figure 16-9, we configure settings that allow *open access* for this folder to everyone on a network. Everyone can open, read, and change the contents of this shared folder. Do this by choosing Read & Write from all three privileges pop-up menus in the Privileges section of the folder's Show Info window.

Figure 16-9:
Allowing everyone access to a folder.

Allow nobody but yourself access

The settings shown in Figure 16-10 reflect appropriate settings that allow *owner-only access,* which mean that no one but the owner can see or use the contents of the shared folder. Choose None in both the Members of Group "Wheel Can" and Everybody Else Can pop-up menus to achieve this.

Figure 16-10:
Allowing no one but the folder's owner access to it.

Allow all users of this Mac access

Check out Figure 16-11 to see settings that allow the group (in addition to the owner) access to see, use, or change the contents of the shared folder. This means no guests can access this folder. Choose Read & Write in the Owner and Members of Group "Wheel Can" pop-up menus and make sure None is selected in the Everybody Else Can pop-up menu to set permissions like this.

Figure 16-11:
Allow one group access to a folder.

Allow others to deposit files and folders without giving them access (a Drop Box)

The settings in Figure 16-12 enable users to drop their own files or folders into a shared folder without being able to see or use the contents of the shared folder. After a file or folder is deposited in this folder, the user who dropped the file cannot retrieve it because he or she doesn't have access privileges to *see* the items in the folder.

Figure 16-12:
Everyone can drop files in this folder.

Read-only bulletin boards

If what you want is for everyone to be able to open and read the files and folders in this shared folder; choose Read Only from the Everybody Else Can pop-up menu. If you do this, however, only the owner can make changes to files in this folder.

One more privilege

The Copy These Privileges to All Enclosed Folders option, at the bottom of the access privileges window, does exactly what its name implies. This feature is a fast way to assign the same privileges to many subfolders at once. After you set privileges for the enclosing folder the way you like them, click the Copy button to give these same privileges to all the folders inside it.

Consummating the Act of Sharing

After you set up sharing and assign access privileges, you can access folders remotely from another computer. (Just make sure that you have access privileges to it first.)

Interestingly, file sharing doesn't have to be activated on a remote Mac to access a shared folder on your Mac. When file sharing is turned off, you can't assign access privileges to folders on that Mac, but you can use it to access a remote shared folder on another machine as long as its owner has granted you enough access privileges and has file sharing enabled on his or her Mac.

If file sharing is turned off on *your* Mac, though, others won't be able to access your folders, even if you've assigned access privileges to them previously (when file sharing was turned on).

If you're going to share files and you leave your Mac on and unattended for a long time, logging out before you leave it is a very good idea. This prevents anyone just walking up to your Mac and seeing your files, e-mail, applications, or anything else that's yours, unless you have given them a user account and granted them access privileges for your files.

Connecting to a shared disk or folder

Now we're going to show you how to access your home folder from a remote Mac, a super-cool feature that's only bound to get more popular as the Internet continues to mature.

To connect to a shared folder on a Mac other than the one you're currently on, follow these steps:

The following steps assume you've got an account on the remote Mac, which means that you have your own home folder on that Mac.

1. **Make sure that you are already set up as a user on the computer you want to log in to (we'll call it "Computer B").**

   If you need to know how to create a new user, see the "Creating users" section earlier in the chapter.

2. **On the computer you're logging in from (we'll call this one "Computer A"), choose Go⇨Connect to Server from the Finder's menu bar.**

   If Computer A is running Mac OS 9. *X,* just use the Network Browser in the Apple menu instead of Go⇨Connect to Server; then log on as you would if both machines were running OS 9. The Connect to Server screen appears.

3. **Click the Local Network item in the left pane of this window, and as shown in Figure 16-13.**

Figure 16-13:
Choosing
the remote
Mac from
the list.

4. **In the right pane of the window, click the name of the computer you want to log in to (Computer B, which is called Shelly's Mac in Figure 16-13) and then click the Connect button (lower-right corner).**

TCP/IP must be active on Computer B. If it's not, you won't see any other machines on the network, nor will you be able to use any remote shared folders. In other words, file sharing doesn't have to be turned on (on Computer B), but TCP/IP does.

The Connect dialog box appears. The person logged in on Computer A's name automatically appears in the Name field (bob1 in Figure 16-14). If that's not you, type your username in the Name field.

5. **Type your password into the Password field and then click the Connect button.**

You would select the Guest radio button if you didn't have an account on Computer B. All you would get to see then are the Public folders of every user with an account on Computer B. A registered user also gets to see their home folder *plus* everyone else's Public folder.

Figure 16-14:
Accessing
folders on a
remote Mac.

The Volume selection dialog box appears.

Volume is the Mac OS X term for all the shared folders on a single disk or volume that belong to that user. You can see a list of volumes in Figure 16-15.

When you log onto a Mac you have a user account on, you will always see a volume with your name (for example, Bob's is `bob1`, in the case of Figure 16-15). You will also see other volumes with usernames of every other user who has an account on Computer B (`shelly` and `frank` in Figure 16-15). If those users have not given you access privileges for specific folders, the only thing you see when you open their volume is their `Public` folder (and the `Drop Box` folder within it). If they've given you privileges for other folders, you'll see those as well.

If multiple items appear in the volume selection dialog box (as shown in Figure 16-15), you may select more than one. Click the first item, hold down the ⌘ key, and click once on each item that you want to add to the selection. After you've selected all the items you want to use, click OK, and they're all mounted on your Desktop.

Figure 16-15:
Choosing a shared folder to connect to on the remote Mac.

6. Select the volume (on Computer B) that you wish to use and click OK.

An icon appears on your Desktop (the Desktop of Computer A), as shown in Figure 16-16. This icon represents a folder owned by `bob1`, which is located on the hard drive of Computer B. Notice that the icon for Bob's volume doesn't look like a drive or folder icon. This icon is what you see whenever a remote volume is mounted on your Desktop. You also see it if you add a server to your `Favorites` folder (more on that later in this chapter) or view a server in the Finder window.

When Bob opens the volume icon (`bob1` in Figure 16-16), its folder window appears (also called `bob1`, with a little house in its title bar because `bob1` is the owner of this volume), as shown in Figure 16-16.

Unsharing a folder

To unshare a folder that you own, change the Group and Everyone privileges to None. Once you do, nobody but you will have access to that folder anymore.

If you're not sure how to do this, see the " Sharing a folder" and "Useful settings for access privileges" sections earlier in this chapter.

Disconnecting from a shared volume

When you finish using the shared volume, disconnect using one of these methods:

✔ Drag the shared folder icon to the Trash icon.

When a disk or volume is selected (highlighted), the Trash icon turns into a little arrow, which represents "eject." Nice touch, eh?

✔ Hold down the Control key and click the volume, and then choose Eject from the contextual menu.

✔ Select the icon and choose File➪Eject.

✔ Select the icon and press ⌘+E.

 ✔ If you've finished working for the day, choose Shut Down from the 🍎 menu. Shutting down automatically disconnects you from shared disks or folders and turns off your Mac.

Changing your password

You can change your password at any time. Changing your password is a good idea if you're concerned about security — if there's a chance your password has been discovered by someone else, for example.

You can change the password for your Mac, or you can change the password you use to connect to your account on a remote user's Mac. We show you how to do both in the following sections.

Changing the password on your Mac

To change the password on your Mac, just follow these steps:

1. **Choose System Preferences from the 🍎 menu on the Finder's menu bar (or click the System Preferences icon in the Dock) and then click the Users icon.**

   The Users pane of System Preferences appears.

2. **Click your account name and then click the Edit User button.**

3. **Type your new password into the Password field.**

4. **Retype your password in the Verify field.**

5. **Click OK to save your changes.**

6. **Close the System Preferences window.**

Changing the password for your account on someone else's Mac

When you log into a remote Mac, you can change your own password if you like. Follow these steps to do so:

1. **Log in to the remote computer you want to change your password on (see the "Connecting to a shared folder" section earlier in this chapter if you don't know how to log in to a remote computer).**

   The Connect dialog box appears.

2. **Type your username into the Connect dialog box if it's not already there.**

3. Click the Options button in the Connect dialog box.

The Options dialog box appears, as shown in Figure 16-17.

Figure 16-17:
The Options
dialog box
offers
several . . .
well . . .
options.

The Options dialog box includes several options for encrypting your password as it is sent over the network. Use the Add Password to Keychain option to store your passwords in a single place on the Mac, meaning that you don't have to retype them each time you access a Mac or other remote resource. Read more about the Keychain in Chapter 13.

4. Click the Change Password button in the Options dialog box.

The Change Password dialog box window appears, as shown in Figure 16-18.

Figure 16-18:
Entering
your old
and new
passwords.

5. Type your current password in the Old Password field.

6. Type your new password in the New Password and Confirm Password fields.

7. Click OK.

Your password is changed, and you return to the Connect dialog box.

8. **(Optional) Type your new password and click Connect to log onto (or into) the other Mac.**

You can skip this step by clicking the Cancel button if you don't need to use anything on the remote Mac at this time. Your password is still changed, and you'll need to use the new password the next time you log into or onto this Mac.

Setting up shortcuts to remote volumes (and folders)

Here are three ways that you can make using remote volumes and folders easier. The first is to use aliases, the second is to use Mac OS X's favorites, and the third uses both aliases and the Dock. The following sections describe each of these methods.

Setting up a shortcut using aliases

After you've mounted (or made visible to your Mac) a volume for the first time, you can make it easier to use in the future by creating an alias for it. The next time that you want to use that volume, just open the alias and the Connect dialog box appears. You type your password and the volume appears (or is *mounted*) on the Desktop. No Connect to Server; no other dialog boxes; no muss and no fuss.

You can do this to any folder within the volume, too. It works just the same with one minor difference: The alias opens that folder, but it also mounts the volume that contains the folder and opens it, too. If you find this bothersome, just close the home folder's window. The folder within — the one you made the alias of and wish to work with — remains open, and you can continue working with it.

Setting up a shortcut using favorites

Here's another easy way to mount a volume: Just click the remote volume's icon (or any folder icon within that volume), and then, while it's selected (highlighted), choose Go⇨Favorites⇨Add to Favorites from the Finder's menu bar. An alias to the remote volume or folder appears in the Favorites folder and on the Favorites submenu of the Go menu.

Setting up shortcuts in the Dock (and on the Desktop)

If you use remote folders often, follow these steps to create a folder that sits on your Dock, ready to call remote computers at your very whim:

1. **Log onto each remote volume (or folder) that you want to be included in the shortcut folder on your Desktop.**

2. **Create an alias for each remote volume or folder you want easy access to.**

3. **Move the aliases you created in Step 2 to a new folder on your Desktop (call it** Remote Folders **or something equally obvious).**

4. **Drag the folder you created in Step 3 onto the Dock.**

There are two easy ways to open any of the volumes or folders in the new folder that contains aliases to remote folders. You can open the folder and double-click any of the aliases in it, or you can click and hold on the folder's icon in the Dock, which summons a pop-up menu that shows all the aliases in the folder. Either way, that volume or folder appears on your Desktop almost instantly.

The road goes on forever and the sharing never ends

In this section, we show you several file-sharing tricks you can use on the road. The first explains how to log onto your home Mac easily from anywhere in the world by plugging into someone else's network. The second is a trick we call "office-on-a-disk," which is a way to take your shortcuts (see the previous section for more info on network shortcuts) with you, even when you use someone else's Mac. Finally, we'll take a look at how to access your files remotely via modem connection.

These techniques are especially useful to iBook or PowerBook users, or if you need to connect to your Mac from someplace other than your home or office network.

Connecting to your home Mac from a remote Mac

In this section, we show how you would make the connection to your own computer with a modem. For example, say you take a plane trip. You bring your PowerBook so that you can work on the plane. When you get to your destination, you want to copy the files that you've been working on to your home Mac to back them up. Well, you can do that with file sharing, and it will be easy for you if you've read about file sharing in the earlier sections of this chapter and understand how to connect to a remote Mac. (If you aren't sure how to do that, please reread the previous sections of this chapter now. If you don't, the following technique will only confuse you.)

If you are the owner of your home Mac, you have full access privileges to both your home folder and also to the rest of your Mac, just as you would if you were working from home. Also, if you own your Mac, you need not make any changes to file sharing privileges in order to log on and use your stuff. If you don't own your Mac (that is, if you are just a user on your home Mac) you will only see your home directory as well as any other volumes or folders that you have permissions to access.

You can connect to your home Mac via an Ethernet network or via modem. We'll talk about Ethernet first, then the nifty office-on-a-disk, and finally we talk about using a modem.

Okay, so you've arrived at your destination. The first thing to do is plug your PowerBook's Ethernet cable into the network and find out what TCP/IP address info you need to use this network (by asking the PIC, or *person in charge;* also sometimes known as the network administrator or resident geek). With those tasks completed, you're ready to do some sharing.

To connect to your home Mac from a remote computer by using an Ethernet connection, follow these steps:

1. **Choose Go⇨Connect to Server (on your PowerBook or other remote computer, of course).**

2. **Type in the TCP/IP address of your Mac at home in the Address field and click the Connect button.**

   The Connect to Server dialog box appears.

3. **Type your username (it may be the same on the PowerBook as on your home Mac) and password and then click the Connect button.**

   The Volume selection dialog box appears. You see both your home folder and your startup hard drive, plus any other disks or partitions that appear on the Desktop of your home machine. In Figure 16-19, you can see Shelly's home folder (shelly) and her hard drive (iMac HD).

4. **Choose a volume and then click OK.**

   The volume mounts on your PowerBook Desktop, and you're in business!

Figure 16-19:
Shelly sees her home folder and hard drive when she connects to her home Mac remotely.

Office-on-a-disk

Here's an even easier way to use your hard drive while working at someone else's Mac. Before leaving your computer, make an alias of your hard drive and copy it to a Zip disk, burn it onto a CD-R, or copy it to your PowerBook's hard drive. At a remote computer, open the alias of your hard drive. The Connect dialog box appears, and as long as you type the correct password, your hard drive mounts on that Mac's Desktop. Neat!

This technique is often called *office-on-a-disk*. If you work in a largish office and find yourself trying to connect to your hard drive from someone else's computer, carry one of these office-on-a-disk disks with you at all times. And if you're using a PowerBook, keep the aliases to your Mac (and any others you use on the road) on the Desktop for quick access.

If you've got no Zip or other removable media disk, don't despair. Still you can use aliases to make your life easier: Just check out the previous section.

Logging on remotely via modem

Mac OS X includes PPP (Point-to-Point Protocol) software that enables you to connect to another computer or the Internet by modem.

With PPP you can access your home hard drive from a remote Mac when you're at another location. You do need a modem, and you also need to configure this modem for remote access, which luckily is a pretty simple process. Because remote access uses the same user and file sharing tools as network file sharing, you should probably bone up on file sharing in the sections earlier in this chapter if you haven't already.

To use a modem to log on remotely, follow these steps:

1. **Choose System Preferences from the menu (or click the System Preferences icon in the Dock).**

2. **Click the Network icon.**

   The Network pane of System Preferences appears.

3. **Choose Internal Modem from the Configure pop-up menu unless you have an external modem; in that case, choose that option.**

   If you've been using Ethernet rather than a modem, notice that two new tabs appear after you choose Internal Modem from the menu: the PPP tab and the Modem tab.

4. **Click the PPP tab.**

   PPP options appear, as shown in Figure 16-20.

5. **(Optional) Type a name for this connection in the Service Provider field.**

This gives a name to the connection information you're now creating so you can easily reuse it in the future. Doing this will make life easier if you need to use this modem connection again.

6. **Type the phone number you want to dial (including any dialing prefix and area code) into the Telephone Number field.**

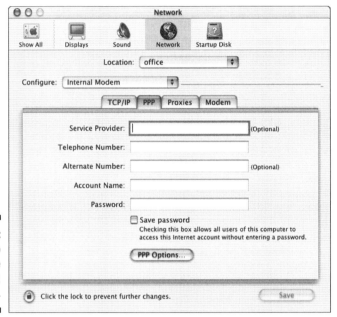

Figure 16-20:
Setting up for remote access via modem.

7. **(Optional) Type an alternate phone number, if there is one, in the Alternate Number field.**

8. **Type your username into the Account Name field.**

9. **Type your password into the Password field.**

10. **(Optional) If you want to log on without having to enter your password each time, select the Save Password check box.**

Selecting this check box means that someone with access to your Mac can log on to your account, so be careful, especially if you are working on an iBook or PowerBook.

11. Click the PPP Options button to set preferences for how your connection is made and maintained.

The PPP Options sheet appears, as shown in Figure 16-21. Of the many options you find here, we point out a few of the most useful in the following list:

- Select the Connect Automatically When Starting TCP/IP Applications check box if you want your modem to connect to the Internet when you launch your browser, connect to a remote server, or retrieve e-mail. This check box must be checked or your Mac won't connect to the Internet automatically when you choose Go⇨Connect to Server.

- Leave the Prompt to Stay Connected if Idle for *x* Minutes check box selected if you're paying long distance charges or Internet access charges. If you don't set this auto-disconnect timer, you could rack up a lot of toll charges if you forget that you're connected and online. If you choose this option, set the number of idle minutes by clicking within the number box and typing the number you want.

- Select the Redial if Busy check box to do just that. You can choose the number of attempts your modem will make if it gets a busy signal instead of connecting.

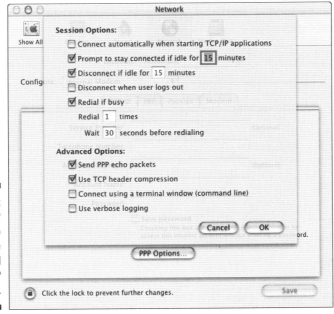

Figure 16-21:
Use PPP
Options to
configure
additional
PPP
features.

11. **When you're done setting PPP options, click OK to close the PPP Options dialog box.**

12. **(Optional) Click the Modem tab in the Network pane.**

    Your modem should be selected in the Modem pop-up menu. If you are having problems connecting, use the menu to find your particular modem and select it.

    You won't need to do much with these settings unless you are having a problem connecting with the modem, but you can set little options here, too. The two options of note are:

    - Choose whether to turn your speaker sound off (to rid yourself of that horrid screeching noise modems make).

    - Choose from tone or pulse dialing, if you need the latter for some strange reason.

    And that's that. Just choose Go⇨Connect to Server and log onto the remote machine. (If you still don't know how, reread the "Connecting to a shared disk or folder" section earlier in the chapter.)

Chapter 17

Back Up Now or Regret It Later

*A*lthough Macintoshes are generally reliable beasts (especially Macs running OS X), someday your hard drive will die. We promise. They *all* do. And if you don't back up your hard drive (or at least those files you can't afford to lose) before that day comes, chances are good that you'll never see your files on that drive again. And if you do see them again, it will only be after paying Scott of DriveSavers Data Recovery Service a king's ransom, with no guarantee of success.

DriveSavers, the premier recoverer of lost data on hard drives, does good work and can often recover stuff that nobody else could. (Ask the producers of *The Simpsons* about the "almost-lost" episodes.) Understandably, DriveSavers charges accordingly. Here's the phone number for DriveSavers: 415-883-4232. Now pray that you never need it — and if you back up often, you won't. But if, somehow, none of this sinks in and you find yourself grasping for straws, tell Scott that we said, "Hi."

In case we didn't stress this enough, you absolutely, positively, without question *must back up* your files if you don't want to risk losing them. Just as you should adopt the Shut Down command and make using it a habit before turning off your machine, you must remember to back up important files on your hard drive and back them up often.

How often is often? That depends on you. How much work can you afford to lose? If losing everything you did yesterday would put you out of business, you need to back up daily or possibly twice a day. If you would only lose a few unimportant letters, you can back up less frequently or even never.

Backing Up Is (Not) Hard to Do

You can back up your hard drive in basically two ways, the brute force method, or the easy way. Read on to learn about both. . . .

Backing up by using the manual, "brute force" method

The most rudimentary way to back up your files is to do it manually. Accomplish this by dragging your files a few at a time to removable disks, such as to a Zip, SuperDisk, or Jaz disk. Or, if you have a CD-R or CD-RW drive, burn a CD with the files you want to back up. In effect, you're making a copy of each file that you want to protect. (See Chapter 9 for more info on removable storage media.)

Yuk! If doing a manual backup sounds pretty awful, trust us — it is. This method takes forever; you can't really tell if you copy every file; and you can't copy only the files that have been modified since your last backup. Almost nobody sticks with this method for long.

Of course, if you're careful to only save files in your Documents folder, as we suggest several times in this book, you can probably get away with backing up only that. Or, if you save files in other folders within your home folder, back up your home folder. As you'll read in a moment, backing up is even easier with back-up software.

Backing up by using commercial back-up software

If you ask Bob, a good back-up program is the best investment you can make. My editor says he never uses it (slacker!). He backs up as he works by copying files the manual way and likes it. Frankly, Bob likes the security of knowing that every document he modifies today is being backed up automatically. And that's what backup software is all about.

Back-up software automates the task of backing up, remembers what is on each back-up disk (if your backup uses more than one disk), and backs up only those files that have been modified since the last backup.

Furthermore, you can instruct your back-up software to only back up a certain folder (say your home folder or your Documents folder), and ignore the hundreds of megabytes of stuff that make up OS X, all of which can be easily reinstalled from the Mac OS X CD-ROM if your hard drive bites it.

Your first backup with commercial software should take anywhere from a few minutes to many hours and use one or more pieces of removable media — Zip, Jaz, CD-R, CD-RW, Orb, magneto-optical disks, or any kind of tape backup. Subsequent backups, called incremental backups in back-up-software parlance, should take only a few minutes.

Be sure to label the disks that you use for your backups because during incremental backups, the back-up software may prompt you to insert specific disks. For example, the software may ask you to Please insert backup disk 7. If you haven't labeled your media clearly, you may have a problem figuring out which disk *is* disk 7.

For some unfathomable reason, Apple has almost never seen fit to provide back-up software with new Macs or to include it with Mac OS. Some early-90s Macintosh Performas had a crummy back-up program, but other than that pathetic attempt, Apple has left millions of Mac owners clueless, giving them nothing more than a brief passage regarding backing up in the Macintosh *User's Guide.* We think information on backing up should be in big red letters, in the first chapter of the guide, and include a warning from the Surgeon General or something. And it wouldn't kill Apple to provide a back-up utility, either. Sheesh, even Windows has a back-up utility, albeit a lousy one. C'mon, Apple, give Mac owners a fair shake. At least include the lame Apple Backup program that some Performa owners got once upon a time.

Fortunately, plenty of very good back-up programs are available for well under $150, including the excellent Retrospect (around $150) and Retrospect Express (around $50) from Dantz Development (www.dantz.com). If you want the most flexible, top-of-the-line back-up software, spend a little more and pop for Retrospect. (Both programs should be available for Mac OS X soon after this book is released, according to Dantz.)

If you have to reboot in Mac OS 9.1 to run a backup program, as Bob had to do during the earliest days of OS X (before a Built for Mac OS X version of Retrospect was released), do it. It's better than remaining unprotected.

Why You Need Two Sets of Back-Up Disks

You're a good soldier. You back up regularly. You think that you're immune to file loss or damage. Now picture yourself in the following scenario:

1. One day you take a SuperDisk or Zip disk to QuicKopyLazerPrintz to print your resume on the laser printer there. You make a few changes while at QuicKopyLazerPrintz, and then take the disk home and stick it into your Mac. Unbeknownst to you, the disk became infected with a computer virus during its brief stint in the computer at QuicKopyLazerPrintz. (We discuss viruses in the "Virus trivia" sidebar elsewhere in this chapter.)

2. When you insert the disk into your Mac, the infection spreads to your hard drive like wildfire without you realizing it.

3. You do a backup. Your back-up software, believing that all the infected files have been recently modified (well, they have been — they were infected with a virus!), proceeds to back them up. You notice that the backup takes a little longer than usual, but otherwise things seem to be okay.

4. A few days later, your Mac starts acting strangely. You borrow a copy of an excellent virus-detection software, such as Virex or Norton Anti-Virus (formerly Symantec Anti-Virus), and discover that your hard drive is infected. "A-ha!" you exclaim. "I've been a good little Mac user, backing up regularly. I'll just restore everything from my back-up disks."

   Not so fast, Buck-o. Some (if not all) the files on your back-up disks are also infected!

This scenario demonstrates why you need multiple backups. If you have several sets of back-up disks, chances are pretty good that one of the sets is clean.

Bob has three current sets of back-up disks going at any one time. He uses one set on even-numbered days, one on odd-numbered days, and he updates the third set once a week and stores it somewhere other than his office (such as a neighbor's house or a safe deposit box). This scheme ensures that no matter what happens — even if his office burns, is flooded, is destroyed by a tornado or a hurricane, or is robbed — Bob won't lose more than a few days' worth of work, which he can live with.

Virus trivia

A computer virus, in case you missed it in *Time* or *Newsweek,* is a nasty little piece of computer code that replicates and spreads from disk to disk just like flesh and blood viruses do. Most computer viruses cause your Mac to misbehave; some viruses can destroy files or erase disks with no warning.

You don't have too much to worry about if

- ✔ You download files only from commercial online services, such as America Online, which are very conscientious about viral infections

- ✔ You use only commercial software and don't download files from Web sites with strange names

You should definitely worry about virus infection if

- ✔ An unsavory friend told you about a Web site called `Dan'sDenOfPirated IllegalStolenBootlegSoftware. com`.

- ✔ You swap disks with friends regularly

- ✔ You shuttle disks back and forth to other Macs

- ✔ You use your disks at service bureaus or copy shops

- ✔ You download files from various and sundry places on the Internet, even ones that don't sound as slimy as `Dan'sDenOfPirated IllegalBootlegSoftware.com`

- ✔ You receive e-mail with attachments (and open them)

If you're at risk, do yourself a favor and buy a commercial antivirus program. On the commercial front, two leading virus-detection utilities are Virex and Norton Anti-Virus (NAV; formerly Symantec Anti-Virus). Each has its advocates. Shelly is using Virex right now; Bob has used NAV for years; and neither of us has ever been infected with a virus. Although you can choose from many shareware and freeware antivirus solutions, none that we know of are as trustworthy as Virex or Norton.

The big advantage of buying a commercial antivirus program is that the publisher contacts you each time that a virus is discovered and provides you with a software update to protect you against the new strain. Or, for a fee, the publisher can send you a new version of the software every time a new virus is found.

As this book went to press, Built for Mac OS X versions of Virex and Norton Anti-Virus had not yet been released and, unfortunately, the Classic versions won't protect you when you're running OS X. So check with both publishers: Built for Mac OS X versions should be available by the time you read this.

Chapter 18

Troubleshooting Mac OS X

*A*s bleeding-edge Mac enthusiasts with almost fifteen years of Mac under our belts, we've had more than our share of Mac troubles. Over those years, we've developed an arsenal of tips and tricks that we believe can resolve more than 90 percent of Mac OS X problems without a trip to the repair shop.

If your hardware is dead, then, sadly, neither you nor we can do anything about it (it becomes a job for your friendly Mac repairman and your check-book). But if your hardware is okay, you have a fighting chance of using the suggestions in this chapter to get your machine up and running.

Dem Ol' Sad Mac Blues

While you usually see a happy smiling Mac face when you turn your computer on, once in a blue moon you may see the dreaded Sad Mac icon (shown in the margin) and hearing that melancholy arpeggio in G minor (better known as the *Chimes of Doom*), or the sound of breaking glass, or any of the other horrible sounds Macs make when they're dying.

The Sad Mac usually indicates that something very bad has happened to your Mac; often some hardware component has bitten the dust. But Sad Macs are rather uncommon — many Mac users go their entire lifetime without seeing one. If you ever have a Sad Mac experience, don't despair immediately. Before you diagnose your Mac as terminally ill, try booting from CD-ROM to try and bring it back to life. If you have your installation CD-ROM already, you can skip to the section "Booting from CD-ROM" a little later in this chapter. If you're not sure about your Mac OS X installation CD-ROM, see the next section.

Better safe than Mac-less

The bootable Mac OS X CD-ROM is soooo important — try to have more than one copy around. That way, if one gets misplaced, damaged, eaten by the dog, scuffed, scratched, or otherwise rendered useless, you won't be out of luck. Bob keeps the Mac OS X CD in his middle desk drawer and several other bootable CDs on the bookshelf. An older version of Mac OS and the CD that came with your computer are examples of extra bootable CDs you may have

hanging around. The Mac OS X installation CD is bootable as well. All of the above will boot your Mac in an emergency, which is why they're so important to have handy.

If you have a removable media drive such as an Orb or Jaz or Zip drive, or a CD-R or DVD-RAM, create a bootable (removable) disk by installing Mac OS X (see this book's Appendix) and stash it someplace safe, just in case.

The ultimate start-up disc: The OS X installation CD

We bet you have a copy of the ultimate start-up disc right there on your computer table — the installation CD in the Mac OS X retail box. You can recognize it by the shiny blue Mac OS X logo. In addition to the system software you need to make your Mac work, this disc also has a copy of Disk Utility, which we discuss in the "Step 1: Run First Aid" section later in this chapter. If you see the flashing question mark, you may need to use the Disk Utility program's First Aid feature to repair hidden damage to your hard drive. And Disk Utility's other feature, Drive Setup, can install new drivers for your hard drive. Read more about both these utilities throughout the rest of this chapter.

If you don't have a bootable CD-ROM, preferably a Mac OS X Install CD-ROM, you can't do the rest of the stuff in this chapter. So if you don't have one handy, go find it now. If you really can't find one, you may want to call Apple and arrange for a replacement — you really shouldn't be without it.

Booting from CD-ROM

To boot your Mac from a CD-ROM installation disc, follow these steps:

1. **Shut down your Mac.**

2. **Insert a bootable CD-ROM (the Mac OS X CD is a good choice).**

   If you're not sure about this bootable CD-ROM business, see the previous section.

3. **Restart your Mac.**

4. **Hold down the C key on your keyboard during startup. Keep holding it down until your Mac either boots from the CD or doesn't.**

5. **If that doesn't work, try holding down these four keys in the infamous four-finger salute: Delete+Option+⌘+Shift.**

   Keep holding the four keys down until your Mac either boots from the CD or doesn't. If it doesn't, try another CD or other bootable disk (Jaz, Orb, and so on). If that doesn't work, you may need to take your Mac in for repairs.

A good way to remember this keyboard combination — which is generally used to force your Mac to start up from a disc other than your internal hard drive, including a bootable CD-ROM — is to think of the mnemonic acronym *DOCS*: *D*elete+*O*ption+*C*ommand (⌘)+*S*hift.

If you can boot from CD-ROM . . .

If you see the Mac OS startup screen when you boot (start up) from your CD-ROM, hope flickers for your Mac. The fact that you can boot from another disk (a CD in this case) indicates that the problem lies with your hard drive or with Mac OS X itself. Whatever the tangle, it will probably respond to one of the techniques we discuss throughout the rest of this chapter.

So your Mac boots from the installation CD, but you still have this little problem: You prefer that your Mac boot from your (much faster) hard drive than from CD. Not to worry. All you need to do is reinstall Mac OS X (see the Appendix at the end of this book).

If you can't boot from CD-ROM . . .

If the techniques in this chapter don't correct your Mac problem, or you still see the Sad Mac icon when you start up with the CD, your Mac is toast and needs to go in for repairs (usually to an Apple dealer).

Before you drag your Mac down to the shop, however, try calling 1-800-SOS-APPL, the Apple Tech Support hot line. The service representatives there may well suggest something else you can try. If your Mac is still under warranty, it's even free.

If you get the Sad Mac immediately after installing random access memory (RAM) — and this is quite common — double-check that the RAM is properly seated in its sockets. *Don't forget to power down your Mac first.* And follow the installation instructions that came with the RAM chips — if they included an anti-static strap or instructions for discharging static electricity, use them.

Question Mark and the Mysterians

When you turn on your Mac, the first thing it does (after the hardware tests) is to check for a start-up disk (something with Mac OS X on it). If your system doesn't find one on your internal hard drive, it looks for one somewhere else — on a FireWire or USB disk, or a CD-ROM or DVD.

If you have more than one start-up disk attached to your Mac, as many users do, you can choose which one your Mac boots from in the Startup Disk System Preference pane. (See Chapter 15 for details.)

At this point, your Mac *usually* finds your hard drive, which contains your operating system, and the start-up process continues on its merry way with the happy Mac and all the rest. If your Mac can't find your hard drive, or doesn't find on it what it needs to boot OS X, you'll encounter a flashing question-mark icon (as shown in the margin) in place of the usual happy Mac.

Don't go cryin' *96 Tears.* This icon means that your Mac can't find a start-up disk, hard drive, or CD-ROM containing valid system software (either Mac OS X or a previous version supported by your particular Mac).

Think of the flashing question mark as your Mac's way of saying, "Please provide me with a start-up disk."

If Apple can figure out a way to put a flashing question mark on the screen, why the heck can't the software engineers find a way to put the words `Please insert a startup disk` on the screen as well? The curtness of the flashing question mark is one of Bob's pet peeves about the Macintosh. We know — you're clever and smart (you're reading *Mac OS X For Dummies*, aren't you?), so you know that a flashing question mark means that you should insert a start-up disk. But what about everyone else?

If you encounter this warning icon, go through the steps we outline in this section. We give you some different options to try, such as rebuilding your Desktop, using Disk Tools and First Aid, or zapping the PRAM. If one doesn't work, move on to the next.

Step 1: Run First Aid

In most cases, after you've booted successfully from the OS X CD, the first logical troubleshooting step is to use the First Aid option in the Disk Utility application.

Every drive has several strangely named components such as B-trees, extent files, catalog files, and other creatively named invisible files. They are all involved in managing the data on your drives. Disk Utility's First Aid feature checks all those files and repairs any damaged ones.

Here's how to make First Aid do its thing:

1. **Boot from your Mac OS X CD by inserting the CD and restarting your Mac while holding down the C key.**

2. **Launch the Disk Utility application that's on the CD.**

   This launches the copy of Disk Utility that's on the CD, and eventually, the Disk Utility window appears. By default, the First Aid option is selected. (If it's not, click the First Aid button on the left side of the window.)

3. **Click the icon for your boot hard drive at the top of the Disk Utility window (shown in Figure 18-1).**

   Your boot drive is the one with the icon that ordinarily appears in the upper-right corner of the Desktop. In Figure 18-1, Bob calls his *X*.

4. **Click the Repair button.**

   Your Mac whirs and hums for a few minutes, and the results window tells you what's going on. Ultimately, First Aid tells you (you hope) that the drive has been repaired and is now okay, as shown in Figure 18-1. If so, go back to work.

5. **Quit Disk Utility (Disk Utility⇨Quit Disk Utility or ⌘+Q).**

6. **Reboot without holding the C key down.**

If First Aid finds damage that it can't fix, a commercial disk-recovery tool, such as Norton Utilities for the Macintosh or Alsoft's DiskWarrior, may be able to repair the damage. And even if First Aid gave you a clean bill of health, you may want to run one of the commercial utilities anyway, just to have a second opinion. (As of this writing, none of these programs were Mac OS X compatible, though they should be by the time you read this.)

If everything checks out with First Aid, try to boot from your hard drive again. If you still get the flashing question mark, proceed to the next section to try to reinstall the drivers that control your hard drive.

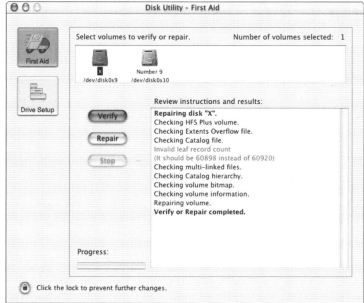

Figure 18-1:
First Aid
repaired this
disk and
gives it a
clean bill of
health.

Step 2: Zapping the PRAM

Sometimes your parameter RAM (PRAM) becomes scrambled and needs to
be reset. *PRAM*, a small piece of memory that's not erased or forgotten when
you shut down, keeps track of things such as printer selection, sound level,
and monitor settings.

Try zapping your PRAM if your Monitors System Preferences or Print Center
forgets your settings when you shut down or restart.

To zap your PRAM, just restart your Mac and hold down ⌘+Option+P+R
(that's four keys — good luck; it's okay to use your nose) until your Mac
restarts itself. It's kind of like a hiccup. You see the flashing question mark for
a minute or two as your Mac thinks about it; then the icon disappears and
your Mac restarts.

One of the things that gets zapped with the PRAM is your chosen start-up
disk. So use the Startup Disk System Preference pane to reselect your usual
boot disk.

Zapping the PRAM returns some system preferences to their default settings (but, interestingly, not the date or time), so you may have to do some tweaking after zapping the PRAM.

Step 3: Reinstalling OS X

The reason that we present the procedure to reinstall the system software almost last in this section is that it takes the longest. We detail this procedure at great length in this book's Appendix to reinstall Mac OS X. Read that Appendix and follow the instructions. If you're still unsuccessful after that point, come back to the following section.

Step 4: Take your Mac in for repair

If none of our suggestions work for you and you're still seeing the flashing question mark, you have big trouble.

You may have any one of the following problems:

- Your hard drive is dead.
- You have some other type of hardware failure.
- All your start-up disks and your system software CDs are defective (unlikely).

The bottom line: If you still see the flashing question mark after trying all the cures we list in this chapter, you almost certainly need to have your Mac serviced by a qualified technician.

If You Crash at Startup

Startup crashes are another bad thing that can happen to your Mac. These crashes are more of a hassle to solve than flashing question mark problems but are rarely fatal.

You know that a *crash* has happened when you see a System Error dialog box, a frozen cursor, a frozen screen, or any other disabling event. A *startup crash* happens when your system shows a crash symptom any time between flicking the power key or switch (or restarting) and having full use of the Desktop.

A startup crash may happen to you someday. We surely hope not. But if it does, the easiest way to fix it is to reinstall OS X from the CD. We detail this procedure at great length in this book's Appendix. Read that Appendix and follow the instructions. If you're still unsuccessful after that point, come back and reread the "Step 4: Take your Mac in for repair" section earlier in this chapter.

Part V
The Part of Tens

The 5th Wave   By Rich Tennant

"...and with QuickTime image-editing technology, we're able to recreate the awesome spectacle known as Tyrannosaurus Gwen."

In this part . . .

These last chapters are a little different — they're kind of like long top-ten lists. Although we'd like for you to believe that we included them because we're big fans of Dave Letterman, the truth is that Hungry Minds, Inc. always includes a Part of Tens section in its *For Dummies* books. This book continues the tradition. And because Hungry Minds pays us, we do these chapters how we're asked. (Actually, it's kind of fun.)

First, we give you the low-down on ways to speed up your Mac experience, and then move on to a subject near and dear to Bob's heart — ten awesome things for your Mac that are worth spending money on.

Next up, how would you like the addresses of ten thoroughly cool Web sites that will help you use and enjoy your Mac more? You want 'em? You got 'em.

But wait, there's one more. Last but certainly not least, we briefly describe some Mac OS X applications that you might someday need (and that we didn't discuss in much detail elsewhere in this book), what these applications do, and why you may need them.

Chapter 19

Ten Ways to Speed Up Your Mac Experience

This chapter is for speed demons only. At some time in their Mac life, most users wish that their machine would work faster — even those of us with Power Macintosh G4s. We can't help you make your processor faster, but we do cover things in this chapter that can make your Mac at least seem faster, and most of our tips won't cost you a red cent.

Use Those Keyboard Shortcuts

Keyboard shortcuts (see Table 19-1 for a way-groovy list of the more useful ones) can make navigating your Mac a much faster experience compared with constantly using the mouse, offering these benefits: Trust us when we say learning the keyboard shortcuts for commands you use often will save you a ton of time and effort.

✔ By using keyboard shortcuts, your hands stay focused on the keyboard, reducing the amount of time that you remove your hand from the keyboard to fiddle with the mouse.

✔ If you memorize keyboard shortcuts with your head, your fingers will memorize them, too.

This table also appears in the cheat sheet that came in the inside front cover of this book. Tear it out and tape it to your monitor or somewhere where you'll see it all the time when using your Mac.

Table 19-1	Great Keyboard Shortcuts	
Keyboard Shortcut	*What It's Called*	*What It Does*
⌘+O	Open	Opens the selected item.
⌘+. (period)	Cancel	Cancels the current operation in many programs, including the Finder. Doubles for the Cancel button in most dialog boxes.
⌘+P	Print	Brings up a dialog box that enables you to print the active window's contents.
⌘+X	Cut	Cuts selected item and places it on the Clipboard. (We cover the Edit menu and the Clipboard in Chapter 6.)
⌘+C	Copy	Copies whatever you select and places it on the Clipboard.
⌘+V	Paste	Pastes the contents of the Clipboard at the spot where your cursor is.
⌘+F	Find	Brings up Sherlock in the Finder, or a Find dialog box in most programs.
⌘+A	Select All	Selects the entire contents of the active window in many programs, including the Finder.
⌘+Z	Undo	Undoes the last thing you did in many programs and the Finder.
⌘+Shift+?	Help	Brings up the Mac Help window in the Finder, or summons Help in other programs.
⌘+H	Hide	Hides the current application. Use the Application menu (the one that reads Finder when you're in the Finder) to Show All applications again.
⌘+Q	Quit	Quits the current application (but not the Finder; the Finder is *always* running).
⌘+Delete	Delete	Moves the selected item to Trash.

Learn to Type Better

One way to make your Mac seem faster is to make your fingers move faster. The quicker you finish a task, the quicker you're on to something else. You get stuff done faster if you're not always looking down at the keyboard or up at the screen when you type. You'll also find that as your typing skills improve, you spend less time correcting errors or editing your work.

The speed and accuracy that you gain has an added bonus: When you're a decent touch typist, you fingers will fly even faster when you use those nifty keyboard shortcuts (we list a gaggle of these in Table 19-1).

Resolution? It's Not Just for New Year's Anymore

Another setting you can change to potentially improve your Mac's performance is the resolution of your monitor. Most modern monitors and video cards (or onboard video circuitry, depending upon your Mac model) are capable of displaying multiple resolutions. You change your monitor's display resolution in the same place that you choose the number of colors you want: the Display tab of the Monitors pane of System Preferences. Click your resolution choice from the Resolutions list, which is located on the left side of this tab.

The Dock by default contains a handy little item called `Displays.dock`. With it, you can change resolutions and color depth without opening System Preferences. Just press the mouse button on the *Displays.dock* icon and hold it down for a moment. A menu will pop up under your cursor, as shown in Figure 19-1.

The Mac is not a typewriter

The Macintosh is more of a typesetting machine than a typewriter. So when you use a Macintosh, you should follow the rules of good typography, not the rules of good typewriting. If you want your documents to look truly professional, you need to understand the difference between inch and foot marks (" and ') and typographer's quotation marks (' and 'or " and "), in addition to putting single spaces after punctuation. You also need to know where and how to use a hyphen (-), an en dash (–), and an em dash (—).

For more on making your documents look more elegant and professional, get a hold of an excellent book by Mac-goddess Robin Williams, *The Mac is Not a Typewriter* (published by Peachpit Press).

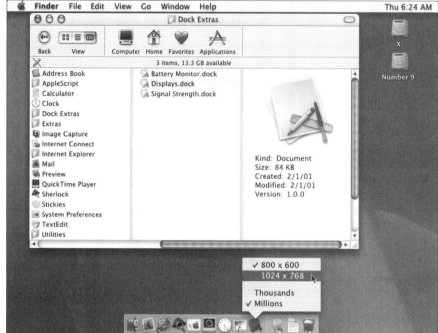

Figure 19-1:
Use the
handy
Displays.
dock tool to
switch
resolutions
right from
the Dock.

Here's the deal on display resolution: The smaller the numbers are that you use for your monitor's resolution, the faster that your screen refreshes. For a computer monitor, *resolution* is expressed as a dimension-type set of numbers (*number* x *number*). The first number is the number of pixels (color dots) that run horizontally, and the second number is the number of lines running vertically. Fewer pixels refresh faster. Therefore, a resolution of 640 x 480 updates itself faster than a resolution of 832 x 624; 832 x 624 updates faster than 1,024 x 768; and so forth.

This isn't true if you have an LCD (flat panel) monitor or a PowerBook. In that case, the native resolution is usually faster. Which is the native resolution? Depends upon the monitor. For the Apple Studio Display 15-inch and most PowerBooks it's 1,024 x 768. If you have a different flat screen, check out the documentation to see what the vendor recommends.

On the other hand, the speed difference between resolutions these days is relatively minimal. In fact, we can hardly tell the difference between one and the other. Furthermore, because you can see more on-screen at higher resolutions, a higher resolution reduces the amount of scrolling you have to do and lets you have more open windows on the screen. Therefore, it could be said that higher resolutions can speed up your Mac as well.

The bottom line is this: Choose a resolution based on your preference rather than which one you think may be faster. That said, if your Mac seems slow at a resolution setting of 1,024 x 768, try a lower resolution and see whether it feels faster.

A Mac with a View — and Preferences, Too

The type of icon display and the Desktop background you choose affect how quickly your screen updates in the Finder. You can set and change these choices in the View Options windows (see Figure 19-1). From the Finder, choose View⇨Show View Options (or use the keyboard shortcut ⌘+J).

The View Options window, like our old friend the contextual menu, is . . . well . . . contextual. Depending on what is active when you choose it from the View menu, you see one of two similar versions: folders in Icon view or the Desktop (left side of Figure 19-2) and folders in List view (right side of Figure 19-2).

The Global and Window tabs of the View Options window have identical options. You use the Global tab to set the default appearance for all your Finder windows, and the Window tab to set up the current window. If you select the Use Global View Preferences check box in the Window tab, the options you set in the Global tab are applied to this window. We discuss the View Options window in more detail in Chapter 7.

Figure 19-2:
Your choices in the View Options windows for Icon view (left) and List view (right).

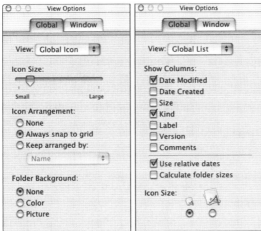

When bigger isn't better

The smaller the icon, the faster the screen updates. In the Icon view of the View Options windows, moving the Icon Size slider to the left makes icons smaller (faster) and moving it to the right makes them bigger (slower). In List view, select one of the two Icon Size radio buttons to choose smaller (faster) or larger (slower) icons. The difference is greater if you have an older Mac.

Background checks

In Icon view of the View Options window, you can choose a picture or color as the background for your Finder windows. Not choosing a picture or color might just save a bit on screen redraw time. Try leaving the default None option selected.

Calculated moves

We recommend that you deactivate Calculate Folder Sizes (that is, deselect, or clear, its check box) to make the screen redraw faster in the Finder. At least to us, the screen feels as if it redraws faster with this feature turned off. This feature is offered only for windows using the List view.

The Finder is kind of smart about the Calculate Folder Sizes option. If you try to do anything in the Finder while folder sizes are calculating — when you make a menu selection, open an icon, or move a window, for example — the Finder interrupts the calculation so that you can complete your task before it resumes calculating. So, in theory, you should never notice a delay when Calculate Folder Sizes is selected.

Try the Calculate folder sizes option both on and off. We don't know about you, but Bob at least finds any noticeable delay unacceptable, and he notices a delay when this option is turned on, even on very fast Macs. Maybe this feature is just annoying and not actually slowing things down, but he can't stand having it on. If you want to know how big a folder is, just click it and choose File⇨Show Info (or press ⌘+I).

Getting ahead-er and other stuff

The Show Columns check boxes in the View Options window for List view — Date Modified, Date Created, Size, Kind, Label, Version, and Comments — have a slight impact on screen update speed when you open a Finder window in List view. The Finder has to draw everything you select here: With fewer items checked, the Finder updates windows faster.

The impact of these items on screen updating is pretty small, so your choice should be made based on what information you want to see in Finder windows, not on whether choosing them slows down your Mac. Play around with these options if you like, but unless your Mac is very slow, you probably won't notice much difference between on and off.

Get a New, Faster Model or Upgrade Yours

Apple keeps putting out faster and faster Macs at lower and lower prices. From time to time, Apple and other vendors offer reasonably priced upgrades that can transform your older, slower Mac into a speedy new one. Check out the latest iMacs — they're usually an excellent value. Or, if you crave portability, iBooks and PowerBooks are rocking good computers. Or consider a used Mac that's faster than yours. The big-time honcho of auction Web sites, eBay (www.ebay.com), has hundreds of used Macs up for auction at any given time. Shopping on eBay might just get you a better Mac at an outstanding price. Give it a try!

Get a G4 Accelerator

An *accelerator* is a card that replaces the processor (CPU) in your Mac with a faster one. Even if you have a G4 in your Mac already, you may be able to upgrade to a faster one.

But before you plunk down the cash for an upgrade, be sure that it's compatible with Mac OS X. Some upgrades only work with older versions of Mac OS, and those won't help you.

Visit www.macworld.com for information on the various upgrade options available and how they compare with each other. Upgrades start at a few hundred dollars and go up to more than a thousand clams. The older your Mac, the more bang you'll get for your G4 upgrade buck.

Get an Accelerated Graphics Card

An *accelerated graphics card* is designed to speed up one thing: the screen update rate. Accelerated graphics cards blast pixels onto your screen at amazing speeds. They're extremely popular with graphic arts professionals who would otherwise suffer slower screen redraws when working with 24-bit graphics. Most of them are also awesome for playing 3D games.

You can use a graphics accelerator only if your Mac has a slot for it; that's where you install one. Currently, you'll need a PowerMac G4 to use a graphics accelerator with OS X.

Visit www.macworld.com for information on the various graphics cards available and how they compare with each other. Cards start at around a hundred dollars and go up from there. And remember, the older your Mac, the more of a performance boost you'll see for your money.

Get a New Hard Drive

Depending on how old your Mac is, a faster hard drive may provide a substantial speedup. If you have a relatively new Mac — any Mac with a G4 processor — the internal hard drive that came with it is pretty fast already. Unless you also need more storage space, a new hard drive may not be the best way to spend your bucks. On the other hand, if you have an older G3 model, a faster (and larger) hard drive may be just the ticket.

Fire Up Your Mac with FireWire

If you really crave speed, get a FireWire hard drive — all Macs released since February 2001 include at least one FireWire port. *FireWire* is the name for the fastest *bus* (or data pathway) on your Mac. FireWire is the state of the art in connecting devices that need fast transfer speeds, and is used to connect devices that require high-speed communication with your Mac, such as hard drives, CD burners, scanners, and camcorders.

In other words, FireWire is the fastest, easiest way to add storage to Macs that include FireWire support. Hard drives that connect via the USB port work fine if you don't have FireWire, but they're as slow as molasses by comparison. So if you have the need for speed, be sure you opt for a FireWire hard drive and not a USB model.

Mac OS X 10.0, the version that shipped in March of 2001, cannot boot from external FireWire or USB drives — yet. This feature is expected to be added to Mac OS X at some time in the future. *So,* before you buy a FireWire or USB drive, check with Apple to see if the current version of OS X will let you boot from it. (Even if you can't boot from a FireWire or USB hard disk, you can connect it and use it for storing any files you like, or for backing up files from your internal hard disk.)

The Software Update System Preferences page will automatically update your copy of Mac OS X for you. Don't forget to run it every so often, or configure it to run automatically. See Chapter 15 for more info on Software Update.

Chapter 20

Ten Ways to Make Your Mac Better by Throwing Money at It

. . . .

In This Chapter

▶ Paying to make your Mac faster

▶ Paying to make your Mac life easier

▶ Drooling over some Mac toys

. . . .

This is one of our favorite chapters. As you've probably figured out by now, we love souping up our Macs. We live to find ways of working smarter, saving time, and saving hand motion, and we revel in tweaking our Mac OS X machines. So it gives us great pleasure to share in this chapter our personal top ten things that you can buy for your Mac to tweak it and make it faster, easier to use, and (we hope) more fun.

The items listed in this chapter are things we have, use every day, love dearly, and would (and probably will!) buy again.

RAM

RAM, or *Random Access Memory,* is your computer's primary working memory. The more you have, the smoother your Mac runs — period. If you have anything less than 192MB in your Mac, you'll like your Mac *a lot* better if you upgrade to 192MB or more. If you like to do a few things at once, more megabytes of RAM will make you a happier camper. (For what it's worth, RAM has never been cheaper than it is today — it's worth every penny.)

Back-Up Software

The only two kinds of Mac users are those who have lost data and those who are going to. If your work means anything to you, get something that helps automate the task of backing up your files. Retrospect or Retrospect Express, both from Dantz Development (www.dantz.com), are the names to trust. And please, please read Chapter 17, which is titled, appropriately, "Back Up Now or Regret It Later." It may well be the most important chapter in this book.

As we write this, Dantz has not released the Mac OS X versions of their software, but has publicly stated that this release will be out soon. One or both products should be available by the time you read this.

A Better Monitor (Or a Second One)

If you have a tiny monitor, get a bigger one. With a larger monitor, you spend less time scrolling and rearranging windows and more of your time getting actual work done — which is a good thing, right? For example, Bob's setup includes two monitors: a 15-inch Apple LCD (a flat-panel, much like a PowerBook monitor for your desktop computer) and a 20-inch Sony Trinitron. It's an awesome setup — one he highly recommends. With two monitors, you can have the menu bar and Finder windows on the first monitor, and document(s) you're working on displayed on the second monitor. Or, when using a program like Photoshop (which has lots of floating palettes), you can put the palettes on one monitor and a document you're working on can be displayed on the big one. And so on.

Flat-panel LCD displays, such as the Apple Studio Display, have come down dramatically in price over the past year. In Bob's humble opinion, LCD displays are brighter and easier on the eyes than traditional CRT (glass picture tube) monitors. If you can afford one, that's what you really want. Alas, owners of most iMacs, as well as iBook owners, are out of luck on this tip — it's not possible to add a second monitor to these models. If you've got a later iMac that includes a video port, go ahead and get a bigger monitor.

A Fast Internet Connection

High-bandwidth connections (that is, fast Internet access) just *rock*. By adding a high-speed Internet connection such as DSL or cable modem, your capacity to communicate electronically will increase tenfold. With this add-on, you can join an online service, surf the Internet, e-mail your friends, and much, much more, at speeds up to ten or more times faster than a 56 Kbps-speed modem. Web pages that once took minutes to load appear on-screen almost instantly. If you can afford cable/DSL (around $40/month in most places) and are in an area where these services are available, high-speed Internet is worth every penny.

Removable Media Drive(s)

Apple stopped including floppy disk drives with new Macs a couple of years ago. So now the only ways you can load new files (programs, documents, games, or whatever) onto your Mac are by copying files from some other kind of removable media (like a Zip disk or a CD-ROM, see Chapter 9), or by downloading from the Internet.

If you want to back up your Mac or hand your buddy a disk with files on it, you'll need some kind of removable media drive. Zip and SuperDisk are the most popular brands; stick with a popular brand because then you'll be able to trade disks with anyone who has the same kind of drive. Perhaps the best choice these days is a CD-R (recordable CD-ROM) drive or CD-RW (with unlimited writing capabilities) drive so that you can make your own CDs that contain files, music, or both!

If you have a relatively new Mac, you may have a built-in Zip or CD-RW drive. If you do (or if you get an external one), for goodness sake — use it to back up your stuff!

Games

Gaming on the Mac has never been better. Shelly has a serious addiction to *The Sims,* while Bob thinks that *Myth II* from Bungie Software may just be the best game ever invented. *Myth III* may even be out by the time you read this. Watch for Bob (he's known as "Wookiee").

Other games Bob *loves* include *The Sims*, *Unreal Tournament,* and almost every game that has the word "pinball" in the title. (For what it's worth, Sierra Attractions has put out a bunch of great ones including *3-D Ultra Pinball* and *3-D Ultra Pinball Thrillride.*)

Multimedia Titles

Many great games, references, and educational titles come on CD-ROM or DVD-ROM these days. You'll love 'em, and so will your kids. Your Mac is more than a computer — it's a full-blown multimedia player. Enjoy it.

Some Big Honking Speakers with a Subwoofer

Face it: Most Macs have crummy speakers (or worse, only one crummy speaker). With a decent set of speakers, games are more fun, music sounds like music instead of like AM radio, and the voiceovers in your multimedia titles suddenly become intelligible. If you're into sound, you'll enjoy your Mac much more if you add a set of window-rattling speakers, preferably one with a massive subwoofer to provide that booming bass you know you crave. So crank it up!

If you have a DVD-ROM drive and one of those gigantic 24-inch monitors, a killer set of speakers makes watching movies on your Mac a zillion times better. Ka-ching!

A New Mouse and/or Keyboard

If you're still using that hockey-puck mouse that came with your iMac, G3, or G4, do yourself a favor and beat it to death with a hammer. It'll make you feel good. Then buy a real mouse. You'll be so much happier if you upgrade to a mouse that's easier to move around and maybe even has two (or more!) buttons. You'll be amazed how much easier it is to work with a mouse that actually fits your hand.

Also, consider ditching that silly Chiclet keyboard if you're stuck with one (you know, those curved, tiny-keyed annoyances that first came with iMacs and that Apple continued to foist on users for many years). Third-party Mac keyboards on the market today are also a huge improvement over what probably came with your Mac.

Bob is partial to so-called "ergonomic keyboards," which he finds more comfortable for prolonged writing sessions. He also thinks he types faster with this kind of keyboard. His current axe is a Microsoft Natural Keyboard Pro. Even though it's a Windows keyboard and the modifier keys are mislabeled and reversed (the Option key is next to the space bar and says Alt; the Command key is where you'd expect the Option key to be and has a Windows logo on it), he still likes it better than other keyboards. Unfortunately, while Microsoft offers excellent Mac OS 9 drivers for it, there aren't any for Mac OS X yet. So, one of the keyboard's best features, the customizable multimedia keys, don't work with OS X at all. If you can get past all that (and, granted, it's a lot to get past), Bob still thinks it's an awesome keyboard. Check it out at the following URL:

www.microsoft.com/mac/products/hardware/default.asp

Also check out the clear Apple Pro keyboard and Pro Mouse if these didn't come with your Mac. They're pretty cool.

A PowerBook or an iBook

Because one Mac is never enough. With a portable Mac, you can go anywhere and continue to compute. And both iBook and PowerBook are capable of using Apple's AirPort wireless networking, so you can surf the Net, print, and share files from the couch or the pool.

A New Mac

If you have any money left, consider upgrading to a newer, faster Mac. They've never been faster, cheaper, or better equipped; if yours is getting a bit long at the tooth, consider a newer, faster model.

Timing can be everything when shopping for a new Mac. Historically, new models are announced at Macworld Expo in January (in San Francisco) and July (in New York City). So it's usually a bad idea to buy a new Mac in December or June because chances are good that what you buy will be discontinued in a month or two. On the other hand, Apple occasionally lowers prices the month before Macworld Expos to clear out old inventory before introducing new models. Keeping that in mind, *Bob's* advice is to wait until after a Macworld Expo to choose your new Mac. But, if a December or June deal is so good you can't pass it up, go for it. Bear in mind, however, that the model you're buying may be discontinued shortly and replaced with a faster, better model at around the same price.

Caveat emptor.

Chapter 21

Ten Great Web Sites
for Mac Freaks

*A*s much as we would love to think that this book tells you everything you need to know about using your Macintosh, we know better. You have a lot more to discover about using your Mac, and new tools and products come out almost daily.

The best way to gather more information than you could ever possibly soak up about all things Macintosh is to hop onto the Web. There you'll find news, free and shareware software to download, troubleshooting sites, tons of news and information about your new favorite operating system, and lots of places to shop. So make sure you read Chapter 11 to get set up for the Internet because the sites in this chapter are the best, most chock-full-o'-stuff places on the Web for Mac users. By the time you finish checking out these ten Web sites, you'll know so much about your Mac that you'll feel like your brain is in danger of exploding. On the other hand, you may just be a whole lot smarter. Happy surfing!

MacFixIt

www.macfixit.com

Frequent *Macworld* contributor and consultant Ted Landau has put together an awesome troubleshooting site to help you solve common problems and keep current on compatibility issues with new system software and third-party products. The site is searchable, too, which means you can find information by searching for a keyword. And Ted's coverage of Mac OS X so far has been stellar.

VersionTracker.com

www.versiontracker.com

Looking for free or shareware stuff? Try VersionTracker. It's one of the best sites to search for software for any version of Mac OS by keyword. It's a treasure trove of software and updates, and worth visiting even if you aren't looking for anything in particular. So check it out and download some games or something. We love this site.

MacInTouch

www.macintouch.com

For the latest in Mac news, updated every single day, check out MacInTouch.com. Authored by longtime *MacWeek* columnist Ric Ford and his staff of news hounds, this site keeps you on the bleeding-edge of Mac news, including software updates, virus alerts, and Apple happenings. We consider this a site that's essential to keeping up with Mac OS X.

MacCentral

www.maccentral.com

Bigger than MacInTouch (though often less relevant and rarely as well-written), MacCentral is another popular Mac news site. Now part of *Macworld* magazine's Web empire, MacCentral is updated several times a day and is one of the best sites on the Web to find rewrites of press releases within hours after being issued.

Tech Info Library

http://til.info.apple.com

Got a technical question about any version of Mac OS or any Apple product — including OS X? March your question right over to the Tech Info Library, Apple's searchable archives of tech notes, software update information, and documentation. The library is especially useful if you need info about an old Mac; Apple archives all its info here. Choose from a preset list of topics or products and type a keyword to research. You're rewarded with a list of helpful documents. Click any one of these (they're all links) to take you right to the info you seek. The site even has tools that can help narrow your search.

The Mac OS X Home Page

www.apple.com/macosx/

Part of Apple's main Web site (click the Mac OS X tab), this section is all about Mac OS X, its cool features, how to get the most from it, what applications are available for it, and so on. Don't miss the Theatre section for quickie mini-tour movies of the features in the Dock, Finder window, Mail, and more. (You need QuickTime 4 or higher to view these shorts, but you can download it from each movie page.) Check in here to see what Apple has cooking.

ramseeker

www.macseek.com

One of the best ways to make your Mac better is to buy more random access memory (RAM). RAM is the readily available memory your computer uses; the more you have, the smoother programs run. While Mac OS X may run on a Mac with only 64MB of RAM, officially it requires 128MB and works even better and faster with more than that. As cheap as RAM is, the price that you pay for it can vary quite a lot. Get the lowdown on RAM prices with ramseeker, which organizes memory prices by Mac type.

Outpost.com

www.outpost.com

This site is all about buying stuff — what big kid doesn't love his toys? Here you can find lots and lots and lots of Mac products, including Apple CPUs, memory, drives, printers, scanners, and other miscellaneous accessories. You'll love the prices, as well as the free *overnight* delivery (on orders over $100) that this site touts.

EveryMac.com

www.everymac.com

The author of this site claims that this site is "the complete guide of every Macintosh, Mac Compatible, and upgrade card in the world." You can't argue with that. Become a member and sign up for forums. Check out the FAQ and Resource sections, too, for your Mac-related questions.

inside mac games

www.imgmagazine.com

This is the best of the Mac gaming sites on the Web (at least in Bob's humble opinion). Order CDs of game demos, download shareware, check out game preview movies, or shop for editors and emulators. Find forum camaraderie and troubleshoot gaming problems, too.

dealmac

www.dealmac.com

Shopping for Mac stuff? Go to dealmac ("Because cheap Mac stuff rocks," this site boasts) first to find out about sale prices, rebates, and other bargain opportunities on upgrades, software, peripherals, and more.

Chapter 22

Ten Mac OS X Apps That You Might Need Someday

. . . .

. . . .

Dig around the Mac OS X Applications folder or take a gander at the System Preferences application's main window, and you'll run across some programs and preferences that you won't use every day but are still kind of cool.

In this chapter, we tell you what some of these items do and whether you're likely to get much from them. Unfortunately, because of space limitations, we didn't talk much about any of them elsewhere in this book. And, we can't really explain how to use each of these potentially useful goodies in much detail here. Instead, our objective is to briefly describe each one and then provide some insights on whether you need it or not.

Almost everything we mention in this chapter includes a Mac OS Help feature. Use it to discover more about how these goodies work. Just search Mac OS Help for the item you're interested in, and you'll get an eyeful. (Some of the apps we discuss in this chapter are also discussed in Chapter 13, where we talk about the applications that come with Mac OS X by default.)

Web Sharing

Web Sharing enables others to share documents on your computer through the Web. You can set up a Web site just by adding HTML pages and images to the Sites folder in your home folder, and then activating Web Sharing in the Sharing pane of System Preferences (which we detail in Chapter 15).

Web Sharing works only while your Macintosh is connected to the Internet. In other words, if you use a modem and connect to the Internet by "dialing up," this application won't be a lot of use to you because your server (your Mac) will only be on the Internet when you've dialed up and made a modem connection. When you're not connected, your server won't be available. That's not to say Web Sharing can't be used this way, but you'll have to tell users when they'll be able to find it, and then make sure you dial up and make a connection at that time.

Furthermore, even if you keep your modem connected to the Internet 24 hours a day with a Digital Subscriber Line (DSL) or cable modem connection, using this feature may violate your agreement with your ISP because some ISPs prohibit you from running a Web site. On the other hand, some ISPs don't care. Check with yours if you're concerned.

Bob sez: I do use this feature occasionally, but because I don't use it 24/7, I never bothered to check with my ISP. Do me a favor and don't rat me out.

FTP Access

FTP (File Transfer Protocol) is kind of like Web Sharing: It allows folks on the Internet to access files on your Mac. The difference is that FTP access is specifically designed to let you make files available for download, while Web Sharing is designed to let people view Web pages.

When you activate FTP by selecting the Allow FTP Access check box in the Sharing pane of System Preferences, users on the Internet have the same access to the contents of your Mac that they would if they were using file sharing (see Chapter 16 for more on file sharing). People who don't have accounts on your Mac can access Public folders and Drop Box folders — or any folder to which you grant everyone access, as we describe in Chapter 16.

Internet users can connect to your Mac with any FTP client application. An *FTP client* is a program that offers FTP features — upload files, download files, and so on. Better FTP clients can also do stuff like rename and delete remote files. Most Web browsers can serve as FTP clients, as well as browsers (although they're mostly good for uploading and downloading, and not much use for deleting, renaming, and other useful functions).

On the Mac, Interarchy (which we discuss in the upcoming pages) and Fetch are probably the best known (and best) FTP clients. You can also find FTP clients for Windows, Linux, and most other operating systems (but because we use Macs, we don't know the names of the good ones).

Interarchy is a great Mac FTP client, one that is also capable of performing many other Internet-related tasks you might someday need. For example, you can use it to search the Internet to find the files you want, provide a wealth of information about your Internet connection, help manage remote servers, and enable you to remotely control your Mac across the Internet. Interarchy is shareware; you can read more about it or download a copy to play with at http://groups.yahoo.com/group/interarchy/.

Applet Launcher

You'll find Applet Launcher in the Utilities folder (in your Applications folder). The Applet Launcher is an application you can use to work with Apple's version of Java. *Java* is a programming language (or a platform, depending on who you ask) that's most frequently used in Web pages you view on the Internet. Stand-alone Java programs, called *applets*, are beginning to become available as well.

With Applet Launcher, you can run programs written in Java on your Mac, with no Web browser required. Mac OS X and Internet Explorer (the browser that comes with Mac OS X) also support Java within Web pages. So you have a choice — run stand-alone applets with Applet Launcher, or have your browser do the work of loading and launching Java programs that are part of a Web page.

ColorSync

From the ColorSync pane in System Preferences, pick a profile, or check to see that the profile ColorSync is using is the right one for your display, input, output, or proof device. ColorSync helps ensure color accuracy when scanning, printing, and working with color images. This package includes ColorSync software, as well as pre-made ColorSync profiles for a variety of monitors, scanners, and printers. If you're not a graphics artist working with color files and calibrating monitors and printers to achieve accurate color matching, you probably don't need ColorSync.

A *ColorSync profile* is a set of instructions for a monitor, scanner, or printer, which tells the device how to deal with colors (and white) so the device's output is consistent with other devices output (as determined by the ColorSync profiles of other devices). In theory, if two devices have ColorSync profiles, their output (on screen, on a printed page, or in a scanned image) should match perfectly. Put another way, the red (or green, or blue, or white, or any other color) you see on screen should be exactly the same shade as the red you see on a printed page or in a scanned image.

To calibrate or not to calibrate?

One thing you might want to try, even if you never plan to use ColorSync, is to calibrate your monitor. This process adjusts the Red, Green, Blue, and White levels, and may make what you see on your screen look better than it does now.

To calibrate your monitor, follow these steps:

1. **Open the Displays System Preferences pane.**

2. **Click the Color tab and then write down the Display Profile that your Mac is currently using (it's above the Calibrate button).**

3. **Click the Calibrate button.**

   The Display Calibrator Assistant appears.

4. **Follow the simple on-screen instructions to calibrate your monitor and create a custom display profile.**

5. **When you get to the last screen in the Display Calibrator Assistant, you can either give your new profile a name and save it by clicking the Create button, or you can click the Cancel button to revert to the way your display was before you adjusted the calibration.**

If you click the Create button and then decide you don't like the results of your calibration, just click the Display Profile you wrote down in Step 2 from the list and your monitor will go back the way it was before you calibrated it.

Image Capture

Image Capture is a nifty little application that enables you to download images from a digital camera to your Mac. You'll find it in your Applications folder. You can use it with all kinds of digital cameras, so if you have more than one, you may not have to worry about installing an application for each.

Unfortunately, Image Capture doesn't work with every digital camera. For example, Image Capture did not recognize Bob's relatively new Olympus digital camera.

To find out if Image Capture works with *your* digital camera, plug the camera into one of your Mac's USB ports and open Image Capture. If the Camera menu at the top of the window reads No devices found, you're out of luck.

Image Capture can automate some parts of the image-downloading process. For example, you can set it up to download all images from the camera into a pre-selected folder, and to open automatically when you connect your camera to your Mac.

You may not want to use Image Capture if you prefer the program that came with your digital camera (the program you use to import pictures from the camera). On the other hand, you may *have* to use Image Capture if that program hasn't been upgraded to support Mac OS X and doesn't run under Classic (some programs just don't work with Classic).

Finally, if the program that came with your camera doesn't run under Classic, and Image Capture doesn't work with your camera, you'll have to reboot with OS 9.1 to run the program. (For more info on running Classic and OS X, and rebooting under OS 9.1, read through Chapter 14.)

Text-to-Speech

Use Text-to-Speech to convert on-screen text into spoken words from your Mac. This application is pretty much unchanged from earlier versions of Mac OS. With a whole slew of voices to choose from, you can have Text-to-Speech read dialog boxes, or even documents, aloud. You can activate this feature in the Speech System Preferences pane. Click the Text-to-Speech tab to check it out.

 Sometimes hearing is better than reading. For example, Bob sometimes uses Text-to-Speech to read a column or page to him before he submits it. If something doesn't sound right, he gives it a final polish before sending it off to his editor.

Text-to-Speech is kind of cool (the talking alerts are fun), but having dialog boxes actually produce spoken dialog becomes annoying real fast for most folks. But check it out! You might like it, and you may find times when you want your Mac to read to you.

Speech Recognition

Speech Recognition enables your Mac to recognize and respond to human speech. With this feature, you can issue verbal commands like, "Get my mail!" to your Mac and have it actually get your mail. You can also create AppleScripts, and then trigger them by voice.

You'll find the Speech Recognition tab right next to the Text-to-Speech tab in the Speech pane of System Preferences. You need a microphone (some Macs have them built-in) to use Speech Recognition. And you'll only be able to talk to your Mac when using applications that support speech recognition.

An AppleScript is a series of commands, using the AppleScript language, that tells the computer (and some applications) what to do. You create AppleScripts with the Script Editor program, which you'll find in the AppleScript folder within the Applications folder.

Bob sez: This application is clever and kind of fun, but it's also slow and requires a microphone. And I've never been able to get Speech Recognition to work well enough to continue using it beyond a few days. Still, it's kind of neat (and it's a freebie), and I've heard many users profess their love for it. So you may want to check it out.

NetInfo Manager

NetInfo is a hierarchical database that contains much of the configuration information needed to manage what goes on behind the scenes of Mac OS X. NetInfo knows all of your settings, who has an account on your Mac, what network addresses you're using, and lots, lots more. With NetInfo Manager, you can view and edit some of this information. Although it has a Mac interface, the database info displayed there will be pretty much incomprehensible to most folks.

NetInfo is a central location for a lot of important information, and by using NetInfo Manager, a savvy Mac user can do cool things that can't be done with the Network or Sharing System Preferences panes. But most average users won't want to play here. One suggestion: If you're at all curious about the internals of the Unix operating system on which Mac OS X is based, start by learning a bit about NetInfo before you dive into the hard-core Unix stuff (see the next section).

Unix Tools (Terminal, Console, and Process Viewer)

Mac OS X is based on the Unix operating system, although its Unix underpinnings are mostly hidden. While most Mac users are grateful to be able to ignore Unix, if you know Unix, or think you might like to, you'll find that you can do a lot of very geeky things with the Unix tools included in Mac OS X.

You'll find all three programs in the Utilities folder within your Applications folder.

Unix is not for the inexperienced or faint of heart. Before you even begin experimenting with it, you should get yourself a good Unix primer and learn the ropes. And as usual, be very careful. Mucking around in the Mac OS X Unix files gives you access to lots of stuff that isn't ordinarily available to you, which can very quickly lead to major problems if you're not absolutely sure what you're doing. For more info on Unix, check out the *Unix Bible,* 2nd Edition by Yves Lepage and Paul Iarrera (published by Hungry Minds, Inc.).

Terminal

Basically, Unix uses a command-line interface. Instead of clicking buttons and dragging icons around the Desktop, you type commands (not in English, by the way) at a command line. To do this in Mac OS X, you use a program called Terminal, which you'll find in the Utilities folder in the Applications folder.

Terminal is nothing more than a single window with a line (or many lines) of very geeky-looking text — there are no menus or buttons to make your life easier. So Terminal is mostly useless to you unless you speak a decent amount of Unix.

Console

Console is another Unix tool that's used to show you technical messages from Mac OS X — in Unix-speak, of course. It shows what Unix processes are running, what devices are in use, and so on. Think of it as a Unix troubleshooting and status-checking tool.

Unfortunately, like Terminal, Console's only window is a wall of super-geeky-looking text — there are no menus or buttons to make your life easier. Which means that Console is mostly useless unless you speak a decent amount of Unix.

Process Viewer

Process Viewer may be more useful for seeing what's going on "under the hood" than Console. That's because it's got a Mac interface, or at least it has some menus, a "find" text field, and columns you can sort. Think of it as another Unix troubleshooting and status-checking tool.

Appendix

Installing Mac OS X (Only If You Have To)

In This Chapter

▶ Installing (or reinstalling) Mac OS X
▶ Setting up Mac OS X with Setup Assistant

*Y*ou will probably never need this appendix. Some of you will get Mac OS X pre-installed on a new Macintosh, and others will have installed it long before buying this book. And so, we expect that few of you will have to refer to this Appendix to install OS X on your Mac for the very first time.

But (and there's always a but, isn't there?), someday something unexpected may happen to your Mac. You could have a hard drive crash, or a problem starting up from your hard drive, or maybe you'll see the flashing-question-mark icon when booting — all meaning that you'll need to *reinstall* Mac OS X. And so, we expect that some of you (and we hope not many) will have to refer to this Appendix, for instructions on reinstalling OS X.

In this appendix, you'll discover all you need to know to install or reinstall Mac OS X if you should have to. We say reinstalling is a hassle because, while you won't lose the contents of your home folder or stuff in your Documents folder (unless something goes horribly wrong), you may lose some System Preferences, which means you'll need to reconfigure those panes manually after you reinstall. It's not the end of the world, but it can be inconvenient. That said, reinstalling OS X usually corrects all but the most horrifying and malignant of problems. And the process is relatively painless, as you'll soon see.

A Mac OS X reinstallation is a drastic final step. Be sure you've tried all the stuff in Chapter 18 before even thinking about reinstalling OS X. If nothing else fixes your Mac, reinstalling Mac OS X may well be your final option before invasive surgery (that is, trundling your Mac to a repair shop). We save this solution for here at the very end of the book because it's the biggest hassle, and you don't want to reinstall OS X if something easier can correct the problem. So if you have to do a reinstallation, realize that this is more or less your last hope.

We'll stay with you through it all; be brave.

How to Install (Or Reinstall) Mac OS X

In theory, you should only have to install Mac OS X once. And in a perfect world, that would be the case. But you may find occasions when you have to install it again, such as:

- ✔ If you get a new Mac that didn't come with Mac OS X pre-installed
- ✔ If you have a catastrophic hard drive crash that requires you to initialize (format) your boot drive
- ✔ If any essential Mac OS X files become damaged, corrupted, or are deleted or renamed

The following instructions do double duty: They're what you do to install Mac OS X for the first time on a Mac, and they're also what you do if something happens to the copy of OS X that you boot your Mac from. That is, the process for installing or reinstalling OS X is exactly the same.

Unlike earlier versions of Mac OS, there is no clean install option for OS X. And there aren't a handful of installation options, either. For the most part, one size fits all.

If you've backed up your entire hard drive, you may want to reinstall from your back-up disk or tape rather than reinstalling OS X from the Install Mac OS X Installation CD. That way, you'll be certain that everything is just the way you left it, which is something you can't be sure of if you reinstall from the Install Mac OS X Installation CD.

Here's how to install (or reinstall) OS X, step by step:

1. **Boot from your Install Mac OS X Installation CD by inserting the CD into your machine's CD-ROM or DVD drive and then restarting your Mac while holding down the C key.**

   When Mac OS X has finished booting your Mac, the Install program launches automatically. Here is where you begin the process of installing or reinstalling Mac OS X.

2. **Unless you want to use a language other than English for the main language of Mac OS X, click the Continue button in the first screen you see; if you do want to use another language, select the corresponding radio button and then click the Continue button.**

3. **Click the Continue button when the Welcome screen appears.**

4. **Read the Important Information screen and then click the Continue button.**

5. **Read the Software License Agreement and then click the Continue button.**

   A sheet drops down querying whether you agree to the terms of the license agreement. If you don't, you can't go any further, so we advise you to go ahead and click the Agree button.

   If you're currently using any version of Mac OS except version 9.1, you may next see a dialog box with the warning that you can't run Classic applications unless you have Mac OS 9.1 or a later version installed. You can't install Mac OS 9.1 right now (you're installing OS X!), but you can click OK and install it later. (Mac OS X includes a Mac OS 9.1 Install CD for your convenience.) If you have Mac OS 9.1 installed, you won't see this dialog box.

6. **Choose the disk you want to install or reinstall Mac OS X on by clicking once on its icon in the Select a Destination screen.**

7. **(Optional) If you want to completely erase the Mac OS X disk, starting completely from scratch, select the Erase Destination and Format As check box.**

   If you choose the Erase Destination option, the disk you selected in Step 6 will be erased! You should only choose this option if you have backed up all your important files. In most cases, erasing the start-up disk is not necessary.

8. **Leave the Mac OS Extended option selected (on the pop-up menu) and click the Continue button.**

   The other menu choice is Unix File System (UFS). Suffice it to say that it's not a good choice. In fact, we'd say that 99.9% of you should not format your disk using the Unix File System. And the other tenth of one percent know who they are and why they need a UFS disk. 'Nuff said.

   Now you have the choice to perform an Easy Install or a Custom Install. The Easy Install copies all of Mac OS X onto your chosen (as you chose in Step 6) hard drive; the Custom Install (click the Customize button at the bottom of the screen) enables you choose to install only the items you want to install.

   For the record, the Easy Install includes four items: Base System, Essential System Software, BSD Subsystem, and Additional Print Drivers. A Custom Install always installs the first two items, but also lets you choose (by selecting check boxes) whether to install the BSD Subsystem and Additional Print Drivers. BSD Subsystem is some Unix stuff you may or may not need (if you don't know whether you need it, we suggest that you install it). Choose Additional Printer Drivers to enable your Mac to talk to a variety of printers without having to install drivers for them.

In almost all cases, Easy Install is the right way to go, and that's what we assume you'll choose for the rest of these steps because you're either doing a complete install or reinstall of your operating system.

9. **To begin the installation, click the Install button.**

   The install process takes 10–20 minutes, so now might be a good time to take a coffee break. When the install process finishes, your Mac will reboot and you can begin using Mac OS X, hopefully, trouble-free.

   After your Mac reboots, the Setup Assistant appears.

10. **Work your way through all of the Setup Assistant screens (you have to before you can begin working in OS X), which we show you how to do in the next section.**

Getting Set Up with Setup Assistant

Assuming that your installation (or reinstallation) process goes well and your Mac restarts itself, the next thing you should see (and hear) is a short, colorful movie that ends by transforming into the first Setup Assistant screen, fetchingly named Welcome.

To tiptoe through the Setup Assistant, follow these steps:

1. **When the Welcome screen appears, choose your country from the list by clicking it once, and then click the Continue button.**

   If your country doesn't appear in the list, select the Show All check box, which will cause a bunch of additional countries to appear in this list. Choose yours by clicking it, and then click the Continue button.

   The Personalize Settings screen appears.

2. **Choose a keyboard layout from the list by clicking it once, and then click the Continue button.**

   If you're an American or want to use an American keyboard setup, click the U.S. listing. If you prefer a different country's keyboard layout, select the Show All check box, and a bunch of additional countries (as well as a pair of Dvorak keyboard layouts) appears in the list. Choose the one you prefer by clicking it and then click the Continue button.

   The Registration Information screen appears.

3. **Fill out the fields (name, address, phone number, and so on) and then click the Continue button.**

   If you're interested in what Apple will and will not do with this information, click the Privacy button on this screen and read the Privacy Policy.

   The A Few More Questions screen appears.

4. **Complete the form and then click the Continue button.**

   The Thank You screen appears.

5. **Click the Continue button.**

   The Create Your Account screen appears.

6. **Fill in the Name, Short Name, Password, Verify, and Password Hint fields and then click the Continue button.**

   Each of these fields has an explanation beneath it. You can't click the Continue button until you've filled in all five fields.

   The Get Internet Ready screen appears.

7. **Select from two radio buttons — I'll Use My Existing Internet Service, or I'm Not Ready to Connect to the Internet — and then click the Continue button.**

    If you choose to use your existing Internet service, you'll see another series of screens in which you provide specific information about how you connect to the Internet, your IP address (if you have one), what kind of connection you have, and so on. If you don't know one (or more) of the items in this series of screens, don't worry. Just leave them blank and keep clicking the Continue button. Later, after the Setup Assistant finishes and you are up and running with Mac OS X, you can ask your ISP (Internet Service Provider), and then put in that information in the appropriate place (the Network and/or Internet System Preference panes).

8. **When the next screen appears, click the Continue button.**

   The assistant will quit and in a few moments, the Mac OS X Desktop will appear. That's it. You're done!

Index

• *B* •

• D •

• T •

Notes

Notes

Discover Dummies Online!

The Dummies Web Site is your fun and friendly online resource for the latest information about *For Dummies* books and your favorite topics. The Web site is the place to communicate with us, exchange ideas with other *For Dummies* readers, chat with authors, and have fun!

Ten Fun and Useful Things You Can Do at www.dummies.com

1. Win free *For Dummies* books and more!
2. Register your book and be entered in a prize drawing.
3. Meet your favorite authors through the Hungry Minds Author Chat Series.
4. Exchange helpful information with other *For Dummies* readers.
5. Discover other great *For Dummies* books you must have!
6. Purchase Dummieswear exclusively from our Web site.
7. Buy *For Dummies* books online.
8. Talk to us. Make comments, ask questions, get answers!
9. Download free software.
10. Find additional useful resources from authors.

Link directly to these ten fun and useful things at **www.dummies.com/10useful**

For other titles from Hungry Minds, go to **www.hungryminds.com**

Not on the Web yet? It's easy to get started with *Dummies 101: The Internet For Windows 98* or *The Internet For Dummies* at local retailers everywhere.

Find other *For Dummies* books on these topics:
Business • Career • Databases • Food & Beverage • Games • Gardening
Graphics • Hardware • Health & Fitness • Internet and the World Wide Web
Networking • Office Suites • Operating Systems • Personal Finance • Pets
Programming • Recreation • Sports • Spreadsheets • Teacher Resources
Test Prep • Word Processing

Hungry Minds™

FOR DUMMIES
BOOK REGISTRATION

We want to hear from you!

Visit **dummies.com** to register this book and tell us how you liked it!

- ✔ Get entered in our monthly prize giveaway.

- ✔ Give us feedback about this book — tell us what you like best, what you like least, or maybe what you'd like to ask the author and us to change!

- ✔ Let us know any other *For Dummies* topics that interest you.

Your feedback helps us determine what books to publish, tells us what coverage to add as we revise our books, and lets us know whether we're meeting your needs as a *For Dummies* reader. You're our most valuable resource, and what you have to say is important to us!

Not on the Web yet? It's easy to get started with *Dummies 101: The Internet For Windows 98* or *The Internet For Dummies* at local retailers everywhere.

Or let us know what you think by sending us a letter at the following address:

For Dummies Book Registration
Dummies Press
10475 Crosspoint Blvd.
Indianapolis, IN 46256

BESTSELLING
BOOK SERIES